W9-AOE-249

Typo

The Last American Typesetter
or
How I Made and Lost $4 Million
(An Entrepreneur's Education)

by David Silverman

Soft Skull Press Brooklyn NY   2007

© 2007 by David Silverman

Soft Skull Press
55 Washington St. Suite 804
Brooklyn NY 11201

Distributed by Publishers Group West
www.pgw.com 1-800-788-3123

Printed in Canada
Book design by Luke Gerwe

Library of Congress Cataloging-in-Publication info available from the
Library of Congress.

For Dan Coyne and my father.
Two men who I once thought had all the answers.
I forgive you.

Table of Contents

We've all been in debt from time to time. Maybe you borrowed five dollars from a friend, or maybe you ran up something on your credit card you shouldn't have, like a bread machine. Who needs a bread machine? If Armageddon comes, you won't need a loaf of homemade rye.

Or maybe you borrowed a couple million dollars to buy a typesetting company in the Midwest with your best friend and mentor and then watched it all go horribly wrong.

Oh right, that was me

—New York City, 2004

Prologue: Driving

August 1999

MY FATHER, STEADY AT FIFTY-FIVE MILES PER HOUR behind the wheel of the Buick station wagon, always flashed his headlights to let the truckers know it was safe to pass at night, and they would blink their taillights in acknowledgement—a secret handshake between the professional big-riggers and my father.

Driving in the black gloom of an oncoming storm, I clicked the lights on my Honda CRV as a Wal-Mart rig roared past me on the big hill that curves down and out of the Central Valley. The eighteen-wheeler switched on and off the running lights that encircled his cab and flat bed. I smiled a little, wishing someone had come with me if for no other reason than to show them that my Dad was right.

I would turn thirty-two years old in three months, but I had long ago absorbed his tendencies—either careful or neurotic, depending on one's feelings about following the rules. As the rain started to fall, I ticked off the same roadside markers he pointed out on every family trip: a small white shield every tenth of a mile followed by a tall green one every mile. I was driving the New York State Thruway the hour and a half due north to our family house in the fifties-era suburbs of the city of Kingston. The foothills of the headlands, as my sister called them, were sandwiched between the Hudson River and the wall of the Catskill Mountains— which aren't really mountains, Dad had often told me, but a tree-covered plateau eroded by rivers seeking the sea.

The late summer storm passed quickly, and when I reached the Plattekill rest area, mile marker sixty-five, the sun had returned, igniting the wet road into mist. I divided my speed, a very un-Dad-like eighty, by the number of miles until marker ninety-two—home. I repeated the calculation with every signpost, plenty of time to wonder why the government spent so much money to neatly mow the median and what I would find at the house I had been born in and not (aside from family vacations) spent a single night away from until I went to college. Although that wasn't entirely true. I remembered as I turned off the highway and merged onto Kingston's lone traffic circle that I had once convinced them to let me go to the state chess tournament in Syracuse my last year of high school. But, according to my father, I had come back so unruly he would never permit it again.

The house, a cross between a ranch and saltbox draped in white aluminum siding on a quiet dead-end street, looked as unassuming as always. But the lawn on our quarter-acre plot was a disaster. After a decade of neglect, dandelions had beaten back everything except the "duck grass" that stayed brown most of the year and my father had never been able to defeat. I sat in the car for a moment. The bottom panel of the screen door was as busted as the day I had kicked it in, clear evidence that everything would be as I left it on my last visit—nearly three months ago. Upstairs my bedroom would be dark with maybe a water glass that had evaporated down to a thin coat of dust. The closet would be stuffed with my unfinished elementary school art projects, old copies of *Byte* magazine, and that dubious peach-colored award for last place in the national college computer-programming contest in Atlanta, 1988.

My father didn't come to greet me, but I imagined him in the driveway, the hood of one Buick or another up as he re-spaced the spark plugs or de-gummed the carburetor's butterfly valve, extending the life of the car another hundred thousand miles. He was an engineer by training and desire, and I remembered him surrounded by parts: the lawnmower blade he re-sharpened every season, the innards of the kitchen clock that kept breaking, or spiced ham for the sandwiches we assembled as a family on Saturdays.

ℓ

Typo

We sat in the spotless living room: me in the blue chair that I sat in for his lectures, and my father, with his thin legs bent Indian-style beneath him on the green shag carpet. His shoes were off, exposing deformed toes that had become crumpled in shoes handed down through four elder brothers.

I saw his bald spot that he combed his grey hair over, the thick white moustache he'd always had, the beard that was starting to grow unchecked after nine years of retirement, the thick PhotoGrey glasses as wide as a windshield, and the nose like mine, a honker. Everything was right except the small glass of Old Smuggler whiskey resting next to his ashtray.

There had always been the one, regular drink after work, and I would never have guessed that such a minor pleasure, a tiny blue dot of ink bled onto the breast pocket of the crisp, white-shirt of a man defined by obligation, responsibility, and a dedication to his family, would overtake him so completely—his concern for me replaced by worries he would run out of whiskey.

I looked at the couch no one had sat on since my mother died two years earlier. My father's health aide had folded her old blanket on one of the grey cushions. Dad's acceleration beyond the one-a-day drink had begun with Mom's Alzheimer's. As her sole caretaker during those years, he had ramped up slowly but steadily, until, by 1999, he was downing a pint of whiskey a day. My business partner, Dan, of the same generation as my father, said that the drinking was simply his cure for the sadness that had become his disease.

Dan, at my request, had traveled to the house a year before. He took a rare day away from work and his family to come three hours by train and another two by car to spend an afternoon with my father—arguing sincerely with him on the front stoop to stop drinking. To become the old Dad—the one who taught me to hang my shirts buttons facing left. The afternoon had stretched into a twenty-four hour ordeal that in the end hadn't changed anything—except for me putting that hole in the screen door and pushing my father a little further into seclusion. The next morning I drove Dan to New York to get him to his train. He rested a hand silently on my shoulder, and I knew he cared about me as much as anyone then.

I had come back to get the money my father had offered to me in earlier, sober days: two hundred thousand in IBM stock that he had acquired—sometimes a fraction of a share at a time—over all those years. But looking at him on the floor, surrounded by a plastic bag full of cigarette butts, junk mail and bits of broken nails he plucked from his toes, I felt less certain.

"How is old Dan?" my father asked.

I looked at the picture of myself on the mantel—a computer printout made of dot-matrix letters arranged to show my Dorothy Hamill bowl cut and my own PhotoGrey glasses.

"Still calling himself a benevolent capitalist?" he continued.

He had kept that photo on his mid-level engineer's metal desk at IBM. In his world, there was no greater good than the old IBM, and it was the same for me. Next to the family Bible on the shelf below my portrait was the familiar black and gold binding of *Think*, the biography of Thomas Watson and the thin blue spine of the *IBM Ethics Manual*.

My father was a firm adherent of the meritocracy those books espoused. For him, advancement in the world was assured via IBM's twin paths to promotion: one for managers who liked to "play politics" and one for engineers who were promoted solely on their intelligence and objective accomplishments. When I was seven, playing a game of "war" with maple branches as rifles, I had proudly told a defeated enemy, "You aren't out. IBM puts you on probation for six months so you can improve your performance. Respect for the individual." I believed it then. I still believed it.

"He says you still love me," I said, unexpectedly, and maybe a little too angry, but his face showed no shock.

My father had retired in disgust when Big Blue had their first-ever layoff. He had been promised a promotion to senior engineer, but his boss of two decades reneged on the deal knowing my father would resign. It gave the boss a needed "chit" in the drive to let go of twenty percent of the employees. After that, Dad had started going to Atlantic City. He'd started fighting more with Mom, and, one terrible night, he'd packed a bag and spent the night at a Super 8 motel, frustrated that his life's work of responsibility had netted him only resentment. I began to sense that I didn't know what the man I wanted more than anything to be, had wanted his life to become. His anger from that night never went away when he chose to take care of Mom's declining health, but he didn't speak directly about it. Instead he scolded us loudly using his I'm-counting-to-three voice that "visiting home isn't about coming here to have fun and go out with your friends. You're needed to look after your mother." And after she died, the anger still emerged when he saw ads for Microsoft—Bill Gates had betrayed IBM—or was reminded about the doctor who had first diagnosed mom with Alzheimer's—"he scarred her and she never recovered from that"—but for most of the time it lay dormant, deep within, covered by a thick carpet of Scotch.

"Of course I do," he said. "You're my son." He leaned to blow smoke into the chimney the way mom had made him—to keep the smell out of the house—and continued, "Now tell me about Clarinda."

"Typesetting," I said, and he watched me intently, the glass by his side untouched, "the process of putting bits of lead together to make pages, is long dead, but the opportunity—" I felt the words coming like they did when I was trying to impress my father about having gotten on the dean's list, a torrent of self-created conviction "—the opportunity to make pages for publishers using computers continues to grow. And editorial services: copyediting, indexing, design—"

He was getting distracted, looking beyond me, and I, nervous, switched direction, "You're getting in on the ground floor of the roll up of the American typesetting industry. First we buy Clarinda, the premier typesetter in Clarinda, Iowa. They've been in business for almost fifty years and Dan negotiated with the bank that owns them to sell to us for almost nothing. Can you believe it?"

He smiled and puffed again. "My son, Mr. Businessman."

"All we need is two hundred thousand dollars," I said, the words coming out of my mouth, while my mind tried to absolve me of doubt. All his savings. All his "bad weather" savings for "just in case." If I lost it, who would take care of him?

He laughed and patted his pockets, "Not here, but you're welcome to whatever I've got. You know that."

"Are you sure?" I asked.

He grinned and took a sip of whiskey.

"You'll pay it back," he said, his yellow teeth showing, "I know you."

"Of course I will," I said. I had to.

"So, if you're going into the kitchen, how about you get me another ice cube. And while you're in there," he said and smiled, like a child expecting another grilled cheese sandwich, "why don't you top off my glass."

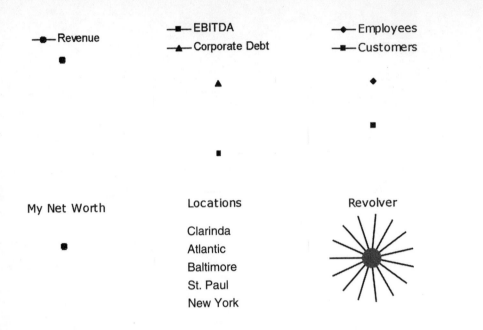

Revenue

EBITDA
Corporate Debt

Employees
Customers

My Net Worth

Locations

Clarinda
Atlantic
Baltimore
St. Paul
New York

Revolver

We bought Clarinda from Household Finance for the "book value" of $2.7 million for land, computers, furniture, and so on, but nothing for "intangible" customer relationships, what's called "goodwill" in merger speak. Or, as Dan said, "A bargain at twice the price."

For **revenue** I've used "future run rate," which is the current month's revenue times twelve. This better represents how well the company was improving (or declining) than the historical 12 months.

EBITDA is earnings before interest, taxes, depreciation, and amortization, which is basically the same as net income before taxes, but sounds cooler.

Corporate Debt is the debt from the acquisition. Monthly debt service was around 5% of the total because our loans were low interest or no interest, which Dan called "pretty darn good if you ask me and you should be asking me."

Revolver Expires refers to the number of months left on the revolving line of credit from Household Finance. It is essentially a corporate credit card that we used to make payroll while waiting for customers to pay their bills. If we didn't replace it or get Household to extend it by the expiration date, then the name "revolver" became apt because without it, we would be unable to issue paychecks and therefore be out of business instantly—like a bullet to the head.

My **Net Worth** is the value of my share of the company minus long-term debt plus any cash I hadn't spent on plush bicycle seats and Pottery Barn sofas.

Clarinda and Atlantic, Iowa, each housed about fifty typesetters, customer service staff and management. St. Paul had about a half dozen copyeditors, book designers and production managers. Those three facilities were the Clarinda company that we purchased. Baltimore was an office with about a dozen typesetters and managers who were essentially employees who had been with Dan through many different companies since the 1970s. Baltimore was currently under the ownership of our former employers, a company called Bembo, but Dan was negotiating to roll it into the Clarinda company. Although Clarinda, Iowa was official company HQ, Dan preferred to be in Baltimore near his family and his trusted staff. Lastly, there was New York, which was, for the moment, just me in my rented one bedroom apartment where I conducted business, day and night, in my underwear.

Benevolent Capitalists

September 1999

DAN AND I DROVE SOUTH THROUGH IOWA on Interstate 29 in our standard-issue rented white Ford Taurus, passing exits for what appeared to be only fields. After forty-five minutes Dan gave in and lit up a cigarette, hanging his arm out the passenger window and trying his best to blow the smoke outside. I coughed, but didn't begrudge my friend, partner, and boss his one weakness. He was, after all, in charge.

Nearing sixty, Dan was an old school, button-down executive and I suspected he hadn't taken off his ancient houndstooth jacket since leaving home in Baltimore that morning. A self-described "wrong side of the tracks Irishman," he looked more like a corporate version of George Carlin than the world's foremost expert on typesetting, and he smelled like a country singer, all hair tonic and Benson and Hedges cigarettes. His bronze-to-grey hair was nearly the same color as his leathery skin and thinning, but not so thin that he couldn't get it puffed up every morning with rigorous combing. He was thinking, as always, about his plans: how to remake the company we'd just bought, how to beat the East Indian competitors, how to take the company public, how to roll up the typesetting industry and make us millionaires.

Those potential millions were both the first thing on my mind and the last—first because, quite obviously, I wanted to be a millionaire, and they would let me pay back my father his retirement money. They were the last because I had Dan, and he had taught me, "millions are easy, kiddo; building a company that will endure is hard." He should know, he had made millions for every boss he'd worked for, but never for long enough to get any of it for himself. We had worked together for more than four years at two companies where he had been my boss and I had been his loyal, tech-guy ward. Both companies had been run by narrow-minded men who had thwarted Dan's typesetting dreams and had been the worst kinds of owners: lying, greedy, and uncaring.

Like my father, he had told me repeatedly that the good guys ultimately win in business. When we closed on the purchase of the fifty-year-old Clarinda typesetting company two weeks ago, the good guys, we believed, were winning. The benevolent capitalist was now the CEO of his own company. Without my asking, he had made me, who had never owned anything, an equal shareholder with him, increased my salary a third over my previous job to a hundred and thirty thousand a year and bestowed on me, who had never been the boss of anyone, the title of President.

We turned off at the green-and-white highway sign for the town of McPaul. McPaul had four pairs of railroad tracks, two houses, a closed post office, closed gas station, and closed antique store. No more than a mile beyond, we crested a hill and then: nothing.

Or rather, my city boy idea of nothing: farmland. From the top of this crest I could see twenty miles and there was only one building: a corrugated steel Quonset hut that had been crushed by some natural disaster, lying in a field like a deity-discarded soda can. Every other corner of the world was corn, soybeans, or sky—a third-grader's watercolor of blue, green and harvest gold.

There must be states covered in tomatoes or cucumbers or radishes or whatever else is in the grocery store because Iowa doesn't have them. I asked a local, "What's that?" "Corn." "And that?" "Soybeans." Aside from the occasional cattle or pig farm that was the only agriculture I saw.

We arrived in Clarinda an hour and a half after leaving Omaha. Clarinda had a town square and a mixture of manicured Victorian and vinyl-sided ranch houses. Just over five thousand people lived in what was the biggest urban center with the only movie theater for twenty miles around. The Clarinda tourism brochure highlighted other distinctions— Clarinda was the birthplace of Glenn Miller (he left when he was two), the birthplace of 4-H (contested by at least one other town, in Illinois), and the home of the largest indoor swimming pool in Southwest Iowa (leaving one to assume that somewhere to the north and east lies a much more substantial indoor pool). Keeping up with the times, Clarinda has staked an additional claim as the locale where the hamburger was invented by a Mr. Bert Grey, who employed a German chef of the eponymous town (contested by just about everybody).

It was nearly ten o'clock, so we went straight to the brand new Super 8 motel at the edge of town. Although chain motels appear to be all the same, I, as an experienced business traveler, could spot the minute gradations in quality the way an Olympic judge could tell the difference between a 9.7 pommel horse routine and a 9.6. Do they serve three kinds of stale muffins for breakfast or two? Is the morning orange drink thicker or thinner than water? Is there a morning orange-flavored drink?

The Super 8 was a looking at a major technical deduction—there was no one at the desk. "Hello?" I called.

"Hello!" Dan said, more loudly, and put his green overnight bag down.

I looked around the corner down a hall of rooms. No one. I went and knocked on the door. "When you find her," Dan said, "I'll be outside smoking," and he walked out, tapping a cigarette box against his wrist.

A few minutes later a young woman came out from the room behind the counter. "Oh hi!" she said, "I didn't know anyone was out here!"

I told her we had reservations.

"Look at that!" she said, turning the pages of the book where my and Dan's names were written with arrows across several pages. "You're staying a long time here. You must love Iowa." She smiled at me. No more than a teenager, her teeth were crooked in as many ways as she had teeth—which were not as many as there should have been. "Just fill out this card with your name and company."

"It's the Clarinda company," I said.

She looked at me blankly. The Clarinda company had been located on First Street for 40 years. "I'm sorry. I'm not from around here," she said. "I'm from New Market." New Market was fifteen miles away.

My room had soap but no shampoo, not even the little ketchup-packet kind that you have to tear open with your teeth, but I didn't deduct any more points. It didn't really matter. Not only did I not have enough hair to warrant a complaint, I was here for much more important business— my future millions. I fell asleep to the lullaby of long-haul trucks on the highway a dozen yards from my window carrying what sounded like giant tubs of loose metal pipes over the rumble strips intended to stop them from missing the lone traffic light in fifty miles.

The Clarinda building had its own loading dock—*my own loading dock!*— a sign—*it lit up at night!*—a cafeteria room with vending machines— *whatever!*—and over 25,000 square feet of office space that was mostly unused—*mine! 50% mine!* All that space was a reminder of just how big the equipment required and how labor-intensive typesetting used to be—not to mention how cheap office space was in Iowa.

Dan greeted the receptionist. I wasn't sure if he said "Mary" or "Carrie," so I just smiled. She beamed back at me, the new boss from New York City with a bicycle messenger backpack slung over his shoulder for a briefcase.

My office had a distinct 70s flavor with a single fluorescent lighting block overhead, paneled walls, and a grey-orange carpet. I had inherited from the former occupant a little round conference table, a credenza—my father worked twenty-five years at IBM before he got a credenza—and a view of a cornfield. Dan's office adjoined mine and was bigger. His desk, unlike mine, was made of solid wood, which, I admit, I would have liked, but his view of the cornfield wasn't as good.

I rifled through the drawers, there were some pens, lots of paper clips, a few dozen rubber bands, some spare change, and oddly, a fly swatter. I put the change in my pocket, and unpacked my office supplies: a copy of the video game *Age of Empires* and a PalmPilot. Now what?

As I sat there tapping my hands, a man walked in, keeping his head down and avoiding my gaze. He had white hair, multi-layered cheeks like a walrus, and gave off an aura of unmistakable Santa Claus-iness. His overall straps stuck to his broad chest like copper bands on a barrel made of jam. He slid behind my chair and stood there. I didn't know what he was doing, but I didn't want him to know that, so I picked up the mail already on my desk, and looked through the invitations to buy monogrammed pencils, umbrellas, and garbage bins for "President, Clarinda Company."

I glanced sideways and saw he had opened a metal boxed that contained a readout like a bomb timer. Increasingly uncomfortable with the man wedged behind me, I picked up the phone, but before I could think of someone to call, he turned, handed me a white plastic card and closed the box. "Yes, sir," he said.

He had already started out, head still down, when I realized I would have to act. "Um, what's this?"

While still backing out he said, "I'm sorry, I didn't want to get in your way."

"It's OK." I said. "What's this card?"

"It's your keycard," he said

I looked at it in confusion.

"To get in and out of the building."

Someone else had already given me a regular old metal key that opened the front door. I showed it to him. Did I need a keycard also?

He thought about this and began scratching his back by rubbing up against the doorframe like a grizzly bear. "Well," he said, "only a couple of people have those." He rubbed up and down one more time, "I was told to give you a keycard."

ℓ

At one o'clock, Dan, wearing a rumpled blue blazer with brass buttons, convened his newly created "Executive Committee" in the large conference room next to my office. The room was cold. Although it was across the hall from the main HVAC unit, it had no heating ducts. Other than that, it was the nicest room in the company. On the front wall a huge whiteboard hidden behind double French doors. The conference table was large and solid, and seated about a dozen people in high-backed chairs, which made the lectern and microphone seem like overkill. There were two windows: one looked out onto a tree and the barren cornfield across the street; the other framed a parking lot. On the far wall a retirement-gift sized pendulum clock ticked away, and interrupted the first minute of the meeting by chiming loudly on the hour. It smelled of cheap paneling and erasable marker ink.

Dan stood at the whiteboard and made a sweeping motion. The dried out pen left a thin green line. He redrew over the first impression, and then again—each time pressing harder and causing a little more squeak—to clearly write one number a foot high on the otherwise empty board: "9"—the number of millions of dollars of revenue he hoped we could get to.

I scanned the room for reactions. At thirty-two, I was a few years younger than Kathy from St. Paul, but more than a decade younger than Sally and Steve, and everyone else in the room had kids my age. With his leathery face, Dan, although younger than half the group, looked like he was old enough to be everyone's parent. However, I was by far the baldest. Maybe living in the big city was more stressful than I had thought.

"If the sales estimate Ron has given me is correct," he said and winked at Ron, who as estimating manager, knew every price the company had ever charged. He also served as the mayor of the nearby town of Shambaugh, a position that rotated among the town's population of 190. "And all the customers that David and I spoke to from our old employer Bembo aren't lying to us, when they say they will follow us to Clarinda, then we will do nine million our first year." Dan's voice reminded me of Walter Cronkite. Warm, sincere, fatherly, and when he talked to you, you felt there was no rush—that the most important thing to him was that you understood and that you told him what you needed to. "Imagine that," he said, moving his attention to the production manger, "Fifty percent more than last year. Can you imagine that, Frank?"

Frank, who was—incredibly—the original plant manager sent down from Chicago forty years before, nodded cautiously. He looked like a Lutheran minister—all humorless straight jaws and elbows—combined with a cowboy, combined with a yellow short-sleeve shirt.

Dan continued, "If David and I are able to get through to some of those venture capitalists, we'll also be buying two or three of our competitors, maybe even as soon as next year. Who knows, we might go public." He smiled broadly, exposing his wide, slightly yellowed teeth. "All of you are going to be part of that. You are going to make this company the best in the world."

I looked out the window at the cornfield thick with green stalks. I had nothing to do except listen to Dan win them over. I'd heard this speech repeated to every potential client, investor, and partner for three years, and could repeat it with my eyes closed, but I still listened as every careful word of instruction reminded me we were going to be millionaires running our own typesetting empire. All I had to do was let Dan make his life-long dream happen—let the plan in his head play out with me quietly at his side.

He walked across the room and dropped the worn out marker in a trashcan directly behind me. "Connie, you're my appointed cheerleader; what do you think about that?"

Connie, the customer service manager who Dan hoped to turn into a salesperson, could not have looked like a less-willing cheerleader. She had sounded so sweet on the phone, but in person was pinch-faced, as if an encyclopedia-sized binder clip was fastened to the back of her head. She smiled, aware of everyone looking at her, raised a loose fist just below her shoulder and said, "Rah!"

"That's the spirit!" Dan said, without the slightest edge of sarcasm. "But the reality is Clarinda hasn't done nine million in years. At this critical juncture, the challenge we have is making it to the end of that first year."

A clerk knocked on the door and handed Dan a stack of pages, which he gave to me to pass around the room. I recognized the list we had gone over on the floor of his Baltimore office the week before: all hundred and eleven employees' names and salaries.

"I've picked each of you to be on this executive committee," Dan said, one hand stretched out on the table, resting palm down on the list, "because you are the ones who run this company. You've all been here while Household danced in one president after another. What were there, five of them in just the past few years?" He turned to Frank, who had been studying his copy.

Frank looked up, chuckled, and said, "More like seven."

"Seven," Dan said, pushing out his lower lip thoughtfully. "And you've lived through all those other companies—"

"Poole Brothers, American Can, Nodaway Valley, and Whitestar," I interjected. I had found an anonymously authored company history in the cubbyholes behind the whiteboard. Frank looked amused. Minnie, the brittle controller with bright white hair, scowled, and Dan continued.

"None of those other owners wanted your opinion, did they?"

Ron leaned back in his chair, his hands calmly in his lap. His mildly happy, wide-eyed stare had never strayed from Dan since the meeting began. "That's right," he said.

I recalled a sexual harassment suit against a former president of Clarinda I'd seen during due diligence. The suit had been dismissed because, as the judgment read, "by all accounts many people found the Clarinda Company President a difficult person with whom to work, regardless of their gender. Both male and female employees testified that he accused them of incompetence, undercut their authority and threatened to fire them."

Dan continued his pitch, slowing down to stress each word of the plan, "But to get to that glorious future, we've got some work to do. As far as the bank is concerned, this is a 'turnaround' situation. But they don't know this business like you and I do. The formula is simple—" he went back to the board and wrote a few numbers "—we needed to get revenues to three to four times labor costs so that, after all of those fixed costs like rent, sales, and all of us folks in management—like you and me—who don't make pages, we will get ourselves a nice, solid, ten percent profit. Follow this tried and true formula and we will show those banks how quick those ten years of losses at Clarinda can be turned around."

He half-capped the marker. "To get revenues up, David and I bring in the customers. To get costs down, we will send some work overseas to Bembo, our production partner in the Philippines, and to Baltimore, and very importantly, we will improve productivity here with technology and training." He looked around the room, as if he were a coach giving his team one last reminder before sending them onto the field "But we have a bigger problem before we can do any of that. We critically need one thing—" He uncapped the marker to write in capital letters. "CASH. We can't do anything without it, and we start today with a credit line and zero receivables. Money doesn't come in till we send out a new bill. When will that be, Minnie?"

Looking pleased to be called on, she responded curtly, "It will be a few months before any new checks start coming in."

"And that check will require that we've completed a job," Dan said, "And when's our first new job coming in, Shirley?"

"Oh," Shirley, the Clarinda plant manager with an unfortunately small and upturned nose, said looking up at the ceiling, as if the answer was there. "The Batson book is coming in a couple of weeks."

"And that means—" Dan said, preparing to explain the time lag between finishing a job and money coming in.

"Oh wait," Shirley said. "I forgot about Donaldson, that's coming in next week."

"That's great," Dan said, "But that still means—"

"They just called me this morning," Connie said. "Donaldson's delayed."

"Well, that's OK," Dan said. "It still means—"

"What about Fredericks?" Ron said, his Midwestern twang drawn out by his speech's methodical cadence, "Isn't that already here? I thought I saw it in the mail, Shirley, did you see the mail today?"

"We can sort all this out, later," Dan said, still even voiced, "But the task at hand is who are we—you—going to hire in our new company?"

The multi-geared pendulum clock swung to the hour and gonged twice. Legally, we were a new corporate entity, and had to hire everyone anew. However, employees who'd been working for "The Clarinda Company" regardless of owner for the past two decades wouldn't see it that way. Dan went to the whiteboard, opened a new blue marker, and began writing in sloppy script next to the faded "9." *750K*, "Payroll," he said. *1.5M*, "Our credit line." He tapped at the board making little blue dots, and said, as if to himself, "If we don't reduce payroll, we'll be out of cash in three months." He turned and slowly scanned the room. A small blue line had been inadvertently scribed on his wrist.

"But without employees, who would do the work?" he asked Sally, who he had hand picked from the typesetting staff to join management.

She looked back at Dan, both hands on the table. She was a hundred pounds overweight, wore a pink "Grandmother" sweatshirt, and was one of the most knowledgeable typesetters in the country, and maybe she was realizing that being an executive wasn't so great. "Couldn't we just cut everyone's pay a little?"

There was a general murmur. Kathy, a Scandinavian-looking manager from St. Paul, who was visiting Iowa for the second time in her five years with the company, said, "My people would never go for that—they have lots of job options in town."

Minnie spoke over her, "I could have Kenny work on the next payroll run. We couldn't cut the pay for this one."

Dan sat down and drummed his fingers slowly on the table. He drummed from thumb to pinky and back with an unbroken rhythm. He used to be a guitar player, or as he put it, "My uncle had an Elvis cover band, and when I was a young man he'd take me down to Baltimore Street where all the strip clubs and whorehouses were, and we'd play 'Blue Suede Shoes' behind a chicken wire fence." He lifted his head and gazed at the far wall, like a politician waiting for the reporters to quiet, watching everyone and no one. "Employees have to feel respected," he said calmly and tented those long fingers against his lips. "A pay cut will make everyone unhappy. We will be fighting every day against negative feelings towards the company. The option we have is to reduce the number of employees now. Then, if we do well—and we will—we'll be able to give raises to everyone and rehire some others back. It's the only way."

Kathy said, "What about benefits? What percentage of pay are they?"

Minnie responded, eyeing Kathy's blond hair with distaste, "We are negotiating new contracts for health care, but we have certain requirements to meet for the State."

In the pause Dan always gave before responding, I spoke up, "We have to cover eighty percent of healthcare, on average, based on our loan from Iowa, but the level of coverage isn't set." Minnie pursed her lips.

"We will be giving everyone the same or better benefits than before," Dan said, giving each word a slight pause at the end. "People expect their vacation and medical coverage. We did an asset purchase, and can set any policy we want, but the employees won't think that way. When they pull that check out of the envelope, they aren't going to care why it's smaller." He put on his drugstore glasses—as a lifetime glasses wearer, I was always appalled to watch him wrap his fingers around the lenses, but he didn't seem bothered by the oily smudges. "Now then, I'm thinking we need twenty." He picked up his list and read, "Applebee."

"Keep," Frank said over his own reading glasses that he had removed from his shirt pocket. More than anyone else in the room, Frank seemed to know that we would have to let people go to survive, or maybe he just had been through layoffs too many times in the past.

"Keep," Dan acknowledged. Frank made a tick mark next to the name.

Over the next hour, we went through the whole list and came up with two names not to be hired. The receptionist I had smiled at that morning, and a maintenance man who had been at the company for thirty-nine years. Unlike my father's unfair boss, Frank spoke warmly about the man, the compassion clear in his voice. "We're good friends and we've talked about this. He's ready to retire and he told me he wouldn't mind if I told him we had to."

Dan sighed and nodded. "He's a good man, and so are you, Frank. But we will have to do more to make sure the rest of us have a job." With another sigh, he flipped his pages back. "Applebee."

At six o'clock we were still going and several of the managers looked restless. "My wife expects me at five," Ron said, uncomfortably, when Dan asked if anybody had to get home. There were other engagements: a bowling league, kids to be picked up from school, Sally's mentally handicapped son had to be driven home from his job at the Pizza Hut.

"Then let's go home. We all have lives to live," Dan said. "We'll meet tomorrow at ten."

I went back to my office to answer e-mails from the handful of customers we had brought with us from Bembo and the telephone calls

Typo

from the local newspapers who wanted interviews. I called my girlfriend back in New York, then my sister, and then tried to talk to my father for a few minutes. "We'll have to have you out here soon," I said. "See what your money bought."

"You know I don't travel so good," he said.

"I know, but you never know about the future. Maybe you'll get a sudden urge to see your son the boss."

"You're probably right," he said. "But I've got a sandwich waiting for me in the fridge."

"Dan would love to see you too."

"Dan? He's out there with you?"

"We'd buy you all the sandwiches you want," I said.

"That so?" he asked, and I could hear the phone rustle against his long beard. "You tell Dan he's all right in my book."

"So you'll come?"

"You know," his voice had become stern and pleading, a mixture of telling me to stop asking and asking for help, "that I don't travel too good."

ℓ

"I noticed the janitor spends a lot of time cleaning up my wastebasket. When I came in this morning, it must have taken him ten minutes to empty that bucket," Dan said at the start of the second day of the executive meeting, and chuckled. "It's OK, I've got nothing to hide. If anybody here wants to go rooting through my desk, go right ahead. Although, I don't know what you're going to find other than a lot of Maalox." He rubbed his hands along his yellow and black tie. "I encourage all of you to leave your doors open too, and leave your desks unlocked. It's the new kind of company we are."

"I can't do that," Minnie said. "I've got everyone's payroll information.

We have laws we have to follow."

Instead of Minnie, Dan winked at Connie, "You're absolutely right, Minnie. There's definitely information we have to keep private and protected. You know I respect whatever you do." He put on his glasses, cleared his throat, smiled, and said, "Applebee."

I listened to the names being read over and over, while I rubbed an impression of the routed edge of the table into my employee list with my pencil.

"Jessie is someone we could let go."

"No, Jessie is the only one who can run the Dylux machine."

"What about Rob?"

"We were going to let Rob go."

"Rob's been with the company a long time, he could learn how to run the Dylux."

"Jessie could learn Rob's job also."

I didn't know these people, and each name wasn't a personal friend, someone I would recognize at the supermarket, or my son's friend's parents. On my mind were the loans that we had used to buy Clarinda. Financing had been maddening—banks had defined us as an existing business or a startup, and based on that definition they couldn't lend to us. Instead, we had to get credit from the company we bought Clarinda from: Household Finance. We owed Household both a $1.2 million term loan from the purchase and the $1.5 million revolving line of credit that we were burning through, as Dan had pointed out, at $750,000 a month. The term loan we had a few years on, but the revolver was due to expire at the end of 2000, only fifteen months away. Household had established the due date because they didn't want to be our bank forever, but this meant we had the combined pressure of reducing cost and getting in revenue to stay within the line while trying to find another lender.

Dan assured Household that another bank would give us credit by then, but privately he told me that only amazing gains in revenue and profit would bring in a new lender. "We'll have to snap this place into shape to convince another bank to let us keep it," he had said. "Or that revolver goes off against our head and we lose."

On my list, I doodled all the other debts we had taken on to buy Clarinda: State of Iowa, $400,000, the city of Atlantic, Iowa $50,000, the Southwest Iowa Coalition Foundation, $50,000. I'd spent the past year stumping around Iowa meeting John Deere-hatted councilmen to get those loans. And then there was all the money I owed my father. I drew a stick figure with a smiley face holding a bag of cash.

What really bothered me though was that Dan and I had been forced to personally guarantee the loans. "Why couldn't we borrow the money like any other company?" I had asked our lawyer in Omaha while signing page after page as he notarized away.

"Nobody just gives away anything in this country," he'd explained. "Without the guarantees you can hide behind the corporate shield. And if the company fails, you could just walk away. They want to know that you have a personal incentive to stick around."

"Losing my job and my father's inheritance isn't enough? They want me bankrupt, too, if we screw up? I thought that was the whole point of incorporating and hiring lawyers."

"Only because in this instance they're calling you a startup," the lawyer had said.

Two hours into day two and the 'no-hire list,' as our attorney called it, or the 'fire list,' as the employees called it, was up to eight names.

I thought about the competition. There were four or five typesetters as big, or larger, than Clarinda and at least a hundred smaller companies. Looming on the horizon were low-cost typesetters from India. Dan and I reminded ourselves and our customers over and over that the Indians' quality was poor and they didn't understand the publisher's needs, but we knew it was only a matter of time before they caught up. I drew a stick-figure map of India—nothing more than an upside-down triangle.

At five o'clock, we had eleven names.

"I know you know what you're doing," Dan said. "You are the

executives and this is your company as much as mine, and I trust you. So I say we stop." He put down his list. "You all have places to be, but I'd like to spend a little more time and go over the incentive plan I'd like you to help me design." He went to the board and started talking about a bonus pool to be made from profits and a stock option plan. He was determined not to let the meeting end on the negative note of the eleven people "not to be employed."

"Stock options?" Minnie asked. "For everyone?"

The next day, I called all the customers on the list Dan had given me before lunch and then looked at the cornfield swaying in the breeze. Shouldn't the boss do something other than just call customers and wait for Dan to tell me how to handle an account, ask me a technical question, or give me another customer?

I needed to see my new company. I walked around the corner from the "executive suite." Some prior manager had put up a wall that separated what were now Dan's office, my office, the conference room, and the HVAC closet from the rest of the plant. On the other side of the wall were customer service's cubicles, the offices of the plant manager, Accounting and Estimating. A door at the back led to Filing and Shipping. All of the actual typesetters sat at long desks in another room beyond that—as far away from the executive suite as you could get. As if nothing could be worse for the boss than accidentally running into an actual worker.

Most employees had been there for twenty years or so and, as I walked, I noticed that the man in the overalls, who worked for Minnie, was relatively well dressed compared to the majority of the staff. I counted seven pink 'World's Best Grandmother' sweatshirts and two blue ones. The desks were decorated in the same style: greeting cards, witty coffee mugs, and plush toys aplenty. Tomorrow, I decided, I would wear blue jeans instead of black ones.

I felt self-conscious walking into the typesetting area. I was out of place among workers who I was no longer one of. Until Dan's insistence had won me the business card title of President, my entire career had been as a computer geek sitting behind a screen, not as anyone's boss. My previous last three job titles had been 'Chief Scientist,' as in 'head of all the scientists'—which sounded great, except there were no other scientists.

The windowless room had five double rows of long tables, the same as in the lunchroom, each with two Macintosh workstations and stacks of manuscripts. Hallways and swinging doors led off to the loading dock, the art room, storage areas, the room that housed the Dolev (a several-hundred-thousand-dollar device for making film as part of the process of making printing plates and—ultimately—printed pages, a machine that was the size of a pizza oven and smelled so strongly of chemicals I wondered how anyone could spend all day in there), and other rooms I wouldn't discover for years.

In the middle of the afternoon most of the room was occupied, but nobody looked up or said "hello." Everyone was focused and determinedly busy, although not too busy—I watched one woman remove a stack of paper from the left side of her desk and put it back again a minute later.

I leaned awkwardly on one of the desks, my fingertips extended to keep balance like a lunar module carefully touching down. I tried to assume the posture of a boss who was easy to talk to, but not imposing. I didn't know any of the production floor employees, so I tried to make conversation while avoiding addressing anyone by name. I felt like a fake when I asked, "So what are you working on?" my voice a little high.

The grey-haired typesetter looked up at me like a grandmother being greeted by her youngest grandchild. "I'm working on first pages for this math book," she said, pointing to the manuscript I was leaning on. The pages were printed in regulation double spaced Times Roman and covered with corrections from a variety of editors, in a variety of colors—red for the copyeditor, green for the production editor, purple from the book designer, and blue from the author.

Typesetting marks abounded: use Garamond 14pt for the equations;

set the baseline 12pts after minor heads; the measure for excerpt examples should be 40ems. There was a handwritten page of material to insert stapled to the bottom. To me, the scrawled edits running up to the edge of the page were hard enough to read and, combined, they rendered the document barely legible, yet the screen in front of the grey-haired lady displayed a complex page with colorful, shaded sidebars, arrows pointing this way and that illustrating a frightening equation, and pictures of smiling puppies that somehow the author thought would help explain polynomials—all in all a beautiful page that recalled my high school math teacher, and proof that making that page required skill and experience.

When she was done, the proof pages would go back to the author and editor for a second, third or even fourth round before being sent to a printer like Quad Graphics in Davenport, Iowa, for printing and binding. It was the cycle of our lives. "We typesetters make the first copy, and printers make the rest," Dan always said.

"That's great! So, uh, who's it for?" I asked.

"The author is Wichowski."

As I would learn, books were always referred to by the author's name. If there were multiple authors, only the first got the honor of having his name bandied about in deepest Iowa. "But who's the publisher?" I asked.

"The publisher. Hmm. Let me check." She flipped through the job jacket and looked through the manuscript. Then she called out, "Josie, who's the publisher for Wichowski?"

"Prentice Hall," Josie said, looking up and smiling at me benignly.

"No, it's Mosby," another lady said, also looking up and smiling twice as benignly.

Josie picked up the telephone mounted on the back wall beneath a sign in large black letters, "NO PERSONAL CALLS!!" "Hi, it's Josie. David's back here and he wants to know who the publisher of Wichowski is. Yes, oh, it is Prentice Hall. I thought so."

I was glad they had gone to the trouble to find out for me, but that wasn't the point. "Prentice Hall is one of our biggest customers. Do you know who their parent company is?" I asked the room, although everyone had gone back to their computers.

The typesetter I had started with shook her head.

"They're owned by Pearson. Pearson also owns Addison Wesley Longman. They represent around twenty percent of our business."

She beamed at me. I felt like the grandchild trying to get his grandmother to really look at the overdue notice from the electric company.

I sat down. Dan had not sent me back here, but I knew he would want me to talk to her honestly. "Do you know how much we charge the customer for that page you have?"

She shook her head again. "I don't think we're allowed to know."

"Well, who's better qualified to say that you can know other than me?"

She looked at me blankly.

"Dan and I own the company."

Nervousness had crept into her expression. This was not my father's IBM. Employees hadn't been respected, and I didn't like it. I explained how each page was worth $25 and how Dan and I intended to use technology to get more pages per hour, and thereby get raises for her and everyone else. Maybe she believed me, maybe she didn't, but it was the truth, and the future, I was certain, would bear us out.

I continued my tour of the plant. On the floor of a storage closet I found a peculiar old machine with a keyboard and a paper tape coming out of it. It was an ancient Fairchild phototypesetter. An operator would have typed a line of type into the machine and then typed it again. If it was the same the second time, a bell rang and the text was encoded as holes in the paper tape. The double-check was required because it had no display of any kind. Another machine would transform the tape into film, which was assembled into pages by literally cutting and pasting. It had been the latest and greatest technology of the 1960s. It had transformed the industry, rendering what had taken days in mere hours. I took the green metal cover off and brought the machine, with its guts exposed, to my office where I placed it on the little table outside. Perhaps I would start a museum of great moments in publishing technology.

During my walk, someone had stuffed the inbox that was nailed to the wall outside my door with a week's worth of status reports. I couldn't imagine how anyone had been able to make any use of the hundreds of pages, and there was only one sure way to prevent the box from filling again: I tore it out of the wall, screws and all.

I looked at the Fairchild with its "trash" folder full of 30-year-old paper holes. I looked at my trashcan stuffed with a plastic inbox and useless reports. Meaningless routing of paper to inboxes was at an end. We were going to change the company like it had never been changed before, including technology improvements as significant as those Fairchild had made.

We were in business.

e

For dinner we selected Brunner's, by far the best restaurant in town. They called themselves a chain because there was another location in the Ozarks, although we only ever saw the one five blocks away on Washington Street.

We ate up front by the bar, rather than in the back dining room, because Jan, the bartender, let Dan change the TV channel to watch his Maryland Terrapins battle some other college basketball team. Besides, the only other patrons this late at night were a grey-haired woman and her aged mother who had an oxygen tank on wheels. I watched her pull out the feeder tube to take a quick puff of her daughter's cigarette.

Dan never understood how I could know the chemical symbol for Tungsten ("W"), but nothing about basketball, baseball, football, golf, or any professional, semi-pro, or college sport athlete other than Lance Armstrong.

"You know who Tiger Woods is, don't you?" he asked.

"Yes," I said and screwed up my face in mock concentration. "He does those ads for American Express." Dan had challenged my expectations about people. Growing up as a nerd who thought athletes were idiots by definition, he had convinced me that a man who was an avid sports fan and former jock in college could not only be my most trusted friend, but also as smart as my father—and in the case of understanding people, smarter.

"Speaking of American Express, was I right that little store would deliver to your father?" he asked.

I nodded. The call had been surprisingly easy. The owner of the deli had taken my credit card number and offered to bring a spiced ham sandwich to my father every day so that he wouldn't have to drive. The same had gone for the liquor store, in whose parking lot Dad had drunkenly broken off the side mirror of the Buick.

"See, kiddo, some people are good and some just don't care." He pushed away the plate and shook his head. "Those bastards at the liquor store were happy to take your credit card to keep him soused at home, but when you asked them to call the cops if your father looked like he was drunk, they pretended they didn't know him. I don't wish them ill, but—" He noticed I was looking sadly at my food. "—well at least he isn't driving and that's the thing."

"Can we talk about something else?" I asked.

"Of course, my boy." He didn't say "my boy" condescendingly, but like a father welcoming his son home after a long trip away, and it always reminded me how much I meant to him. "So what have you learned about our dear Clarinda's technology?" he asked while pointing at his beer glass. Jan promptly deposited a fresh Bud on the table.

I explained that the entire company had just one dial-up line to connect to the Internet.

He nodded. "I'm not surprised."

I told him the Internet is more than e-mail—although customers expected that too—but more importantly we should be researching software and typesetting issues. And we should be trying to get rid of the pile of those ancient dictionaries with the moldy bindings I had seen in the proofreading area. As for me, I told him, my girlfriend and I resolved Scrabble challenges online (stuck in Iowa, I was reminded that I should have been proud of her for beating me, rather than sulking all night when I lost).

"I thought you also said the Mac G3s are old hat," he said, his eyes on the TV. "Why don't you come up with a plan to buy all new computers?"

That caught me off-guard. I had just been thinking about a faster Internet connection.

"I was speaking to Luke at Household on Tuesday, and told him that you found out the computers were old. I also told him that the roof in Atlantic is leaking. Did you know that?" he asked.

"No," I said. How would I?

"I told Luke he'd sold us a bill of goods," he said and lit a cigarette. "He gave me $50,000 back, and we can spend that on whatever we like. That's our money." He held the cigarette away from me, propping his elbow on the empty chair next to him. "So why don't we start with $20,000? What will that buy in the way of new equipment?"

I could do that.

The next day, I called a meeting with the two tech support people, excited for my first chance to use my little conference table. A half-hour before they were due to arrive, Minnie came to see me. She had never gotten a financial degree, but she had outlasted every other person in the accounting department until she became the boss. She wore a lilac jacket with a large brass brooch.

"I thought you might want to take a look at this," she said, handed me a glossy file folder-style brochure from IBM, and sat down, hands clasped. Her nasal voice had a distinct undertone of reprimand and she smelled like menthol. How did she know I had worked at IBM? Or about my father bringing home tractor-fed scrap paper from work for me to color on as a child? Or my love-hate feelings for the company that betrayed my father's ethical beliefs, which they had created in the first place?

"I saw there was some extra money coming back from Household," she said, "and I thought we could finally upgrade the accounting server." The brochure suggested we could upgrade our System 36 to a used AS/400 for just $20,000. She couldn't read minds: she could read bank statements.

But why would I want to spend my entire equipment budget on the accounting department? Dan called all accountants "bean counters," and had warned me, "spend your money on bean counters, and there won't be any beans to count. I'd be perfectly happy to let them use yellow legal pads and pencils."

"I don't know," I said, flipping through the brochure—the AS/400 had beaten the 8100 system my father had pushed for in IBM's internal competition and cost him a promotion—"Isn't there a PC-based accounting system we could switch to?"

What I didn't know at the time was that the System 36 required a $50,000-a-year programmer to keep it running—the nice man who had given me my keycard.

"All the previous owners listened to my recommendations about technology," she said and frowned.

"Dan's pretty serious about only spending money on production. Have you talked to him about this?"

"He told me to see you," she said.

"Oh," I said, and fidgeted with the brochure. Another thing I didn't know: Minnie had already scheduled the IBM salesman whose card was stapled to the front to come see me.

"There's another matter," she said, and handed me an expense report form.

I hated expense report forms, and I had looked forward to being the boss so I never had to fill one out again. Did Bill Gates have to separate out his telephone bills from his room charges on his hotel receipts?

"I need receipts by law," she said, and poked at the form.

"Look," I said, trying to follow Dan's lead to be reasonable and not dictatorial, "I've got a lot of work to do to improve the company, and I don't want to waste time filling out expense reports. I know what the IRS needs, so this is what I'll do: Anything on my corporate American Express is a corporate expense. If I pay cash, I won't expense it—after all, the company or me, it's both my money. How's that sound?"

She frowned more severely. She reminded me of a landlady I once had who had threatened to withhold my security deposit because I had failed to dust the spot between the windowpane and the storm window.

Just then Jim, who had come down from Atlantic, and Penny, who had walked across the plant, showed up. As Minnie left, she made a, "un-hunn" sound as goodbye.

Jim wore a flannel shirt and with his full brown beard he reminded me of the sidekick guy from the television show *Home Improvement*. Penny was a short woman with a mass of waist-length black hair like that worn by the kind of people usually seen enjoying Renaissance festivals, except she didn't appear to enjoy anything.

The three of us in my orange conference chairs were cramped much closer together than I had expected. "I've got $20,000 to spend, how does that sound?" I asked, trying to keep my pen out of Penny's hair.

Jim made a soft "whoo-eee," and put his hand on his head.

"What I need from you both is a shopping list. What have you always wanted?"

Jim's shook his head as if I had just told him the price of corn had doubled.

"Apple's got a new operating system and servers, what do you think about those?" I asked.

"We just bought a Sun server," Penny said. "We've always had bad luck with the Apple servers."

"Well, it's just something to consider," I said. "We'll be buying new stuff every month. How about some of these?" I showed them the scroll wheel mouse I had brought with me, rolling through a few web pages. "Might make things easier for the typesetters,"

Jim nodded approval. "Pretty nifty."

"But they won't work with the old machines," Penny said. "And there'll be a lot of envy if some have it and some don't."

"Well," I said, wondering why it was so hard to convince a technology person to buy some technology, "The main thing is that I want to get Internet for everyone."

"All the service people?" she asked, pushing her hair out of her pale face.

"Sure," I said. "Everyone."

"What if people start downloading things?" she said. "You don't understand the people here. They don't know how to use computers."

"Well," I said, "Then we'll just have to give them instructions not to download anything." But what I wanted to say was, "If they don't know what they're doing, isn't that your fault?"

The next day Connie and Frank dropped by to discuss my plan for universal Internet access. Connie looked pained. Frank looked dragged along. "Is it true?" she asked.

I told them, yes, it was true that I didn't care what employees did with the computer when they weren't on the clock. As long as the work got done, why not let them use our equipment to advertise their garage sales or e-mail photos of their kid's last wrestling match? Even if they played a game online, they were still learning something about technology.

"People will get upset if they see someone else playing a game," she said.

I suggested that worrying about what someone else was doing was the only guaranteed waste of time, and Frank, against Connie's dour disapproval, smiled.

A month passed during which I visited customers and spent a few days at home in New York. Then I was back in Iowa. At the Super 8, the local youths were having a keg party.

"Beer cans float in the pool. In the Jacuzzi, they explode," the orthodontically challenged desk clerk said. "You know, I'm getting kind of sick of them coming over here and having parties while I have to stand over here working." She had been sleeping on the counter when I arrived.

She gave me the key for the "hot-tub honeymoon room" advertised on the sign outside. It was a twenty-by-twenty carpeted room with a four-person hot tub in the corner—as if someone had dropped it there. With no regular shower available, I would be reliving some Iowan's wedding night dream every morning.

At the office, someone had installed a replacement inbox on my desk and filled it with reports. On top was my expense report that I hadn't filled. Minnie had her clerks call up the airline, get copies of my tickets, staple them three-a-page to a sheet of paper, and present the assembled report for my signature. I toyed with the idea of writing: "What's this item? Please clear with management." But I knew my joke would not be appreciated, so I glumly signed it.

Wanting to focus on something positive, I headed for Penny's office to see how our plan for buying new computers was going. Her windowless room adjoined the network closet and both rooms were jam-packed with filing cabinets, blinking-light rack-mounted things, tapes, and cables, cables, cables. Tiny, cramped, and scented with computer fan exhaust, the room was, however, the most organized and tidy I'd ever seen. There wasn't even dust on top of the five-foot-high filing cabinet, which was impressive because it was taller than her.

To my surprise, Penny and Jim hadn't been able to come up with a single item to buy.

"OK, let's say five new G4s with all the software," I said.

She punched it in the computer and then went to her adding machine.

What's up with the adding machine? I wondered. I looked over her shoulder. She was using Quark, the same software we used to make pages, for her spreadsheet.

"Why don't you use Excel?"

"I'm comfortable with Quark."

"But it doesn't add numbers."

She rolled her shoulders. "I guess I'm a little afraid of it."

What kind of tech support person was afraid of Microsoft Excel?

l

When the new computers showed up, all $20,000 worth, the UPS guy piled them in a Pharaonic pyramid in the shipping area. He must have thought it was quite funny because it had been very carefully done. At least that's what I imagined, because Dan, who was in Iowa while I was home in New York, told me about it.

"How did you get me to come out here by myself?" he asked.

"I had to go to the doctor, and the only appointment—"

"What's that sound?!" Dan shouted.

"It's a fire engine and an ambulance, going opposite ways!" I responded. My apartment in downtown Manhattan lay at the intersection of Bowery and Houston Street. Every emergency vehicle going East or West, uptown or downtown got stuck at the traffic lights under my apartment. Through some perverse law of acoustics, the sound became louder as it rose, ricocheting off surrounding buildings until it came blasting into my apartment. The time for a siren to approach, deafen, and then die out was twelve minutes; more at rush hour. Over time, I became accustomed to the sounds, and therefore less and less able to take it.

"Did I tell you the boxes are still piled up?" Dan shouted.

"I e-mailed Penny," I yelled back. "She said she was installing them." I picked up a piece of lint. I had hated it when my mother swept dust up with her hand, and now here I was doing it—wiping my fingers along the low counter that separated my couch and the stove. "Open kitchen," the real estate person had called it.

"She's chipping them off the pile like they're made of marble. I've never seen it take so long to get a computer installed. Now what's that sound?"

It was the Thursday afternoon Krishna parade of tambourines and chants. "I'll call her," I said.

"Good man. Now, what do you think about opening an office in Syracuse?" Dan puffed on a cigarette. He allowed himself to break the rules and smoke inside. "I've been talking to Art, up at Gryphon Printing, and he tells me that they are thinking of getting out of typesetting and focusing on printing. He might be able to swing some accounts our way and I told him we might want to hire some of those good typesetters up there. We could put in a few computers, rent a little space. Art could sell for us, he knows a lot of publishers, and they owe him a few favors—"

I was glad that, unlike yesterday, I hadn't been in the tub when Dan called. Getting out would have made a splash he would have heard, even over the sirens. I'd sat there until my teeth chattered. Today, I sat down on the couch, feet up, for the rest of Dan's morning lecture.

When he finished, I called Penny.

"I've got to do a burn-in test, David," Penny said, annoyed that I'd interrupted her day. "Sometimes they're not configured right and I've got all the software to install."

"Can't anyone help you? Maybe Jim can come down from Atlantic?"

"What's that sound?" she asked. It was Friday, and the Lubovitcher Jews were rolling a dozen mitzvah tanks (Winnebagos with loud speakers) blaring *Hava Nagila* into the traffic jam.

"Jim doesn't understand my process," she shouted.

ℓ

Back in Iowa with Dan, I had one good box waiting and many bad ones.

The good one contained a bicycle. Dan had suggested I buy myself a reward for taking over Clarinda. Growing up, my father had required me to make a spreadsheet comparison a la Consumer Reports—which he subscribed to—to buy anything from a video game system (denied) to a Radio Shack electricity lab (approved). So at the bike store, I felt a rush of freedom, like turning on the air conditioning with the car windows rolled down, when I asked. "What do you have for a newly minted millionaire?"

The bad boxes contained half the new computers still in a pyramid. While I unpacked the bike on the floor of his office, Dan fumed. "That little troll is killing us!" He raised his voice, "are you paying attention to me or the bike?"

I reluctantly put down my Allen wrench and apologized.

I reminded Penny how important the new computers were to productivity and how important that was to profit and, ultimately, to her and everyone else's pay. I mentioned the Indians. She repeated, "I'm working as fast as I can."

How was I supposed to change the company if I couldn't get one employee to do what I asked?

ℓ

At Brunner's, Dan was only able to eat half of a small filet—he'd recently gotten his bad teeth replaced with dentures that constantly hurt him. He probed the inside of his cheek with his tongue while watching me eat my double-fist sized pork tenderloin. Nearby Villisca proclaimed itself the Pork Capital of Southwest Iowa on an enormous iron pig at the Route 71 junction.

"How is your old dad doing?" he asked.

"Three bottles a week," I said flatly.

"I know you're feeling like he's let you down, kiddo, but he's not doing this to hurt you."

"What am I supposed to do? Keep calling him when he's too drunk to talk? Go out there and fix him?" I couldn't help feeling instantly angry whenever Dan suggested my father—who had raised me to remember to refill the humidifier every week—was not responsible for his own actions.

"My boy, you'll never know what your old man went through with your mother—taking care of someone for all those years changes a person."

"So I can't change him back?" I cut the mandatory pineapple slice that came with the pork into tiny pieces with the edge of my fork.

"Would it make you happy if I called him tomorrow? Let him know he has someone near his age to talk to if he wants? Tell him how good we—you—are doing?"

I nodded.

He pushed away his plate, and upended a Benson and Hedges pack to get the last cigarette out. "Here, this should amuse you." He fished a yellow Post-It out of his pocket. "This is a personal trip to Las Vegas, please remit cost to the company," it said.

Dan's last ticket to Iowa had been issued from TWA's reservation center in Vegas. Apparently that confused Minnie into thinking Dan was spending company money on personal trips to Nevada.

He crumpled the note in his ashtray. "Did you know she told me I shouldn't get reimbursed for my time out here because Iowa is company headquarters? She said I can't submit an expense report for travel to HQ! I asked her if I should be submitting my expenses for Baltimore then, and she said, 'you should take that up with Household.' She still has the unmovable belief that there is some higher authority at the company than you and I." He finished his beer and Jan, unprompted, brought another.

"Thank you, Hon." I used to think Dan was being old-man sexist saying, "Hon," but then I spent a day in Baltimore where every waitress, tour-guide, or bus driver called me, "Hon." "Inmates my boy. The inmates are running the institution. Minnie still thinks her job is to protect the employees from the 'bad men' sent in from the evil bank. She can't accept that the company's money is our money, any more than she can accept we are good to the employees because we want to be, not because Household gave us a loan.

"My boy, she thinks this is her company. When I asked Edna for sales reports, she checked with Minnie if it was OK to give them to me. And think about this, kiddo, Minnie's got four other clerks working for her. Do you have a secretary to run around the plant carrying out your orders? No, you're too busy being chided by the janitor for leaving a dirty cup in the sink—you didn't think I'd heard, did you?"

My face reddened. "So why don't we just fire them? Why spend so much time trying to convince them to listen to us?"

"We need her and everyone else to do their job. If she doesn't run payroll, who will? You?"

"Maybe," I said defensively.

He stubbed out his cigarette. "My son Ben loves me. He such a good kid and he doesn't like that I'm out here all the time now, but he trusts me to keep loving him. He knows how much he means to me." He searched the pack with a long finger for a potentially missed cylinder. " But the people here don't know us. They don't know how much you love your father. They don't know that they can trust us." He pulled his finger out—there was nothing left—and crumpled the box. "Kiddo, we did not build this, we inherited it, and it's up to us to change it. Are you with me?"

"You know I am," I said. Why did he think he had to ask?

"That's my boy," he said and smiled, showing his shiny white dentures, and rubbing at his leathery cheek to dull the pain.

ℓ

The challenge was to break Clarinda's union-shop-without-a-union production system. Each book required a job estimator, a customer-service person, a setup person, a keyboarding manager, outside keyboarders, one or more typesetters, an art specialist, a "proofer" (it took me a while to figure out this was the person who ran the laser printer), one or more quality-control people, a system-setup person (a whole position to set up file folders on the system), a technology specialist for when things went wrong (they always went wrong), a production supervisor, a plant manager, a shipping clerk, and a biller. Clarinda was known for its quality because their wildly redundant process caught mistakes before they got to the customer. There had to be a better way.

I decided to implement my "Great Idea" program I had been thinking of for years. It would give money directly to employees who made process improvements and institutionalize a culture of innovation through reward. I knew it was a good program because it wasn't my idea—I'd stolen it from IBM, where they called it the "cost effectiveness program." My commemorative plaque and CD player for four consecutive cost effectiveness ideas was among the items in the closet in my father's house.

I told Dan that the Great Idea had been my dream as an employee, and Clarinda's employees should already know how to fix their company. He indulged me, "You're fired up. See what they make of it."

What they made of it? How could anyone resist cash?

I posted a five-page submission guideline, complete with examples, in the lunchrooms of the Atlantic and Clarinda plants. When I got my first Great Idea submission I wasn't terribly surprised to see that it was one of my examples. I decided to be generous and rewarded the three employees who had copied it—at least they were trying. There followed a flurry of a couple dozen applications. It was a stretch to consider any as productivity improvements, such as one suggestion to unbend staples for reuse, but I accepted most of them on the principle of not squashing initiative. And then the suggestions stopped. Nobody could think of anything, not even a scam. Passing through the lunchroom some time later, I noticed someone had quietly replaced the Great Idea information on the bulletin board with a calendar featuring pictures of kittens in baskets. Maybe Dan knew something I didn't.

Shirley, the Clarinda plant manager, knowing I was looking for employees interested in technology, told me of a proofreader with a personal Web page. Intrigued, I sought her out in the middle of her shift: midnight. Pages and plants surrounded her. We had an informative discussion about selecting ferns that could thrive on fluorescent lighting. I said I'd seen her web page and would happily get her any software or training she wanted.

I got her the software, but when I checked back a week later, she hadn't opened the box. As I trudged to my office through the dark corridors, I was disheartened. The next day, Dan corrected me, "What's important, David, is that you showed her, and anyone she talked to, that we are willing to support change, whether or not she was ready to start making web pages. We will lick this thing."

$$\ell$$

We had to. Our competition in India worked for one-thirtieth the pay of Iowa. Dan planned to do some of our work in Manila with our old employer Bembo—who still had the Philippine typesetting operation he had built for them—but he intended to keep growing our American plants as well. "We will be a low cost provider, not a cheap one," he said, "If we do our work right the first time, we will make a profit."

"That sort of sounds like 'no duh'," I commented. "I mean, isn't it obvious?"

"Not in Clarinda," he said. "Or have you seen us do an alteration?"

Alterations were the gravy of the typesetting business. When a manuscript arrived from a publisher it was supposedly a finished work, yet after the author and editors reviewed proof pages there were invariably changes. Typesetting companies charged for these "by the line," at a typical price of $1.25 per. For example, if you deleted the word *changes* from the above sentence and four lines changed because they wrapped differently, Clarinda would charge $5.

The reason for this excessive calculation goes back to when lines had to be remade by hand with either a hammer on lead or an X-Acto knife on film. Using a Macintosh there was no such issue, and far fewer Band-Aids. However no typesetter was about to tell the publishers it was a scam akin to charging for shipping on an electronic download (we did that, too). Given that a good operator could do fifty to sixty alterations an hour, that's pretty easy money, and should have been our highest-margin work.

Some publishers ran their own alteration rip-off. For new writers who didn't know better, they charged the alterations back to the author at double our price. Some of the India-based typesetting companies—not knowing a good thing when they saw it—had started offering alterations for free, cutting the cost of a book in half and killing the American typesetting company's profits. Publishers who got the free Indian deal were careful not to tell their authors.

At Clarinda alterations were not only unprofitable; they were universally loathed. Dan invited Frank as general manager, and Ron as estimating manager, to explain Clarinda's correction process at his slightly-larger-than-mine conference table. Ron, who had just come back from his weekly haircut, began, "Well, first Customer Service counts 'em."

"How does Customer Service know how many lines will be altered? They aren't making the changes." Dan said, sitting at his desk, rolling and unrolling the end of his tie.

"I always wondered that, myself," he said.

Dan chuckled. "Well, I've been wondering too."

Frank gave a small "huh," which, for him, was like doubling over on the floor.

"Then maybe we should change the process?" Dan asked.

"Well, I don't know," Ron said. "Who would count the alts?"

"At every company I've ever run," Dan said, "The changes come in. A typesetter gets right on 'em. They make a little tick sign on the bottom of the page for each." I slumped lower in the chair. I had heard Dan's plan so many times, but he liked me by his side while he drove them towards his goal—and nothing but the most detailed self-examination would get them to understand.

"Well, I don't see why not," Ron said. At least Ron, who now reminded me of a retired Merv Griffin-era talk show host, always agreed with Dan.

"That's an option," Frank said.

"How do you think Shirley would feel about that, Frank?"

"That's a point," Frank said. I liked Frank. I really did, and not just because Dan kept telling me how much I liked Frank. He was so calm and never angry. And how can you hate someone who hardly says anything?

"Let's get Shirley in here, then. David, would you page her?" Dan asked.

I quickly deferred. Paging meant dialing a code on the phone that connected you to every loudspeaker in the plant. I had no desire to be broadcast my voice over the intercom system. Ron made the call.

Shirley sat down next to me, and got halfway through her explanation before becoming uncertain, "you know, I'm not sure what the typesetters do with the rundown. I know they need it. I can call Sally, if you like."

"Get her in here," Dan said.

We rolled a chair in from my office for Sally. "…and that's it. Then it goes back to service."

"And what do they do with it?" Dan asked.

"That's Connie's domain."

Connie moved some of Dan's papers off a chair he had been using as a filing cabinet to the floor. We were now seven in an office meant for two or three. "…Then I give it to accounting for billing," she said.

Dan nodded to Ron.

"I'll get Minnie," he said.

Minnie chose to stand in the doorway. "Jess puts them in the System 36."

In sum, the Clarinda alteration process was:

1. Alterations arrive from the publisher. If the overnight delivery was late, the package sits for a day.
2. Every page is stamped with a consecutive number. In other words, give the book our own redundant page numbers.
3. A customer-service rep records every page with an X or an OK on a "rundown" form.
4. The rep counts the number of alts, making their best guess since they aren't doing the typesetting.
5. The typesetter (who does the actual work) goes through every page looking for alterations—ignoring the rundown form.
6. Quality Control (QC) checks the alts. The QC person makes a personal rundown and sends just the error pages back into production by separating them from the job.
7. A typesetter fixes the errors and sends them back to QC.
8. The QC person checks the pages again, fixes their rundown form, and puts all the pages back together.
9. Billing takes the Customer Service count and bills.

Our process was, technically speaking, madness, because alterations are always rush jobs. Dan's preferred way of solving a problem was not sweeping action, but to talk slowly, clearly, relentlessly. His tide of words went on for hours. One by one people escaped, but it wasn't league night, so Frank was stuck, and Ron's hair was already sharpened to a point, so he had no excuse either.

Dan's style reminded me of the way my father corrected my behavior as a child. He would sit down by the fireplace, motion me over to the blue high-backed chair, and talk at me until I agreed with everything he said about finishing my homework or not biking over my mother's peonies, and the pain of listening to him tell me how I was wrong over and over from every angle made me want to avoid those lectures at all cost. I excused myself and went next door to my office to continue listening at a distance while answering some email.

The meeting went on past sunset. I started up a game of *Age of Empires* and took over the ancient world twice before I heard Dan on the phone with Helen and his teenage son, Ben. At the Ice House—too late for tenderloin at Brunner's—he re-emphasized his plan as if he had read through my silence in the meeting to my frustration with the need to endlessly repeat.

"There is no point in reprimanding an employee or just demanding things be done my way without their understanding," he told me over a brown-at-the-edges salad. "They won't work any better or faster. If you reprimand or demand, they will never listen. You might as well fire them—and if we fire them, who will do the work?"

Dan was right. My father had been right. The Pennys, Minnies, and midnight proofreaders of the world could only be reformed, slowly, with respect.

$\mathcal{l}$

"David," Dan said, "I want you to come in here and see what you think of my idea."

"Just a second—" I was at last on the phone with the Clarinda *Herald*, filling them in on the details of our acquisition of the company. When the issue appeared the next Wednesday (the *Herald* printed once a week), I planned to clip out the article and mail it to my father. "—Yes, Iowa will always be headquarters. Yes, thanks. Always glad to let you know what we are up to."

I walked into Dan's office.

"Sorry to interrupt you, my boy. I didn't know you were on the phone with the press." I was aggravated for a moment, but his "my boy" was said so warmly, that I was left with only anger at myself for the insubordination of feeling bothered.

"How did it go?" he asked.

"Fine. No problems."

"No lynch mob coming to get us?"

"I don't think so."

Waiting for the banter to finish was Sally. Since she weighed over two hundred fifty pounds she had been careful to sit in a chair without arms that might, as I had seen happen once, become unmanageably difficult to get out of.

"Good. Sally and I were just discussing starting a real training department. The first in the company's history, and putting her in charge of it."

Sally and I had first met during our initial "due diligence" visit in the summer of 1999. She had told me then, after a few standard niceties, all the things that were wrong with the company. I had liked her instantly.

"What do you think of that?"

I told them I thought it was a great idea.

"What I'd like you and Sally to do is find a spot to put the trainers," he said.

Over the years, her skill and speed had gotten her attention, and attention got her demoted because of her constant insubordination. Once a former owner had yelled at her about a customer complaint.

"It's a problem with the Chakin font, not us. I already sent a fix, Mr. Blowhard," had been her response.

"Well, don't let it happen again," was all the flustered man could say.

While it was true she'd fixed the problem, there was no Chakin font. She'd made it up because he'd pissed her off—and if he ever repeated the problem to someone else, which he did, he would look like a fool, which he was. The only reason she didn't get fired was because she was the only one who could fix the tough jobs. She had survived by being indispensable. Although, before Dan had decided to put her on the executive committee, she had been shuffled off to a workstation in a far corner, curtained away from everyone by several rows of high-walled booths.

"Sally may be the only Iowan who understands irony," Dan said and winked at her. "But that hole they've got you in just isn't going to cut it anymore. Not for our number one trainer."

Sally clasped and unclasped her hands: she wasn't used to the praise.

"How about the hall next to the proofreaders?" I suggested.

"You mean the one where the Audrey and her staff sit?" Sally asked.

"Sure," I said. "I mean, shouldn't Audrey be closer to her typesetters anyway? She's got three doors and the Dolev room between her and her employees."

"Sounds like a plan," Dan said.

The next week Frank moved Audrey and her staff to the production floor and moved training in. One of the rooms was a maintenance closet full of tools with a shower stall. We ripped it all out, carpeted, painted the walls, and gave Sally her first real office. The other offices were for trainers yet to be hired and two classrooms.

I found her plugging in machines in the big training room, a software install CD clenched between her teeth like a scabbard. She wasn't going to wait for Penny.

"Next week, first class," she muttered, lips still around the disk.

It wasn't my Great Idea. It was better.

ℓ

On a cold Monday in December I was back at home in New York. Over the previous weekend, my girlfriend had arranged a surprise party for my 33rd birthday, which was a surprise because my birthday is in November. But all of November had come and gone with me in Iowa—including the first Thanksgiving that I hadn't spent with my sister and father since my mother died. As I walked between appointments I thought about my call home that day. My sister, Carol, had picked up the phone, "How's the turkey in Iowa?" she asked.

"Corn fed," I said. "How's dad?"

"Drunk."

I told her how sorry I was she had to go without me.

"Are you a millionaire yet?" she asked.

"On paper."

"Well, that's something, right?"

Walking the crowded streets in New York, going from Oxford University Press to Thomson and now to McGraw-Hill, brought an excitement of success I had begun to lose driving through the barren winter fields of Iowa. The meeting at Oxford arranged by our new salesperson Larry—who played up his getting fired by our Indian competitor, Bookers, to get the appointment—had gone well: we would be starting a multi-volume encyclopedia worth nearly fifty thousand dollars—five times more than an average textbook. At Thomson, I visited an old friend who managed one of their legal publishing divisions. We played ping-pong in his office. As I checked in with McGraw-Hill security at One Penn Plaza across the street from the General Post Office engraved with the slogan, "Neither Wind Nor Sleet Nor Snow." I was, in my opinion, the very model of American entrepreneurship—self-made achievement consisting of loyalty, ethics, and good grades in school. I only wished my father could truly be proud of me.

McGraw-Hill had, as Dan said, "Not a mountain, but a mountain range of books." Hilda, our salesperson, visited them weekly, and had, at last, landed a small amount of work. I had been called in to discuss Clarinda's year 2000 readiness (the millennium bug! Run for your life!)

I looked in the mirror as the elevator silently whisked me to the 38th floor. I was wearing my New Yorker uniform: black dress pants and a black sweater. I straightened my wire frame glasses. When the doors opened on a dimly-lit lobby full of plush but empty chairs, and a frowning receptionist in a suit, I started to feel unsure.

"Hilda spends a hundred dollars on dinner every time she goes to visit them," Dan had told me. "I thought it was for dinner with the customer, but it's just for her and her fat face, alone."

"Why don't we fire her, if she won't listen to you?" I asked.

"That's not the way, kiddo. It's the wrong message," he had said. "And who else will sell to McGraw and Mosby?"

The receptionist ushered me into a conference room also dimly lit—what did they think they were? A posh boutique on Madison Avenue? The walls were lined with elementary school textbooks and in the chairs were two dour managers. I wished I'd worn a suit.

A lumpish man with the large jowls of a friendly used car salesman had on a brown suit—the color preferred by businessmen who like to say, "I'm from Missouri. That's the show me state." The other was the large VP of production who looked alarmingly like Hilda. She was wearing what I surmised to be her best suit and a thick plastic badge with her name and the words "VP of Production." I'd never seen a badge on any other McGraw employee. She must have had it specially made.

The consultant unfurled his millennium questionnaire. I'd already responded to it, and this meeting was to go over my answers. McGraw and other publishers spent untold sums on consultants who in turn sent surveys to the likes of me about year 2000. We laid out book pages. What exactly might go wrong with a book page when the clock ticked over?

"Let's discuss your disaster recovery plan."

I guessed what they might like to hear, which I admittedly was making up as I went. I finished with, "If something goes wrong it's because all of the computers are fundamentally unable to operate in 2000, and if that's the case, there are probably a lot bigger things to worry about than badly kerned text."

They were not amused.

At that point, I thought I should try turn a bad meeting about vaporous computers into a good meeting about selling them on Clarinda. I told them we were investing in new equipment and our employees. I explained how we would give back to our American employees because of our Manila plant versus our competition in India who was simply looking for the lowest-cost labor. "We have to win your heart as a customer. We hope that by making ourselves the best company in the world with the most knowledgeable staff and competitive pricing that you will come to us and stay with us. We know we can't hold onto you like we did in the past just because we have your old film for reprints. We have to earn your business."

"What's that about film?" the VP asked.

Film is used to etch printing plates, and also for reprints. Often we would get jobs just because we had film stored in Iowa. We had a couple of Dolev machines that churned the stuff out.

"Oh, you know," I said, launching into Mr. Technology Guy mode, "direct to plate is coming along so film will likely be dead in five, maybe ten years at the outside. We are focused on services that are going to be important to you. For example, PDF files. Many of our customers are asking about them and we are already buying equipment—" I stopped. The VP didn't look well. She leaned forward on the table, her badge waving from its pin.

"We have several large film projects with you! Don't you know that?!?" she stammered.

I was confused. I didn't know they had film with us, but I didn't see any problem. I was just talking about the future. It wasn't like the several-ton Dolevs were going to wander out of the plant. They were sitting there humming away turning out film.

The next day, I took a train down to Baltimore. As I walked into Dan's office, he said, "What on Earth were you wearing yesterday? I'm hearing you put Johnny Cash to shame. 'The Man in Black' is all Hilda can talk about."

Too nervous to sit down, I shifted from foot to foot recounting the meeting, when the phone rang. It was Hilda, and Dan put her on speakerphone. "I just spoke to Loni. I've convinced her not to pull the project, but she doesn't like us anymore. She had millions of dollars of film to send to us and David really ruined it."

"Millions of dollars of film? Huh." He puffed a cigarette. "That's not good, of course, but film is low-margin work we can only do in Iowa. What about some nice juicy high-margin typesetting that we can do anywhere?" he said.

Unfortunately, Hilda's commission plan wasn't based on margin. "But they have typesetting vendors. It'll be at least a year to hope for anything after David's visit," she said, unaware Dan was making me listen. "He doesn't understand business. He should not be talking to customers."

Dan calmly listened to Hilda complain more about me—his lips pursed contemplatively. After hanging up, he said, "The man in black. You could have worn a suit, my boy. What were you thinking?" He stubbed out the cigarette in a chipped coffee mug. "I know. I know. Who can be expected to wear a suit to meetings nowadays? Right? Half the publishers don't wear them anymore. You couldn't have known what that VP was all about." He put on his reading glasses, picked up a report that he scanned for a few seconds and then put down. "She was looking for a reason to get rid of us. It was my fault for not going over what the meeting would be about beforehand. But I know you won't make this kind of mistake again," he said and picked up the report again. "What's done is done."

I felt like I had just run over my mother's peonies with my bike. I had let him down. Hilda was horrible, but it didn't matter. I'd lost business, and Dan had taught me better.

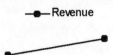 Revenue

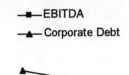 EBITDA
Corporate Debt

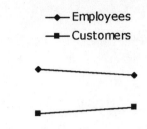 Employees
Customers

My Net Worth

Locations

Clarinda
Atlantic
Baltimore
St. Paul
New York

Revolver

Revenue	$8,000,000
EBITDA	$0
Corporate Debt	$2,000,000
Employees	100
Customers	50
My Net Worth	$100,000
Revolver Expires	9 Months

Returning to Manila

March 2000

I GOT OFF THE PLANE IN MANILA, DAZED. There was the fourteen-hour flight, of course; then, Mr. Important Business Man that I was, I had bought myself a first class ticket, which backfired the instant the "no smoking" sign blinked off and the man behind me lit up and maintained two cigarettes, one in his mouth and one in his hand, for the rest of flight. Contributing further to my irritated disorientation was the fact that I wasn't supposed to be here and I wasn't supposed to be picked up by the man frantically waving me down after I exited customs.

But Dan wanted me here, now, so I forced a smile and made my way through the swarms of Filipinos reuniting with their families and hundreds of ubiquitous Shetland pony-sized *balikbayan* cardboard boxes of treasures like microwave ovens and religious icons sent home from overseas. A third of the nurses, many ocean going crews, and virtually all cruise ship dance bands in the world are Filipinos who send their wages and knickknacks back to their families.

'The Betrayer,' aka Anthony, grabbed my luggage, a single duffel bag. Just under five feet tall, with slicked back hair and dark sunglasses, he sported a Dan-inspired button down shirt and khaki slacks reminiscent of a salesmen trying to hustle a convenience store owner to buy an off-brand of cheap Eastern European cigarettes.

We walked silently across the horizon-less airport parking lot. His rust-red Toyota was littered with baby toys and cassettes of 60s psychedelic music, which he pushed out of my way before we began the hour drive through city streets and alleys to get from Manila airport to Manila itself.

"Just like I remember it," I said, as I tried to un-wedge my feet from the jam of foot-well plastic.

This was my third trip to Manila. The previous ones were for Datadata, a keyboarding company that retyped law books into CD-ROMs in the early 90s. It was at Datadata that I had first met Dan and where he had pioneered his "offshore model" as head of the publishing division: a typesetting operation in Baltimore complemented by a keyboarding and typesetting facility in Manila. Central to our dream for Clarinda, therefore, was just such an overseas group—which we had with our previous employer, Bembo, but things there were getting complicated.

The Betrayer and I were magnificently stuck in traffic. Manila jams lasted twenty-three hours a day—there must have been at least one hour of empty streets. Around us, the highway appeared to be the last resting place of all Japanese, Korean, and Chinese buses, as well as that peculiar Filipino transport, the *jeepney*, which used to be a stretched out WWII jeep. Nowadays, Filipinos made new ones out of highly buffed corrugated steel and painted the travel routes in garish yellow, orange, and green. "Makati, Laguna, Manila City" said the one we'd been stuck next to for an hour. Dozens of men and women squished together wearing pressed long-sleeved white shirts because the ride cost a nickel a mile, compared to twenty cents for a crumbling, but air-conditioned, Chinese bus.

As we inched forward a few feet per minute, I had plenty of time to contemplate benevolent versus non-benevolent capitalism. Outside, the wealthy business district of Makati was crowded with skyscrapers, but underneath the elevated "South Super Highway" we rode along, and squeezed between a concrete wall and the railroad tracks, was a miles-long, twenty-foot wide shantytown where people lived in tin huts with dirt floors and hung their laundry in the shadows of the glass and metal buildings.

"What is Dan planning for me?" he asked as the Doors' "Light My Fire" blared reed-ily from the one working speaker.

Dan and I had left Datadata in 1997 to pursue our typesetting dreams at Bembo, another Philippine-based keyboarding company. Anthony, who had been the manager of the typesetters at Datadata in Manila, had come along with us. About the same age as me, he too was a young man on the make. He was also a Dan favorite, and Dan had frequently counseled him on personal problems and bailed him out of gambling debts—so much so that Dan was the godfather of his baby son.

"Why don't you tell me what you want, Anthony, and I'll see what we can do."

The plan had been for Bembo to buy Clarinda with Dan and I as the managers, but when they had trouble coming up with the money, Anthony had panicked and fled, taking half the staff with him to a competitor—jeopardizing relations with the customers and potentially scuttling our dreams.

"I want to work with Dan again."

"Well, don't we all?"

The rest of our trip was spent discussing Anthony's family and my airplane ride. I wouldn't let him know what I was really thinking.

After we bought Clarinda on our own, Bembo had remained our Philippine partner providing critical keyboarding and typesetting, but now that relationship was deteriorating geometrically and my reason for flying to Asia was to see if we had to make our own facility.

That's why Anthony was my escort. I thought I'd never see him again, but Dan was always ready to forgive. "We might have a use for him, yet. Best to keep him around," he had said, ever hopeful Anthony would remember all he had done for him.

$\mathcal{L}$

That night, at the aptly named Shangri-La hotel, my room was appointed in modern American-mini mogul with a marble bath and separate shower, but I didn't enjoy the fine linens. Unable to sleep, I recalled my last visit to Manila. Datadata had saved money by using a corporate apartment. One night I looked into the extra bedroom, which was bare except for an upturned television box. I turned on the light. I picked up the box—I knew I shouldn't, but I was compelled. Instantly bugs of every size, from little crawly ones to Hollywood horror film specimens, darted for the darkness of the corners. I dropped the box, turned out the light, and slept with the bulb on in my room and a hammer—the only effective insecticide—in my hand.

In the morning, I didn't feeling very prepared to meet with Jose Bembo, the father of the brothers who ran the company and the money behind it. It would be the first time I had ever spoken to Jose, and I didn't have high hopes. He derailed the purchase of Clarinda twice. The first time he had spooked the venture capitalists with his unusual accounting methods—he didn't like to pay social security taxes in the Philippines or the U.S. "If an employee needs money, they can come see me," he was rumored to say. The second time he'd broken his promise to personally put up money to buy Clarinda if the VC deal fell through.

I was kept cooling my heels for an hour. Not easy in an un-air conditioned anteroom in the withering Manila summer, but good for reflecting on a partnership that mirrored the psychosis of our being former employees who bought the former employer's largest customer, and now used them as a vendor. Our arrangement was magnificently roundabout. Dan still sold keyboarding work for Bembo for a commission (including sales of keyboarding from us at Clarinda). Bembo also paid him to manage the Baltimore office he had created, where the half dozen or so typesetters were paid by Bembo, but essentially worked for Clarinda. Dan was negotiating an official transfer, but there was the matter of the equipment, which Bembo had bought, and the lease for the office itself. Absolute cooperation from Bembo was required, lest we risk losing customers by disrupting their work—like repaving a highway still open to traffic.

At the same time, Clarinda needed to send a lot more keyboarding and typesetting to Bembo or we would be unable to compete with India. And we couldn't ramp up with the relationship in limbo. Not that Bembo was the only challenge for sending work overseas. Despite the fact that Dan expected to use those profits to grow Iowa—an average book sent to Manila could keep an American employed for a month—Iowa employees routinely foiled the process. Pages were sent to Manila without instruction, and color-coded corrections faxed in black and white. Work sent from Iowa to Baltimore suffered the same errors, but the Baltimore employees weren't afraid to complain if something was wrong. The Filipinos figured it was their job to try to puzzle it out without asking questions.

Nevertheless, Bembo had taken the position that, as Dan said, "They know we are over a barrel and are seeing what happens if they kick it." Work was shoddy and late. Payrolls in Baltimore and the Bembo typesetting division in Manila were late. Dan was not getting any of his promised commissions. It was their way of negotiating.

At last I was ushered in. Jose's office was a large open space, bigger than the one that housed thirty Filipino typesetters outside, and surrounded by senior staff in pressed white shirts who ran his various enterprises—everything from steel to imported copiers. They eyed each other and me from their spotless desks like courtiers waiting for the best moment to ease a blade into someone's back. In the center, Jose's enclosed office was as luxurious as the antechamber of his sycophants was sparse. He wore a simple white shirt that silkily conveyed it was much more expensive than anyone else's simple white shirt.

"How are things in the States?" he asked.

"Great, um great," I said. Thick gold rings set with stones adorned each of his fingers. But the question in my mind was why would such a wealthy man, who had flown to the U.S. more than once for doctor visits and paid to have his children educated at top American universities, have such copious ear hair?

He smiled broadly. "There is a bright future in typesetting. My son tells me he is very hopeful for what this business will bring us," he said.

"Yes, um, the thing is we've been having some trouble with the work—"

Did he know I was here considering starting our own typesetting division? I wondered if I should bring up that or perhaps start with my own final Bembo paycheck, which had bounced.

"A very bright future indeed," he said and looked out the window. He held the pose and I looked too, wondering if the bright future might be there.

"That's great, but—"

"Great, yes. I want you to know that we are very interested in your input," he said and before I could respond, a man in a white shirt was at my side. My audience was over. I was no longer his employee—I was the president of his largest customer—but I was back on the production floor of keyboarders that stretched to the horizon without having been able to ask one question.

For a potentate like him—he had been close with Marcos—Bembo was nothing but a plaything for his sons. His conception of our meeting was more like a peasant visiting a king: I was there to kiss his rings.

I was not going to kiss anything. Outside, I called Dan from a KFC— the only nearby place with air-conditioning. He suggested again we find an established company and partner with them. Ideally, he wanted both a production and financial partner, like Bembo was supposed to have been, but I'd had enough of Bembo risking our future. I wanted our own Manila operation.

To me, all the offshore companies were just a variation on the exploitation theme. I reminded him "5-1-5" was still common practice. After six months of employment, Filipino companies were legally required to make pension and benefit provisions. The easy way around this was to hire for five months, fire for one and then re-hire. I didn't see how he could let companies like this become part of our benevolent capitalist empire.

"Don't be hasty, my boy. Who's going to run this plant of yours?" he asked. "If you're so hot to do this without Bembo, how about you give Anthony's new boss a chance? What's his name? Pierre? Jacques? Or how about I just call him the Frenchman? If you go meet with him maybe he'll give you a croy-sant. You like those, don't you?"

I hated that Dan didn't seem at all worried when our entire future was in jeopardy, and I knew his mis-pronunciation was calculated to defuse my anger, but I did not want it to.

"Qua-*san*," I corrected.

"See, you're even talking Frenchy."

ℓ

Dinner of coq au vin, French wine, and cheese was served in the Frenchman's high-rent gated compound. We sat on the veranda looking at the walls that separated him and his neighbors from the locals. Anthony hadn't been invited—either because the Frenchman suspected his motives, or more likely because he was a native Filipino. Our conversation was a bit like a foreign film with out-of-sync subtitles.

"Dan would like to partner with you. He wants you to invest in our plan to buy more typesetting companies and not just be a vendor to us," I said.

"We would be happy for you to invest in us."

"Um, no, you would invest money in our joint venture. We will all be shareholders."

"I see! That's wonderful! We need twenty new computers."

The next morning, I told Dan again that collaboration wouldn't work.

"Call Anthony again."

"But he betrayed you!" I said.

"Are you loyal to me, my boy?"

"Of course."

"Then do me this one favor. I taught that boy everything and he called me up last night after your meeting. He was hurt that he wasn't invited. He knows Frenchy doesn't love him and I do—almost as much as I love you. And he suggested that he might be able to set up that operation you want so much. How about that? You know Anthony knows how to manage those people."

It was true Anthony knew a lot about typesetting, and I was glad Dan was trying to find a way to make me happy. If he could forgive Anthony, I could try.

On my way out, I found a note slipped under my door: a phone number, Anthony's signature, and a little smiley face.

"I'll be right there," he said.

The Shangri-La's doorman frowned at the Toyota in the opulent driveway, and reluctantly grasped the side door's handle, which didn't work. Anthony popped the door from the inside. "I've got something to show you."

We headed north to a section of town I'd never seen, an elaborate and spare industrial park.

"I've got a new partner for you and Dan," he said, pulling in front of a building so clean and shiny it was as if Microsoft's grassy campus had been airlifted to the spot, and, decidedly unusual for Manila, there was no one in sight.

"I thought you were going to help us build our own plant."

"This is much better," he said, leaning over to pop my door.

Inside, I was surprised to see Lisa, an ex-Datadata manager and also an ex-pat from Michigan.

"Good to see you! I hear you'd like to hire Barnes and Noble," she said, and registering the unease on my face, "Anthony's filled you in, that I'm running things for them here, right?"

Anthony proceeded to tell me his mad scheme, while giving me a tour of the most beautiful keyboarding operation in the world—everyone had his or her own desk instead of being crammed at long tables like lumberjacks at dinner. Apparently and incredibly, Barnes and Noble had started an electronic publishing group in Manila. They were planning to reprint classic books like *Moby Dick*, and resell them under the B&N label, which required re-keyboarding the text and typesetting pages to the new book design. They had hired Lisa as the production chief, and she had hired Anthony.

"I thought you worked for the Frenchman."

He shook his head.

"But you were his manager. Did you know you were going to come work for Lisa before I flew over?"

He shrugged his shoulders. "This is good for you and Dan. We can now partner with Barnes and Noble."

"Partner? Why did Lisa say 'hire'? Is this what you told Dan last night?"

Slowly, and with much badgering, he revealed that by "partner," he meant that we would have him run a typesetting group out of Barnes and Noble's offices without their knowledge—a little business on the side for Anthony and Lisa. Dan finally had to admit that we could not trust him or anyone else. We needed our own group.

Dan suggested Fanta, the former quality control manager at Bembo who had also been betrayed by Anthony. He had encouraged her to quit with him—hoping the pressure of losing another manager would put pressure on Dan to put him in charge, and when that didn't happen, he had promised her a job with the Frenchman, which also never came. She had ended up without any income for months, and so was likely to be interested. I tracked down her home phone.

"Fanta, Clarinda is finally going to open its own plant, but without Anthony. Dan and I want you to be the boss."

Her voice faint on the bad connection, she said, "But I have accepted an offer at Barnes and Noble."

I called Dan at home in Baltimore. Although it was midnight on Saturday, Helen didn't sound surprised to hear from me. "How are the Philippines?" she asked.

"Hot," I said.

"You knew I'd be up, didn't you kiddo?" I pictured him sitting on the paisley sofa in his rented townhouse attached on both sides to other townhouses just off the Baltimore beltway. He probably had on a golf shirt, having hoped, but failed, to get to the course because Brenda, Ben or someone else in his family needed him to counsel them. He was everyone's therapist—everyone's father. "We've got to get this sorted out. Give Fanta whatever she wants," he said.

Sitting on the edge of my high-sheen bed comforter, I found myself in a bidding war. Filipinos don't negotiate in the way I was used to. I made her an offer, "Ten thousand," and her response was silence. Was I giving too little? Too much? She wouldn't say. With CNN playing silently on the TV I tried to read between two blank lines of silence.

To manage a Clarinda-Manila staff of ten people, I offered her double what I guessed Anthony had proposed: twelve thousand dollars per year—not much compared to an Iowan, but in Manila she would be able to afford a maid, a cook, and a driver. I asked, "Is this good for you?"

She responded quietly, "Well, it's not bad."

We had a typesetting manager. That solved half the puzzle. Now we needed to replace Bembo's keyboarding operation—the first step in the typesetting process, and not something Fanta knew how to do—with someone else, find office space, and solve the small matter of how Clarinda could legally hire people in Manila.

The answer for keyboarding was Mai, another of Dan's old managers from Datadata who he was very fond of. She had started her own keyboarding company, M&T. When she arrived at the Shangri-La she seemed very slight, even for a Filipino, but very well dressed, wearing diamond earrings, necklace, and rings, and smelling of several pints of perfume—the doormen beamed at her.

She had brought along her niece, who sat by her side crayoning in a *Little Mermaid* coloring book. "A day of shopping, for us, you don't mind?" Above our heads, a Filipino band played discreetly on a balcony behind the chandelier. They shifted seamlessly from "Lucy in the Sky with Diamonds" to "Achy Breaky Heart" to what must have been some Chinese standard, because a Chinese businessman near us hummed along.

She told me what had happened at our alma mater, Datadata. After the Manila plant unionized, they built a plant in New Delhi where labor was cheaper. Her job over the previous year was to move the remaining work, fire the three thousand employees, and then let herself go.

Other than reminiscing about how Datadata had not made either of us millionaires—my fifty thousand Datadata stock options (after several reverse splits) were worthless—the meeting did not go well.

"Dan wants this?"

"Yes."

"M&T to do keyboarding for a plant run by Fanta? Dan wants this?"

"Yes, and also keyboarding for Iowa."

"Anthony is gone? Dan wants this?"

"Yes, for good."

"And Bembo is no more? Dan wants this?"

"Yes, as soon as we can."

"Dan wants this?"

"Yes, and me too."

"I don't think we can help you."

She had been watching me intently, but now appeared to lose interest and began playing patty cake with her niece. The Chinese businessman turned to watch.

I was on the phone to Dan again.

"I talked to her, my boy. Right after she left you, she called me from the cab. Everything's all set up. We've got her as our vendor for the keying to feed both Fanta's new Manila typesetters and the Iowa ones too. Keying. Subletting Fanta space. And she'll have her admin do all our payroll. We won't have to do any of that stuff to open our own business in Manila—she'll handle all the gritty details for us. Bing, bang, zoom, home run."

"Then what was that meeting all about? Why did she tell me 'no'?"

"She didn't understand that we're partners, kiddo. She doesn't know you speak for me. She thought you might be up to something."

"Like Anthony?"

"You know she was always one of my favorites and she needed to hear me say it. I should have known that and saved you the trouble."

"But she'll listen to me now?"

"Kiddo, I'll make sure she does."

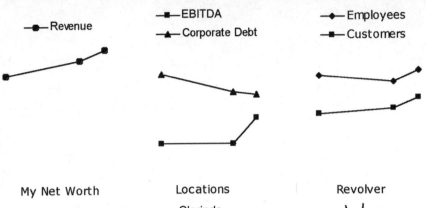

—■—Revenue

—■—EBITDA
—▲—Corporate Debt

—◆—Employees
—■—Customers

My Net Worth

Locations

Clarinda
Atlantic
Baltimore
St. Paul
New York
Syracuse
Manila

Revolver

Revenue	$9,000,000
EBITDA	$1,000,000
Corporate Debt	$1,900,000
Employees	120
Customers	70
My Net Worth	$3,500,000
Revolver Expires	7 Months

Selling

May 2000

I WAS SPENDING WEEKS AT A TIME at the Clarinda Super 8, my unbendable-foam-pillow-unwrinkleable-sheets-tiny-bar-of-soap-but-no-shampoo home away from home. Rather than carrying all my belongings in my luggage, I had begun leaving piles of underwear in a filing cabinet at work, although I still had to take them in and out of the Super 8 every trip. Dan also wasn't a fan of the place. As a smoker, he was relegated to designated rooms on the first floor where there were always bugs coming in from the cold or the hot or just to visit and, as he said, "do a little dance on the carpet—no extra charge," which reminded me that despite our month-long visits, we got the "standard" corporate rate. You'd get the same if you stopped in for a night and simply drove a car, AAA, were old, AARP, or just asked.

This was a problem—or as they say in corporate speak, "opportunity"—and I had two mad schemes to solve it. The first idea was buying a house. It would have to accommodate Dan, me, and at least one visiting employee, so we needed at least a three bedroom house with as many bathrooms and enough space to let Dan puff his Benson and Hedges and allow the visitor the privacy to stay up late eating ice cream like they could at the Super 8. Given the preponderance of mid-century—nineteenth century—four bedroom, one bathroom Victorian structures in rural Iowa this was not going to be easy. The homes I toured at lunchtime with the increasingly frustrated, but still trying to smile when he saw me, real estate agent included a farmhouse on a hundred acres of corn that we plowed straight through in his four-wheel drive minivan. But unfortunately, in Iowa a corporation cannot own a farm. I also considered a former funeral home in Villisca, but the front of the house neon-lit "viewing room" with a trap door for raising and lowering "clients" to the tile and steel tub room in the basement that was the only "full bath" in the house dissuaded me.

The second idea was buying mobile homes and anchoring them in the half-acre backyard behind the plant. I found a variety of single and doublewide trailers on the Web, but complications of weatherproofing and images of Dan coming to the screen door in t-shirt and boxer shorts, frying pan with eggs in hand, ended that one.

Then the morning of our First Annual Sales Meeting, Dan called me in his office. "You know who I was just talking to?"

"No," I said, smacking an insect off of his blinds—the beautiful tree outside our window was infested with box elder beetles. They were known locally as Democrat bugs although no one could tell me why, nor was there any evidence of Republican bugs. Nearly an inch long with red and black markings, they were far less intimidating than the insects that invaded the Super 8 or the nightmare-inducing ones from Manila. The Democrat bugs could fly, but preferred to walk sluggishly. I spun the lethal plastic fly swatter I'd discovered in my desk like a six-gun and whacked a half dozen of the lethargic critters.

"The Celebrity Inn," he said. "I know how unhappy you are and I thought, let's give the local guy a chance." Dan tented his fingers under his nose. The Celebrity lay across Highway 71 from the Super 8, and advertised a game room, as in a room with a hose and a wood-slat floor for cleaning the kind of game you shot with a rifle.

"I told the owner how much time we spend out here, and how many people we bring out to visit, and he was intrigued. He's finishing up a major renovation and he could put a refrigerator in our rooms, a microwave, and a hair dryer for me. You know, David, this guy knew how to sell."

"And why wouldn't I want a hairdryer?"

Dan looked at my buzz cut, like my dad did when I first began to lose my hair in my twenties—as if he was surprised to see me getting old. "You can have all the hairdryers you want, my boy." He rustled together the pile of sales forecasts on his desk. "Now, let's go get 'em."

The First Annual Clarinda Sales Meeting was held in our favorite conference room. Arrayed like a wide-lapelled Lawrence Welk fan club around the table were regular management: Kathy, Frank, Ron, Connie, Steve and Minnie; the new salespeople: Beth from Datadata, Larry from Bookers, Jeff who used to run his own book design and editorial group, and Al from our new five-person Syracuse office; and last, and most certainly least, the Clarinda salespeople we inherited: McSwenson and Hilda.

Nearly seventy years old, with a combination of unnaturally jet black hair and a pallor of skin that led Dan to refer to him as "the cadaver," McSwenson had been with the company since before it began. He'd been a typesetter at Poole Brothers in Chicago when he became the first salesman for their new Clarinda subsidiary in 1959. He had avoided moving to Iowa by establishing an early precedent of working from home. His salesman's uniform was what appeared to be his original brown suit.

Hilda, she of my skirmish at McGraw-Hill, was the only other Clarinda salesperson Dan had retained out of an original staff of four. Overweight in a way that made you want to avoid cottage cheese, she wore a "business muumuu" imprinted with a pattern normally found on fuzzy bathroom wallpaper from 1972.

"I bet you're wondering why I made you all come out to Iowa," Dan said. "Well, next year, when you all sell a million plus, we'll meet at some resort where we can get a little golf in." He winked at me as he began retelling his sales mantras and stories:

"You're either bringing in revenue, or you're cutting costs, or you're the problem."

"Typesetting is like a game of catch. They throw us one book. We throw it back done right, and they throw another."

"Good salespeople are good managers, and visa versa."

He told us about his first job selling ad space for *Time*. The sales manager had commanded a cavernous room of new reps to stand on their folding chairs, slap a rolled newspaper into their palms, and chant as loud as they could, "If you act enthusiastic, you'll be enthusiastic!" I looked around the room wondering if anyone felt like jumping on a chair.

When the catered lunch of Subway sandwiches—all with their trademark glutinous cheese—arrived, I was relieved that I could talk at last. I chatted with Larry, who used to work for our competitor Bookers—the largest typesetting operation in America. He'd lost his job when they had been sold to an Indian firm the year before. He was a Mormon, and true to form was an unceasingly nice person with a dozen children who all did missionary work.

"Dan was the first guy to even take my call after I lost my job," he said, arranging potato chips on his plate. "I told him, 'look I don't know if I can sell any of my accounts away from Bookers,' and he said, 'You're ethical and people respect that. They also respect that Clarinda is a great company with good prices. You'll get the work.' There aren't too many like Dan left."

He turned to Kathy who had been cornered by Minnie at the buffet table. Minnie, who wore dingy white loafers, was frowning at Kathy's sneakers and complaining about invoices. "I hear your full service group is the best in the business," Larry said to Kathy, ignoring Minnie.

"I'm sorry you haven't gotten the invoices. I'll get right on it when I'm back in St. Paul," Kathy said to Minnie, brushing her hair out of her face, and turned to Larry, "Well I don't know. We make our share of mistakes."

"That's the spirit," I said sarcastically, and gestured with my turkey sandwich. "At Subway our sandwiches are mediocre. Some people like them, but some people don't. To be fair, we're not any better than anyone else—and our cheese tastes like office drawer lint."

"I'm sorry," she said and then tried to sound enthusiastic. "Dan says I'm supposed to say 'We're great!' But it feels too salesy."

Larry smiled, a small Mormon smile. "I've got a customer I'd like to talk to you about later, if that's OK?"

Kathy nodded and tried to get some chips using the tongs that Minnie had put in the bowl.

Larry followed me to the table. "Dan tells me nobody knows more about the technology than you. Back at Bookers they were advertising something about full XML production. Do you know anything about that?"

"I know exactly what they're up to. It's all lies. XML isn't directly composable into pages—"

Dan cut me off as he reconvened the meeting: "The traditional typesetting sale." He thumped his briefcase on the table. "I, Mr. Vinne Boombatz the salesman show up at the door carrying a bag and wearing a suit. In the good old days I'd get a book sooner or later. Am I right Larry?" Larry hurriedly tossed away his plate of chips and nodded. "But now," Dan continued. "Mosby, Saunders, Academic Press are all Harcourt. Macmillan and Addison-Wesley have been swallowed by Pearson. Everyone has bought everyone and it's only going to get worse. Boombatz is out of the game if he doesn't sell up from the buyer to the VP, and we are too. We need to do a team sell."

On the whiteboard he wrote "9" and "1"—our much-hoped-for revenue and profit projections—and launched into the discussion of our dreams for acquisitions, Manila, training, and on and on that he had given the executive committee. I silently mouthed his speech along with him because my job was to sit by his side like a politburo member behind Gorbachev, silently adding my support with my staunch expression and natty beaver hat, except I didn't have a hat.

Promptly at five, we caravaned to the Ice House for onion rings after which I collected my belongings from the Super 8 and moved across the street to the Celebrity. The owner, a tall man with vertically blown dry hair shook Dan's hand and made a half-nod towards me. The game room was gone, but the rest of the renovation consisted primarily of an Archie Bunker-style reclining chair in every room. Mine was prom-suit blue and Dan's mud-brown.

I suspected this was not their first home. Falling asleep was difficult. The hallway floor reverberated like a drumhead. Footsteps anywhere in the single story building bounced through my bed un-muffled. Despite those flaws, the owner-operated Celebrity did feel homier than the delivered-on-a-flatbed-from-a-factory Super 8 with its central-office designed efficiency.

The second day of the meeting Dan began, "The more technology and Indian competition make typesetting a commodity, the more we can differentiate ourselves only by better service and technical knowledge." He pulled out a stack of paper and read, "Pearson. Columbus, Ohio. One million. Our biggest customer. Still happy with us, McSwenson?"

Pearson was McSwenson's primary account. The commissions netted him $125,000 a year: the highest-paid employee in the company, making almost double Frank's production chief salary. Dan had remarked before the meeting that McSwenson did very little work. "Whenever I call him, he's always in his car heading to pick up his daughters from ballet, ice skating or flying lessons. I would like to take my son to flying lessons. Wouldn't you like that David, to take your son to flying lessons? Oh that's right, you're always moving from girlfriend to girlfriend so you don't have a son. Someday, my boy. Someday."

"Red is still my friend," McSwenson said, "But he's been wondering when the new owners are going to visit. I've asked you a dozen times."

"We'll get there and talk to Mr. Red Bones at Pearson. Don't you worry about that," Dan said, moving his pencil down the list. "McGraw Hill, Dubuque. That's yours too, isn't it? $150,000 in 1999 for your old friends at Household. What's our projection this year for your new friends Dan and David?"

McSwenson gently touched his solid black hair. "Nothing." Dan peered over his reading glasses.

"After Jack went in there from Household and told them how to run their business. I can't get them to return a phone call."

"What did he do?" Dan asked. "Shit on the table?"

"No, no, he told them they needed to fire some of their buyers," McSwenson said. "I'm surprised you didn't hear about it."

"I didn't," Dan said and crossed out the line on his spreadsheet. "But that doesn't mean you can't give them another call. How about SRA? They're also a McGraw division. We have that big film project going on now. Can we expect the same for this year? Or do they hate us too?"

"I've got a very good connection there," McSwenson said.

"And he's promised you work?"

"I have an appointment with him next week."

"To get a project started?"

"He's been telling me he's waiting for me to visit," McSwenson said, getting a little agitated with Dan's questions.

Dan made a note. "So we'll see next week then. Mosby?"

Hilda answered, "We're still trying to recover from letting Betsy go."

"That's why David is going with you in two weeks to visit them. Do you think we might be able to get back up to a million again after everything else that's happened on that account?"

"That's up to you and David," Hilda said. "My relationship is still really solid."

"It's good they like you. Apparently, charm is our biggest selling point," he said cheerfully, and with a hint of growl in his voice, like my father getting to "two-and-three-quarters" in a count of "three." "But maybe we could remind them we also do pretty damn good typesetting?"

Hilda frowned. I could tell she was still angry about the film fiasco at McGraw, which Dan pointedly didn't mention. Had he warned Hilda beforehand not to bring it up?

Dan proceeded through the rest of the list and salespeople: TPC (me), Oxford University Press, John Wiley, all the Kluwer companies: Lippincott and Raven, Ovid, Plenum and Dan's old firm Waverly, and all of Thomson's divisions: Delmar, Wordsworth, Gale (Larry); Addison-Wesley, now a division of Pearson, Academic Press, now a division of Harcourt and Imperial Printing (Beth); Harcourt General in Texas (Connie).

We ate another round of sandwiches as Dan went through the list before shifting to hand out new accounts. "There are several publishers in the Chicago area we aren't calling on. Would you like to take them, McSwenson?" If Dan could get the Cadaver to sell to a few more customers, he might begin to approach justifying his extravagant base salary.

"Don't you think you and David should visit Red, our most faithful customer, before we start spending too much time building new ones?"

"Of course," Dan said. "You're right. Build the customers we have first. Then the new ones. But I'm holding you to your promise to start working on the new ones after we sell Red." Dan smiled, but without a laugh. McSwenson smiled back. I liked that Dan had demanded a "promise." McSwenson was now honor bound to do actual work.

"Are there any questions?" Dan asked, standing up from the table.

"How is this team selling thing going to work? Are we splitting commissions?" McSwenson asked.

"McSwenson is referring to his unique arrangement where Beth helped him sell to Pearson in New Jersey," Dan said, still standing and putting his fingertips on the table. "As you know we have done a lot out of Columbus thanks to his relationship with Red, but almost nothing out of New Jersey."

"I've sold plenty to New Jersey," McSwenson said.

"Then you'd better take that up with Minnie. Her records show just two books." Minnie and McSwenson traded frowns.

"As I told you then, and I repeat in front of everyone now, you will get your full commission. But you are bringing up an excellent point." McSwenson eyebrows moved upward into his pompadour—as if to say, "*of course my point was excellent—what exactly was my point?*"

"Team selling means you are going to have help from David and me. We want you to sell more, and David's the technical guru who will win the VP's hearts." Larry smiled at me.

"Like at Mosby in two weeks?" Hilda asked.

"Like at Mosby, or Pearson, or TPC, or any of our customers. There are vice presidents of production who hold the keys to Clarinda getting more business, and David's personal mission, which I am assigning to him now, is to befriend them."

Dan closed the meeting and I followed him back to his office. I was worried, primarily because I had no idea how to do that, and secondly because of the disaster at McGraw. What did these VPs want?

"Forget that woman at McGraw," Dan said. "Executives are like anyone else, my boy. They are either trying to get promoted or, like most people, like the buffoons we had with us today, they are trying to hold on to what they have. You will succeed with the ones trying to get ahead."

Back at the Celebrity the maid had ignored my "Do Not Disturb" sign. The bed was vacuum-sealed in new (or maybe they weren't new) sheets and the sign itself had been placed on the bathroom counter. At the Super 8 when I had put out the little plastic "Do Not Disturb" signs on our doorknobs, the maid had gladly ignored my mess. I went to talk to the owner.

"Can you ask the maid to stop making up my room when I have the 'Do Not Disturb' sign left out?"

"I'll talk to her," he said.

I ran out the rest of my week's stay and the sign remained on the knob outside, but the maid decided that it variously meant: empty the trash, turn off the air-conditioner, turn on the air-conditioner, unplug the air-conditioner. Being treated like an intruder rather than a customer disturbed me, and I asked the owner again if she could stop.

"I'm out here for weeks at a time and it feels more like home and less like travel if the bed isn't made up every night."

"I'm sorry," he said, standing behind the counter and sounding more angry than sorry, "but I can't stop her from making up your rooms. She gets confused and will end up not making up any rooms if I force her to stop making up yours."

In a technical knockout, the Super 8 had won us back.

David Silverman

The whiteboard was imperceptibly smaller than it should be—like a door frame in a colonial house that you keep hitting your head on during the tour of historic Williamsburg—because it was proportioned for a closet-sized conference room that sat four Midwesterners uncomfortably, much like the interior of my dad's 70s Opal subcompact.

"Training, American Expertise, Manila Advantage, Employee Respect," I wrote on the board in thin blue ink. Mosby's markers were even drier than Clarinda's. Mosby's chief buyer, Geri, a middle-aged woman who could have been one of our typesetters, eyed me just as dryly, pushed herself a millimeter away from the table—which was as far as she could go with the wall directly behind her—grunted, and looked at Hilda for guidance. Geri's two employees sat quietly and tried to look pleasant without giving me the impression that they were being friendly, in the way a banker looks at a vagrant who has come in for a free toaster.

Hilda tilted her head in my direction and smiled by lifting the left half of her sealed lips toward her squinting eye. I read her expression as "this is the first time I've heard him say something rational, and I can't quite believe it myself."

She wore a flower print muumuu and, God help me, looked like a parade float coming down the hall, her feet hidden by cotton irises and chrysanthemums. I was, unlike last time with a Hilda customer, fervently overdressed in my Armani suit, a dark blue Armani shirt, and the tie that had caused Visa to put a hold on my card—"A hundred and forty dollars for a tie?" the Visa service person had asked me, unable to believe even a paper millionaire would be so extravagant, but then she wasn't trying to prove to the world that she had made it as far from her father in Kingston as he had from his in Brooklyn. Geri and her staff wore matching khaki pants and white blouses.

That morning in the breakfast nook of Hampton Inn on the outskirts of St. Louis, Hilda had explained the challenge that lay ahead, "Mosby's not pleased with you and Dan. When you fired Betsy, you really made them very unhappy. They really liked Betsy." Each "really" punctuated with a sharply pointed thumb. "I don't want a repeat of the 'Man in Black' ruining my commissions again."

"We didn't fire her," I said, ignoring, or at least not commenting on the reference to McGraw. "The executive committee picked Betsy. If Dan had known she was so important to the customer we wouldn't have let her go," I tried out my best Dan, we're-the-good-guys chuckle, which came out half earnest, half uncertain.

He had been over the situation at Mosby with me before my trip. A decade ago, the medical publisher Mosby had been Clarinda's biggest customer: the Atlantic plant opened in 1977 just to serve them. During Household's reign, they had slid to a million a year. Still a lot of money, but only a third of what it had been.

Then, over the summer before we bought Clarinda, Harcourt bought Mosby and Saunders and joined them under one chief. Unbeknownst to us, this VP (Geri's boss' boss) decided to drop Clarinda—a decision that would leave us scrambling to fill the gap with new customers.

"Hilda, can you explain to me what happened with the VP in Philadelphia?" From what I had pieced together from Dan, Ron, and Connie, I thought I knew, but I wanted Hilda's version.

"He found out we were giving a discount to Mosby and not Saunders and wanted us to fix it," she said, sipping a glass of grapefruit juice.

"That wasn't us, Hilda, that was Household—a different company," I said. "So what did they do?"

"Luke split the difference. He lowered Saunders and raised Mosby."

Luke had been the last president under Household, a finance man sent in by headquarters to clean things up and sell the company.

"And?" I asked.

She smiled with all her teeth. "Geri told me she wouldn't pay more and the Saunders buyers said it was proof we'd been ripping them off all along. Really, I don't know why Luke did what he did. It cost me a lot. I told Geri I wanted to believe you were different, but—"

I didn't like it. Luke would have asked Hilda's advice before changing pricing. Since her commissions were based on sales, doing the right thing— lowering Saunders' prices to match Mosby—would cost her thousands. Greed would have encouraged her to come up with the Solomon-like price splitting. However, Luke wouldn't admit it was Hilda's fault, most likely because he was embarrassed to admit that by listening to her he had lost the customer, and much of the value of the company he was selling us.

"That was bad enough," she said, "but when you came along and fired Betsy, that really did it. Did you know they hired her? I saw her in the parking lot yesterday. Of course," she said, looking at me with worry for the first time, "I didn't say 'hi' to her."

"Why not? It's not like she's the enemy. Dan will be glad to hear that she found work."

"Well, really," she said, her worry quickly vanished, "I'm concerned you won't be able to overcome the Betsy issue. Geri wants to buy from me, but she doesn't know you and Dan like I do."

"You're absolutely right, Hilda," I said. How many times had I watched Dan disarm an opponent by agreeing with them? "And that's why I'm here. To convince Mosby that we are different."

In the tiny conference room, I wrote on the whiteboard "9" and "1," our old familiar sales forecast and expected profits. I told Geri we hoped to give everyone raises. "Profits depend on us being able to win back valuable customers like you. As you know, we let Betsy go. That was a mistake. Dan and I didn't know how important she was to you."

"You didn't know?" Geri asked. As she said it, I could see her realize, as a manager herself, how it could happen, and also that Hilda had told her the opposite.

"We had to let some people go or not be able to make it through our first year. Now that we are financially stable, we don't plan to fire anyone ever again. In fact, if we can build some business with you, we'd be happy to hire Betsy back. I apologize for our mistakes and promise to personally consult you if we ever have such a serious decision to make again. I know trust is won over time, but lost in a moment." It was a surreal experience having to invalidate what my own salesperson had said about me.

After the meeting, Hilda pulled Geri and me aside. "I really had my doubts about Dan and David," she said, "but I was impressed with him today. He's more honest than we thought—isn't he? And so smart! I'm willing to give him another chance, and I think you should too."

Her sales technique had been just as Dan had explained: cry on the shoulder of the buyer about the bad bosses—who doesn't like to talk about how bad the boss is? It did bring Hilda closer to Geri, but it didn't sell anything. Why buy from someone whose boss is a moron?

Before I left, Geri took me into her office and pulled out a pile of manuscript. "I was going to give this book to Clarinda before you bought them. I told Hilda I'd wait and see what kind of people you were, and I was honestly about to send it somewhere else." She pulled off the cover sheet, which said, "Graphic World," and handed the manuscript to me, "give me a good price."

One book. It would be a long way back to a million dollars, but it was the right direction.

ℓ

Dan and I sat with McSwenson, who looked more cadaverous than usual in the sunlight streaming through the window, at the Applebee's in Columbus, Ohio. The paid check lay with the receipt sticking out of its pleather folder surrounded by crumbs.

"Let's go," McSwenson said.

"I haven't finished my beer yet," Dan said, but made no motion to drink.

Glancing at my watch, I saw we were a few second hand sweeps away from our appointed time with Red Bones at Pearson, and we had to get to the parking lot, into the car, and drive across the street—Dan's ankles were far too weak from years of playing basketball in bad sneakers to attempt walking.

"Red is expecting us at noon," McSwenson said.

"I know," Dan said and still didn't raise a hand to his half-full glass. Was Dan trying to show Red, by showing up late, that we were glad to come, but that we were strong enough to be a few minutes late? Or was he showing McSwenson that he was the boss and not Red? Or was he just pissed off at McSwenson for refusing to put on his seatbelt on the drive from the airport and thereby subjecting us to a constant "beep beep" alarm? Maybe it was all three. Dan didn't do things randomly. "Well, let's not keep Red waiting," he said, and got up. The beer remained on the table, going flat.

At five minutes past noon, McSwenson skidded his rented Lincoln into the parking lot. We dashed for the building with Dan coming up slowly— lifting his leg from the knee to avoid putting too much pressure on his ankles, and flicking his cigarette out in the street after one last puff. "I can't even get a cigarette finished," he muttered.

In the elevator, a flustered McSwenson forgot which floor Red was on. "We're going to be late," McSwenson said, scanning the buttons. Dan leaned on the handrail and stroked his chin.

At the Pearson reception desk, we were told: "Mr. Bones is in a conference, please have a seat." Fifteen minutes later, Red came out, shook our hands, said, "Sorry for the delay, I was held up on the phone on with my staff in New Jersey."

If you called central casting for a publishing production manager, you would have gotten Red Bones. In his nice—but not too nice—suit, he was just enough shy of six feet to still appear significant when he stood up. He had a narrow waist and looked a lot like the cartoon character Archie without the freckles. He had lips so thin his mouth was a virtual gash below his nose.

Red directed part of what had been the Macmillan division in

Columbus, which was one of four divisions of the higher education group headquartered in Upper Saddle River, New Jersey, which included the former Prentice Hall and Addison Wesley, and this group was, in turn, part of Pearson Education, a component of its parent, Pearson, which also owned the *Financial Times* and Penguin publishing. Worldwide, they spent more on toilet paper than on typesetting. Yet Red's infinitesimally small group in the scope of the company represented one million, or more than ten percent of our business—and we were just one of a dozen vendors. He was, to us, a big man on a campus of giants.

His side-of-the-building office with windows that looked towards Applebee's was full of memorabilia: Lucite award cubes for book production, golf balls from courses around the country, a desktop bicycle model, and the requisite wall of textbooks his group produced.

Red began by quizzing Dan about his background. I listened for the ten thousandth time as Dan recounted Waverly Press, Penta Composition, Datadata, Bembo, Clarinda, and then compliment me and the entire company in his gravelly voice.

Next, Red asked for my history. I went through my tale of growing up true-blue IBM, and fleeing the small town of Kingston for New York City. McSwenson shifted uncomfortably in his seat. His salary and his daughter's ballet lessons lay in our hands.

"You know, I used to live in New York," Red said, "back when I worked for Macmillan." Dan mentioned some executive from those days when I had been in elementary school. He and Red reminisced while I maintained my smile. I found it odd McSwenson had no idea who they were talking about.

Red took us for a tour and then to a conference room to meet his staff.

"You have employees here and in New Jersey?" I asked.

"I split my time between the two. Most of my buyers work here, but a couple of them are in Upper Saddle River."

"Don't you find all that travel exhausting?"

"I've gotten used to it," he said. "It comes along with the responsibility."

His main buyers, who managed a staff of another dozen or so underlings, arrived. All of them reminded me of our service manager Connie—sad-faced, with pins holding their hair. McSwenson greeted them more warmly than he greeted Dan and me at the airport.

The first buyer grimaced, dumped a stack of manuscript on the table and said, "Felso Volume Two still has the wrong art. I've called Connie four times, talked to McSwenson about this and emailed. I have a copy of all my emails," she pulled the top sheets off the stack and made to give them to Dan and me.

"Maybe we should all go around the room and introduce ourselves first," Red said, with an un-lipped smirk. "There will be plenty of time to get all your production concerns to Clarinda's new owners."

"Of course," the buyer said, blinking a few times and putting the manuscript down, "Hi, my name is Edith."

After introductions Red said, "As you know, the reason we like to use Clarinda is because of McSwenson here who has been making sure our concerns are taken care of for, what now, twenty years?"

McSwenson's face cracked like a vampire who had a wooden steak wrenched free from his heart, and proudly responded, "I try to do what I can for you with the plant."

Red continued, "And all the business you get is because of Kathy's full service group in St. Paul. They do an excellent job of project management for us and we have recently started to use you for typesetting as well. While some things are going well, you've got a long way to go there before you're as good as our other vendors." Despite his condescension it was hard to not become mesmerized by the soft voice coming from his lipless face. "So I want to make sure you understand how important Kathy is to you. We've had some cutbacks here." All the buyers nodded with their eyes down. "And your group there in St. Paul allows us to keep getting our books done."

That's what Dan had told me. "Kathy's group does what their production people do: copyediting, sending specs to printers, book design, rights and typesetting management. Our project manager is a replacement person for the publisher." This explained the bad blood between St. Paul and Clarinda. It wasn't just blond hair that made Minnie decry Kathy's expenses. It was because St. Paul project managers couldn't help treating Clarinda typesetters the way these buyers had started the meeting treating us—like mentally challenged orangutans who kept putting in the wrong art.

We moved on to the complaints. After a few minutes, Red left without comment while the buyers showed me proof pages that had the wrong shade of pink in the heads.

"Cyan five percent, not ten percent!"

On our way back to the parking lot, Red said goodbye in the reception area.

"How about we meet you in New York one of those times you're out in New Jersey? It's only a hop, skip away," Dan said, shaking his hand. "We'd be glad to take you out to dinner. And I don't know about you, but personally I've been a big fan of the Four Seasons for years."

Red grinned. "That's an excellent idea."

In the rental car, McSwenson was relaxed, his hands dangling loosely on the wheel. "You guys did a good job. Red really liked you," he said as the seat belt warning beeped. "He doesn't come out to see everyone off like that." Beep. "And a meeting in New York." Beep. "That's something."

"Why don't you put your seatbelt on?" Dan asked.

"Oh, right," he said. "I didn't mean to get on your nerves."

ℓ

Dan and I stood outside the Four Season's restaurant on 52nd street in Manhattan. He wore his blue blazer with the brass buttons and I had on my best suit and the hundred-and-forty dollar tie I had worn to St. Louis. "Sharp tie," he remarked as we waited for Red Bones to arrive in the Lincoln Town Car I had ordered.

The operator, either one man or one of several men who all sounded angry and Egyptian, had been reluctant to take my request to send a car to New Jersey. "What was the name?"

"Red Bones."

"No sir, your name?" I had hesitated. The car service was reliable, but the drivers always liked to discuss Palestine with me, and I suspected my name would ring on the wrong side of the equation for them. "Oh, Mr. Silverman! Of course! You are very good customer." In New York, money ultimately trumps most bias.

"Well my boy, we are finally here," Dan said. "What do you think?"

All I had seen so far was the brass plaque that read, "Four Seasons" and read the Zagat review: "It's not the power place to dine that it used to be, but the Pool Room remains one of America's foremost locales. Nowadays nobodies can get in—if you're willing to wait three weeks."

"You know, McSwenson really had a fit when I told him not to come," Dan said, lighting another cigarette. I moved upwind. "Sorry," he said, and switched the cigarette to his far hand. "I said, 'We're dining late. I don't want you to feel put out. You've got your family to consider.'"

It was true, McSwenson refused to travel overnight, alleging his wife didn't like it. He'd also refused to call new customers like he'd promised at the sales meeting, but why his wife wouldn't approve of that, I didn't know.

"That really roasted his giblets," Dan said, laughing and hacking. He bent over at the waist, hacking some more, but kept the cigarette aloft. A couple in appropriate dinner attire made a wide circle around him. "It's that damned cold," he said, "You know, I think I've had it since we came back from Iowa. I always get one on the plane."

I didn't ask what kind of cold makes you cough but not sneeze. I'd gotten used to the hacking and knew from experience it made him more upset if I commented. "Was McSwenson more pissed off than when you told him that Beth would be calling on New Jersey?"

He righted himself and took another puff. "Oh no. Having a meeting without him just makes him nervous. Beth scares the crap out of him."

In New Jersey there were three other VPs with book lists as big or bigger than Red, and nothing made Dan angrier than a missed sales opportunity.

"You know that cocksucker would rather see Beth fail than let a book get sold that he didn't have something to do with? He's tried to piss a circle around Pearson and he's mad at me that I won't let him. Did you know Beth used to work with two of the VPs in New Jersey?"

I didn't.

"They love her. You know, she tells me they actively loathe McSwenson? And I'm letting him get commission on whatever she sells. Pay two salespeople commission. Am I a softy or what?"

"You're doing what you think will work," I said, hoping he wouldn't light another cigarette, which was already in his hand. "At some point you won't pay him for things she sells, right?"

"And then you know what he does?" He waved the cigarette violently. "He goes in there last week and walks over to the other VP's offices and tells their buyers that he's the go-to-guy. He tells them he doesn't know what Beth is doing, but if they have a problem, they should go through him. He tells them she's not their salesperson; he is." He threw the un-smoked cigarette to the ground and stomped on it with one of his worn cowboy boots that were high enough to keep his ankles from bending. He started hacking again. "That <cough> cocksucker. She sold a book in there and <cough> he comes in and pisses all over the <cough> place." Tears from coughing were coming to his eyes. "You know I had her <cough> on the phone for an hour calming her down." He wiped the tears with his handkerchief. "I'm telling her, 'Yes, I know. I support you. You know I love you, kiddo. Just work with me through this.'" He looked so weak. "And you know I do. I love her and you and all of you who have come into this with me. Like your Dad...Hey, I'm sorry. I haven't asked you for a while. How is your old man?"

"He seems to be doing better," I said. "The health aide comes every day."

"And?"

"Do we have to talk about this right now?"

"Give him time." He wiped his handkerchief across his mouth. "You've just got to give him some time—" Before I could ask how much time I was supposed to give when his drinking kept landing him in the hospital, the town car pulled up and the driver jumped out to open Red's door. Dan stuffed the handkerchief in his pocket. "Red! Are you ready for the best meal of your life? Have you been here before? No?! Well I'll bet after tonight you'll want to come back whenever you can."

You know you're in a fancy place when real estate is several hundred dollars a square foot and there's more water than tables. The tennis-court-sized central pool was dotted with small fountains lit from underneath. Their trickling water focused Dan and Red's voices while blocking off the conversations of the diners wedged up against us—because even in this opulence, the floor space that wasn't under water was fully used.

Red didn't mention business, so neither did we. McSwenson had commented that Red lost weight biking, so I mentioned I enjoyed riding instead of my other primary interests—watching cartoons and eating sandwiches.

"I'm thinking of going to Cuba to bike across the island." He took a sip of wine. "Pack a tent on the bike and see the real Cuba. Maybe you'd like to come with me if I do that?"

Dan stopped his fork in midair.

"That would be great," I said, imagining few things more unpleasant than cohabitating in a tent with Red for a month. "If we can arrange it."

As the plates and all the various silverware were being cleared, Red finally said something about work. "Guy Delaco is emerging as the senior vice president from our group. He's very technical, a real expert. He wants us to start using FUN coding for all our books. What do you think of it?"

"We know all about FUN. Our Manila and Baltimore staffs have worked with the system for years." Dan said, and without irony added, "We love FUN."

Red nodded. "That's what I wanted to hear."

After dinner I took Dan to the train station in a cab. "You always told me that FUN was garbage—little more than 'coding stolen from the old Penta system.' I thought you hated it."

"I did, my boy, and Red doesn't really like it that much either. But it's political. Guy is moving up, and Red just told us how to back both of them. It's our ticket in. Besides, FUN requires Superleaf and Superleaf is production gold for us. What have I been saying since the beginning? Superleaf. Now the Iowans have to learn it. Use Superleaf or we won't be able to work for Pearson."

ℓ

"What do you think?" Guy Delaco asked. He wasn't much older than me, with an 80s Roman-style comb-forward, a denim shirt, and khakis. He was shorter than average, but I could see what Red meant by his comments that Guy was moving. When I arrived, the secretary had nervously approached his fishbowl-like office, while motioning me to stay out of view behind a column until she could demurely semaphore my presence with hand signals. And he had a minion at his side—only up-and-comers had minions—who was tapping quietly away on a PowerBook—the same model that I had brought along.

"You know, I don't want to sound overly opinionated." I touched the knot in my tie to verify its slight askew-ness—business appropriate while indicating my technical bent. "But I wouldn't consider doing a book of any length in Quark without Superleaf." I had taken Pearson's FUN consultant to lunch to pump him for information the previous week. "And when it comes to XML and coding schemes in general—" I had read the article in *Publishing & Production Executive* that profiled Guy Delaco. "I think that a typesetter would have to be out of their minds nowadays to not be going to a code-based automated production platform that could produce print and electronic books from a single source."

"Hopper says you guys are on the ball," Guy said. "He was really impressed with your operation and your staff."

It was true Hopper, the one-man show who made Superleaf from his home in New England, had bonded with Sally and the other typesetters. They had been a committed and interested class. But it hadn't been easy to get him to do the training in Iowa. Hopper had always refused to teach classes until Dan had used his charm, a $20,000 software order, and a $6,000 check Hopper got when he walked into the plant, to convince him. The result was another voice recommending us to Guy, and not just about technology. Another thing Hopper couldn't stop talking about was the taxi we'd arranged from the airport. The driver had brought along his cousin, and she had spent the ride leaning provocatively over the seat, smiling toothlessly, and pressing a bottle of Jack Daniels into his hand. Afterwards, I'd never seen someone so effusive about Clarinda, Iowa.

"What about TeX?" Guy asked.

"I'm sorry, I can't help myself," I said. Guy edged forward on his seat. "I just can't stand TeX. It shouldn't be used to lay out books if at all possible."

"Many of our authors use TeX," Guy said, and grabbed an executive-squeeze toy from his desk—pumping it in his fist.

"And so do the Indians. It doesn't mean I have to like it. I prefer SuperMath, as long as the developer includes a real TeX engine in the next release like he keeps promising."

"Exactly!" Guy said.

It was a truth of selling, and I had at last learned to wield it, but it still never failed to amaze me—quote someone's words directly at them, and not only will they fail to recognize the plagiarism, they will think you are a genius.

The minion looked up from his computer. "That's what I'm fighting with right now," he said, "a damn TeX file. I can't even get it to print."

"The author used his own macro set?" I asked. The minion nodded in agreement. As a child I listened to my father's record album of bad Jewish jokes. My favorite groaner was: "How do you like your son's new boat, dad? It's something, isn't it! And look, I've got a Captain's hat. Your son, the captain!" The father responds, with a thick immigrant accent: "Hmm, yah. Look son, I vant you to know, to your mother, you're a cap'in. To me, you're a cap'in. But to a cap'in, you're no cap'in!"

That's how it was discussing technology with publishers like Guy. They had no idea. FUN was half-baked and Superleaf a necessary kludge because Quark was a hack. The only reason we used any of it was because Microsoft didn't feel that the typesetting industry was a big enough market to make a decent product for, and therefore had never added the half a dozen features Word needed to swallow everyone in the business.

What did I know about TeX? What I'd read in Internet discussion groups. At best I'd seen a file once, and yet, because my father had bought me an IBM PC when I was twelve I knew more than both of these guys and anyone else in the industry, but that didn't matter. They thought they were the smartest guys in publishing and what kind of salesman would I be to dissuade them?

"Forgive me again, but I don't know how to say this." I knew FUN was difficult, but I also knew what was more important: that every other typesetter who had sat in this chair had told Guy they worried about the costs of implementation. "In Iowa, I've been saying this over and over and it's a little embarrassing."

Guy squeezed his toy expectantly.

With absolute gravity, I uttered the magic phrase Dan had prepped me with at that dinner at the Four Seasons, the phrase none of our competitors were willing to say: "Clarinda loves FUN!"

A few weeks later I was in a conference room in New Jersey with thirty buyers, three more patched in via speakerphone, and Guy and Red in the back, smiling serenely at me. We had achieved a level of recognition at Pearson unique among our competitors, and along with it would become the only typesetter doing work for all four divisions.

"Go ahead," Guy said, "Tell them what you told me."

l

I lost the after-dinner air hockey game to Jackie Dee, who was not thin, but not really overweight. She had brown hair—kind of curly but kind of straight. No more than average height and vaguely nothing in particular she looked, well, like a manager. We had driven to San Antonio's Dave and Buster's in her Ford Bronco SUV with mid-level styling, leather seats, but no GPS.

This restaurant's poolroom contained pool tables—dozens of them. There were also acres of video games, roller coaster simulators, shuffleboard courts (indoor shuffleboard? Only in Texas.), and the air hockey table with a whirling red light that spun whenever she scored.

Jackie, the vice president of production at TPC, The Psychological Corporation (a great name, isn't it?), had changed into blue jeans and a polo shirt for our dinner. Her four project managers came along to take Steve and Jo, from our Atlantic plant, and me out on the town.

The traditional place to take visitors in San Antonio is the famous River Walk. I was puzzled why people wanted to dine on what was basically a two-car-garage wide culvert buried a story and a half beneath street level— the murky water complemented by watered down Tex-Mex food, drunken conventioneers, and slow-milling tourists with disposable cameras. We had opted instead for the giant Dave and Buster's by the airport.

"Oh, David, you let me win," she said in her perfect upper-middle-class mid-Texas accent, a de-twanged drawl, and winked at me. She was our largest customer—twice as much revenue as Red— nearly the entire Atlantic plant was dedicated to her, so of course I had thrown the game. But I didn't have to lose to make her happy. It had been quite a successful day.

That morning when I walked in the conference room at TPC's offices in their faceless corporate building that was surrounded by a high, black iron fence, in a bad part of town—their neighbors a worn-out little park of scrub and dirt and three cheap taco places—I received two big shocks. The first was their whiteboard markers worked. The second was they were happy to see me. A whole conference room full of buyers, smiling, happy, and when I finished writing numbers on the whiteboard, they applauded!

TPC makes school tests. Other than the famous SAT test (made by their competitor), I had no idea that testing was such a large industry. They provided standardized tests for students in Virginia, Florida, Massachusetts, Texas, Delaware and many more states. They had started working with Clarinda in 1997 because they had a new production manager who—in an effort to get another promotion by cutting costs—fired their typesetting staff and moved the work from Texas to Iowa.

When he got promoted up and away, Jackie Dee took over. She reportedly had a good relationship with Luke from Household, so, to ease the transition, he and Dan had gone down to visit. I never got a clear report on the meeting. Dan said she wasn't a good manager; Luke said Dan had been condescending and called her "honey." This was the first I'd ever heard anyone, much less a customer, have anything negative to say about Dan, and I worried that if she had not understood Dan's sincerity, that she would be hard to win over. Regardless of what had transpired, she had become my account as a result.

The day after air hockey, Steve and Jo walked around their facility being good customer service people. All our customers had dedicated service people or, like Pearson, project managers in Kathy's group, but the level of service we gave TPC was unprecedented. Every month Steve, Jo, and frequently another service person, came down for three days of meetings. I hadn't seen anything wrong with giving our best customer a regular visit, but Dan had complained, "A trip every month. They better be our biggest customer."

On the way back to Jackie's office, we stopped in the lunchroom. She got a coffee and bought me a peanut butter cup from the vending machine.

"I just had an idea that it might be nice if you could maybe put one of your people here in San Antonio," she said, pushing around the orange-and-black wrapper from my candy. "Your putting an employee here might be a good way to give us both a higher level of partnership. Maybe one of your people would like to move to San Antonio? It really is nice here in the winter."

"I guess I can ask around," I said.

"It's just an idea," she said. "Just a thought I had."

We went to meet the recently hired VP of test development. Another Hilda look-alike, she shook my hand with the tips of her fingers. "I'm not sure why we're meeting," she said. "But Jackie thinks it will be good for you to understand what we are planning, although—" she leaned back in her chair, which threatened to topple with an angry squeal. "I don't really see how you would need to be involved other than just doing what we tell you." She handed me a document. "There's the whitepaper, why don't you try to read through that first before I have to explain more?"

The whitepaper was a marketing pamphlet about a database that had started life as a project at Thomson Publishing, and then gotten funding to go it as a freestanding venture.

A friend from Thomson told me "I can't understand why anyone would buy that piece of crap unless they had never seen a database in their life."

I gave my best smile.

Back in Dan's office in Iowa (go directly from San Antonio to Iowa, do not go home, eat only Subway sandwiches, do not pass Go), I was feeling pretty good about my successful trip. Jackie had decided to expand her business with us. We would be composing tests for elementary school students in Delaware. As I recounted the tale of the other VP, Dan shook his head.

"The database isn't about making a workable system, is it?" I asked as I realized the question was rhetorical. "It's about politics. She was using me to gather information to make the other VP look bad."

"Stocking up on bullets," he said, "You're learning, my boy. But this employee onsite in San Antonio!"

"She just said it was an idea," I said.

"No typesetter on Earth has staff in the customer's office. She wants this and <cough>." He took a swig of Robitussen and then one of Maalox from his briefcase, which had recently been marred with a large red stain from a bottle that had not been closed properly. "She needs this politically." He carefully screwed the cap back on with his long fingers, not moving his wrist, and wiped the chalky residue from his lips. "And it's going to cost us a hundred thousand a year. Mark my words, my boy, a hundred thousand or more. And who the heck is going to want to move from Iowa to San Antonio?"

"She only said it was a thought she had," I repeated. I felt my inexperience compared to Dan—like a child struggling with scales watching Horowitz at the piano.

"She will not let this request go, kiddo," he said. "She will not let this go and we have no choice."

"Should I ask around to see if anyone wants to move?"

"I don't know what else you would do," Dan said and picked up the ringing phone. "Hello, McSwenson, yes, Beth is doing what? Yes, I was the one who told her to have Kathy call Tammy at Pearson. Yes, and what's that? The Mikalson book is screwed up because of that call? Screwed up how—"

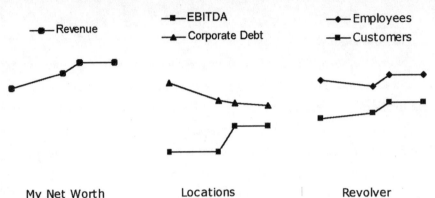

Revenue

EBITDA
Corporate Debt

Employees
Customers

My Net Worth

Locations

Clarinda
Atlantic
Baltimore
St. Paul
New York
Syracuse
Manila

Revolver

Revenue	$9,000,000
EBITDA	$1,000,000
Corporate Debt	$1,800,000
Employees	120
Customers	70
Revolver Expires	3 Months
My Net Worth	$3,600,000

The System 36

September 2000

"CONNIE KEEPS TELLING ME SHE DOESN'T KNOW who to trust," Dan said.

My girlfriend waited in the car while I stood alone on the green carpet of my father's living room, the cell phone battery burning against my ear—emblematic of what had become my social life. A month before we had gone on a hike and while she admired the view I had gone behind a rock—so as to avoid bothering the other hikers—to talk to Dan.

"Connie says you tried to force Jo to move to Texas," Dan said. "I told her you would never do such a thing. Now she says she doesn't know who to believe."

I was in Kingston visiting my father in Benedictine Hospital. It took another trip to the hospital to find the time to get to see him. He had gotten pneumonia again, probably from the aide who came to clean the house—although all the Old Smuggler whiskey shouldn't be discounted. By the bottles in the recycling bin, I estimated he was downing three to four liters a week.

"But Jo is in Atlantic and works for Donna, doesn't she?" I asked. "I thought you were making Connie VP of sales and reorganizing customer service." The living room was so quiet I could hear Dan pause to puff a cigarette in his office in Baltimore.

"They're like schoolgirls, David—little schoolgirls in the playground throwing mud." I imagined him at his desk; the disorganized stacks of paper everywhere, some of it years old; all of it covered in bits of cigarette ash or Maalox drips—yet somehow comforting in its reliable disarray.

"All I did was ask Jo if she wanted to take the job," I said.

"Connie says you tried to force her."

"Why would I do that, Dan? What was I supposed to do? Ask Connie if I could ask Jo? I was just trying to see if she would be interested."

"I told you, my boy, schoolgirls. Can you believe Connie? She doesn't know who to trust: me or Jo. Jo is saying you threatened her. We're going to have a hell of a time with this."

"I didn't threaten anyone!"

"What did you say, exactly?" he asked.

"I said, 'Jackie asked me to see if anyone wants to move to San Antonio. I already talked to Steve, and he's just built himself a new gazebo so I was talking to you, Jo, to see if you wanted to work down there.'"

"You told her about Steve?"

"I'm sorry," I said, picking up my father's whiskey glass from where it sat by the fireplace, "I knew that should have been confidential."

"Hell, they all talk up there. She probably knew about Steve. You know that, don't you? They all talk all the time. Like they've got nothing better to do."

"What do you want me to do? Call Connie? Explain to her?" I rolled the glass in my hand. It had gotten foggy with age.

"No, don't you trouble yourself. You've got your father to go see."

"I already saw him." My father had loved the hospital. Before I left, he had said, "You know I never liked cling peaches when your mother served them. But *these*. These I should take for when I go home. And did you see that nurse when you came in? She brings me extra." He had winked at me—his hair a wild gray mess.

"I was about to head back to the city with my girlfriend when you called."

Typo

"Well, don't worry about Connie," Dan said. "I'll take care of it."

I didn't bother to ask if he would fire her. Dan didn't fire people. He lectured them. I sat down on the blue chair by the fireplace. Wasn't the president of the company allowed to call an employee and ask them if they wanted a job in San Antonio? Had they just been waiting to set me up? Why had I just gotten a lecture from Dan? Did employees not trust management no matter what I did? What had happened to making the company I'd always wanted to work for?

"Dan, one more thing."

"What is it my boy?"

"What about our line of credit with Household. Are we going out of business in three months?"

"Is that what you worry about kiddo?"

"Yes."

"Well, there's no point. It's too late to find another bank and so I've been talking to Luke about getting it extended if we hit our targets."

"And he'll give us more time?"

"That's up to him. The only way to be sure we fail is to give up now. Are you planning on giving up?"

I looked again at my father's living room. What would happen if I lost his life savings?

"No, sir."

"Then get yourself back in that car and come help me teach these people how to run a typesetting business."

ℓ

Back in Iowa, Red Bones' e-mail informed me, "I am very concerned about Clarinda's scheduling and quality. How are you going to resolve the open issues?"

What open issues?

"You weren't listening to me when I said that we were having trouble making schedules, were you?" Dan asked. Probably not, I thought, swiveling back and forth in a chair. He said a lot of things. Lately, many of them were threatening yet vague such as "we're going to have trouble, just you wait," that he uttered like a Greek oracle or a doom-focused fortune cookie.

"What were the open issues?" I asked again.

"I demoted Connie from head of customer service to just in charge of service in Clarinda. She's not going to be getting the big sales VP job I had promised her. Did you know that she transferred the Harcourt accounts I gave her to Larry?" He turned his forefinger against his ear, scratching the cavity intently. "You know, my boy, that means we're going to have to pay commission on those house accounts now—doubling the cost—and she just handed them over."

I didn't know.

"What was she thinking, trying to come between us?" he put his hand on the ringing phone but didn't pick up.

"I don't know, Dan. What are the issues with Red Bones' books? I can't fix them if I don't know." The receptionist paged over the intercom, "Dan, dial 106. Dan, 106."

"You can't fix them, my boy. We are too far into the season," he said, his thin, tanned hand still on the receiver. He had ignored the ringing too long; the receptionist stalked in.

"I've been paging you. You've got a call on 106."

Dan looked up and blinked. "Who is it?"

"I didn't ask," she said. I'd heard him request many times for her to find out who was on the phone before she paged him, but she didn't seem to like doing that. "Are you going to pick up?" she asked.

"As soon as I'm done here with David," he said. She remained in the doorway. He looked at her wearily. "Well, my boy, I guess we're done for now. It's the System 36, it runs this damn place. We're done for the rest of the season." And with that he picked up the phone, his voice returning to its vigorous salesman mode, "Hank! How goes that lovely little editorial company of yours we are still hoping to buy? Good! No, I didn't hear from the bank about loaning you some equipment for the McGraw job. I'm sorry, I was held up a bit in a meeting with David. You remember David, don't you? Yes, he's one of my favorite people too," Dan winked at me, and the receptionist left her perch at the door. "Maybe my favorite of all time, but you're up there too, Hank …"

Dan's conversation would go on for at least an hour, and a stack of phone calls would be waiting for him when he was done. I wouldn't be finding anything out about Red's issues from Dan today. I went to my office.

It was already noon and neither of us had eaten yet. I didn't feel like going to Subway again. The two semi-retired women they employed were always trying to put cheese on my sandwiches and getting Dan's order incorrect. "Tuna, extra mayonnaise, lots of salt and pepper, no, more pepper than that, yes, really more pepper, I know, it's weird."

I glumly pulled two cans of Campbell's soup from my filing cabinet, and poured them into a disposable red plastic bowls. While the first spun lopsidedly around the microwave, I called the cadaver, McSwenson. The line was full of static.

"I'm…daughter from…skating lessons. But I'm…you got me. We're late on the whole Fin… series and the …lkers book with …ed." The line snapped into clarity. "Didn't you get my e-mails?"

I pulled up his dozen e-mails: a huge chain of forwards and replies. There were issues about missing files, comments about fonts; but nowhere could I find mention of a book being off schedule.

"What are you going to do to make Red happy? He's ready to throw us out."

"I don't know, McSwenson, this is the first I've really understood what's going on. And I don't really understand." I said. "I've got to talk to Frank. I'll get back to you as soon as I can."

"Can you do it before the end of the week?"

I had forgotten. "Next week is your trip to see the Pope?"

"If you can get me something to get to Red before I leave—"

"I can always call Red by myself, can't I?"

"Oh, well, of course," he said. "But he's going to want to know that I've gotten things fixed for him, and…" he trailed off into static.

The soup had heated and gotten cold. I ran the microwave another couple of minutes and called Connie. She arrived in the doorway, her hands clasped in front of her black calf-length skirt. She smelled like smoke and looked especially grey, with skin the color of an unwashed ashtray. I often saw her huddled on the loading dock on the north side of the plant with the other smokers, flicking their ashes onto the ground instead of into the long-necked yellow ashcan designed to keep the butts from being blown in the breeze.

I took the soup out of the microwave and put some crackers on a paper plate. She looked unhappily at the crumbs on my table.

"Well, how late are we?" I asked.

"I can get you a report."

"Don't you know?" I offered her a Saltine. She declined.

"I have to ask Shirley. Is there anything else you need, David?"

"Is there a status meeting going on today?"

"At three."

I made a little 'oh' sound, and she walked off.

I brought Dan the second bowl of soup. Still on the phone, he pushed a stack of paper aside so that I could put the bowl down. He put his hand over the receiver. "Thank you, David. You knew you had to put it in front of me to get me to eat, didn't you?"

Connie came in. She had walked out of my door, down the hall, and into Dan's far door rather than follow me through the connecting one. "Oh Connie, is it one, already?" Dan said and flipped his wrist to examine his watch. "I'll be right with you." He put his hand on my arm, "Thank you again for the soup, my boy." Connie managed to look unhappier. She could not avoid having to watch one of us eat, and reluctantly sat down on the edge of a chair.

ℓ

At five minutes to three, Frank, Ron, Shirley, Connie, and Lorraine, the Iowa scheduling woman, began passing by my door on their way into the conference room. The job of scheduling in Clarinda meant reviewing 106 pages of tractor feed paper spat out by the System 36. The meeting flowed along: Frank asked about a book, Shirley said something, and Frank and Lorraine made notes, everyone head down, poring over their individual copy.

"Do you print the whole thing out for every meeting?" I asked.

Frank paused mid-scribble and looked up, "We print it every day."

"Every day? How do you get the changes you marked into the system?"

"Jess enters them," Shirley said, happy that I had asked a question she could answer easily. So that's what the woman with the dinner plate eyeglasses was doing every night outside my office till midnight.

"How do you know if a book's going to be late?" I asked.

Frank held his pencil still above the report. Shirley smiled at me the way my mother had smiled when I asked how she knew what was a weed and what was a flower. "It's in the schedule," she said and went back to the missing artwork for an Oxford book. "Did Sally say she's sending it?"

"Yes," Connie said, "it will be here on—" she looked through her folders and pulled out a memo. "Thursday." Frank wrote it down. Lorraine wrote it down. I looked at my schedule.

"Where does it say this book is going to be late?" I asked.

"We know it's going to be late—" Frank said, moving a finger across the report, "Because we discuss it here and I make a note." Lorraine and Connie put down their pens. The meeting was normally three hours long and I was making it longer.

"And then what happens?"

"And then we change the date," Ron said, his voice at first worried that I was upset and then ending on a happy note—my confusion most certainly solved by his explanation.

"But if you're not at the meeting," I said, "you wouldn't know if the book was going to be late because the due date has been changed to reflect our delay."

"Yes," Frank said, poking the lead of his pencil slowly into the tip of his opposing index finger.

"But people know," Connie said, "Because they see the changed schedule."

"But what about me?" I asked. "How would I know?"

I always thought it was odd that Frank, the production manager for the whole company, had a tiny windowless office in the back of customer service and Lorraine, the scheduler, had an "executive" office in the front that was bigger than mine and had a larger window.

His office just fit his desk and one guest in an un-wheeled chair. On the paneled wall behind him hung a calendar and a circular saw blade painted with an idyllic scene of a fisherman casting a net from his boat.

"I used to have Lorraine's office," he said, "Before Jack demoted me."

"You must have had a lot of offices in forty years."

"No, just these two."

"Oh." I tried not to bump anything off his desk as I crossed my legs. "And after you left Chicago, you never wanted to move back?"

"Nope."

"Have you been back at all?"

He put his thumb and fist up to his chin as he thought. I'd heard from others that they were afraid of Frank, which I didn't understand. His voice was soft like a Lutheran Mel Torme, and I never saw him angry.

Customers could be on the phone screaming and he would remains as mellow as if he had swallowed a tub of Prozac. "Twice," he said.

"Don't you miss it?"

"My daughter likes it, but it's too noisy for me," he said and chuckled. He didn't need Prozac; he had the ultimate barbiturate—Iowa.

"Does anything exciting ever happen in Clarinda?"

He considered this as seriously as he did every question. "We did used to do work for Playboy."

"Playboy?"

"We did final film for them years ago. I've got the proofs in my closet." A couple of late nights would be spent by me looking through all the places in the plant that could be considered "Frank's Closet"—I never found them.

"Well," I said. "So what is going on with the Pearson books?"

He unfurled his status report again. We weren't just having problems with Pearson. For schoolbooks to be ready for the fall, they must be printed in the late summer, which means that typesetting happens during a four-month period starting in February and ending in June. This is *the season* and by April of 2000, we had hit it like Wile E. Coyote hitting a brick wall in pursuit of the Roadrunner—nearly every book was off schedule. "I told all this to Dan," he said after going through the last page. "Didn't he tell you?"

"Not exactly."

He explained that the System 36 managed our schedule by multiplying the amount of time required to, say, scan a piece of art by a job difficulty factor, and that factor was determined by…he was interrupted by Dan's appearance at the door.

"Frank! You're here late! Has David been holding you hostage?"

"I've still got a few things to catch up on," he uttered mildly.

"Well, I need David right now. Can I take him away from whatever you two are up to?"

"Of course," I said. I would have liked to finally figure out was wrong with the Pearson books, but it looked as if that would have to wait.

"Come to my office, my boy. We've got a customer to talk to."

ℓ

Standing behind his desk, Dan picked up the phone. "Still there?" I noted the untouched bowl of soup still on his desk. "I hope I can make this work." He pressed down the hold button and then the speakerphone. "Hello?"

"Hello?"

He fumbled with the receiver. Instead of returning it to the cradle before pressing speaker, he reversed the process, which would hang up. I jumped to grab the phone while trying to keep silent. He often wanted me to listen without speaking.

"Ooops," he said, lighting a cigarette, "I almost hung up on you there, Red. David here saved the day."

"David's there with you?" Red Bones asked.

"Hello." I said meekly.

"Are you getting any biking in?" Red asked.

"Oh, I try."

"He bought that fancy bike and he never gets to go pedaling it," Dan said. "It's such a waste. A pretty purple one it is. You've got a bike like that, right Red?"

"I've got a Cannondale."

I rubbed my hands along the armrests of the chair and Dan took a drag on his cigarette and then winked at me.

"But that's not what we're talking about today, is it, Red?" Dan asked.

"You guys made such a good impression out here. Now I'm wondering why I backed you—my staff says everything with you is late."

Dan shuffled some papers. "I have a report that Connie prepared for David. It looks like we're a week late on a couple of titles. Two weeks late on another couple and all the rest are ahead of schedule or held up waiting for your art."

There was a click like we were being put on mute. Dan pursed his lips and raised his eyebrows. Another click and Red said, "Those two books that are the latest are our triple A titles. The triple A books are two thirds of our revenue. You're close on books that aren't important to me."

"And our people understand that?" Dan asked.

"They should."

"McSwenson has talked with you about this?"

"That's not the point, Dan. I need to hear what you, the owners, are going to do."

"We're going to get right on it," Dan said, crushed out his cigarette and leaned forward on his elbows while clasping his hands together in a ball.

"Kathy is coming out to see you next week, isn't she?"

There was some faint muttering on the line.

"Red, is that you? Are you still there?"

"Oh," Red said, "I was just checking with Henrietta, she's, uh, just walked in."

"Hello," came a voice even meeker than mine.

"Hello, Henrietta, always glad to hear from you," Dan said. "And now McSwenson doesn't have to make an extra call to let you know David's going to be coming out with Kathy and make certain that you are getting our best work."

There was some whispering from the speakerphone, and then a couple of clicks of the mute button being switched on too late.

"Well, that's all well and good and we look forward to seeing David," Red said. "But what we want to know is how you're going to get the books back on track."

"That's what David will be there for. He's the President of the company and he's your man."

There was more whispering.

"Henrietta will have a report for David when he gets here."

"That's great." Dan said. "He's looking forward to it."

"I certainly am!" I said.

After the call I threw away the soup that had congealed into a thick-skinned lump. "I guess I'm going to Columbus." I said. "But how am I going to fix the problems?"

"There's nothing you can do, my boy, but wave the flag."

Red met with Kathy in the morning, but by the time I arrived in Columbus, he was long gone. Kathy and I adjusted our chairs in the windowless conference room where we had been selling the "new Clarinda" only a few months before. There would be no whiteboard talk of financial dreams today.

Henrietta, the senior buyer, began. She was an apple-core-doll faced woman wearing a long yellow skirt and open-toed sandals, who flipped through pages of manuscript and yanked out one error after another. She slid a page under Kathy's nose. "I corrected this in pass three, but here it is in pass four." I leaned over to observe the mark that indicated a hyphenated word should not be broken. "No more than two hyphens in a row is our house style. Your people should know that."

Being careful to not overuse hyphens to break words that did not fit at the end of lines was a hallmark of a well-typeset book versus one made with, say, Microsoft Word. It was no small matter to editors—who had to find something to pride themselves on—and the makers of QuarkXpress and other typesetting software crowed loudly about their advanced H&J (hyphenation and justification) algorithms. Quark will also hang the hyphens into the margin area, a detailed carryover from the days of hot lead—as if anyone in the world who has ever read a book noticed. (And younger editors will mark the hung hyphen as an error, almost guaranteeing that whichever method you use, someone will think it an abomination.)

Kathy examined the page like an archeologist dusting off a ten-thousand year old Aztec pottery shard. "I know," Kathy said. "You made the style change last year. I don't know how this got through."

"Here's the e-mail I sent," Henrietta said, handing it to me.

Sure enough, there was something about hyphens and referring to the style guide. They were right, but it was just a hyphen—a millimeter of ink that no one other than Henrietta and our typesetters would ever care about—potentially costing Clarinda, which meant Dan and me, hundreds of thousands of dollars.

"The other problem I have is that I can't get a straight answer on schedules from Connie. She tells me it's going to be a day, then I call her, and then it's another day or two days. She has no idea. I don't know what's going on in Iowa, but I need straight answers."

"Of course," I said.

After Henrietta was done pummeling us, she got Francine.

"I don't even know why I'm talking to you," was how Francine, an editor with pens in her grey-brown hair, greeted us. "There's no way you can catch up on the schedule now. The author is beside himself."

"If we can't catch up, then maybe we should send you the book back," I said, trying to be helpful. I didn't want her mad at us.

Francine froze. "You can't do that! You want to send it back?! Whose going to do it then? All the other vendors are full up!"

"No, no, I'm sorry," I said. "I was just trying to do what you wanted. Of course we would prefer to finish it."

Francine sat down, the look of horror still in her eyes.

Kathy and I remained in the room without lunch, editors following buyers, until we ran for our plane at five. In the cab I said to Kathy, "What was that all about with Francine? Why did she threaten to take the book back and then freak out when I suggested we do just that?"

Kathy stuffed the stacks of manuscript and reports into her leather bag. "What they don't tell you is that they're complaining about everyone. Red told me that even their best vendor, Corsairs, is having trouble keeping up with the season." She forced the bag shut with a grunt. "And he told me confidentially we aren't the worst."

"Oh, thank God," I said.

"He said we were close."

Columbus was only the start. I spent the coming weeks visiting Mosby, Oxford, McGraw-Hill, Thomson and even TPC for days on end of chewing out. "OK, Buyer One is done, now Editor Two wants to tell you about how you were late with her books." Each Post-It note of error peeled from the page proofs during the meetings felt like a bandage being ripped from my chest.

$$\ell$$

I paced the parking lot of TPC in San Antonio. It had been a long day of Jackie Dee and her managers complaining. At meeting after meeting, I apologized as the president of Clarinda, and they folded their hands and smiled, satisfied we had been castigated. Then we shuffled to the next conference room for another lashing or waited in the same one while the current band of project managers collected their papers and others squeezed into the still warm seats.

At lunch, as a reward, Jackie took me on a tour of the warehouse where hundreds of temporary employees sorted the arriving batches of number 2 penciled-in tests. The women pressed shoulder to shoulder at the long tables could have been in one of the plants I visited in the Philippines. Never had I imagined that my student hours of testing torture in the hot summer led directly to hours of torture for underpaid Mexican test-scorers.

Now at the end of my day I waited for a cab, and, of course, called Dan. TPC's bored, eye patch-wearing, security guard armed with what looked like a real gun watched me with faint hope I might give him a reason to use it.

"We are falling behind on Red's work again," Dan said.

"But I sent out an e-mail that any messages about delays had to go through me."

"Welcome to my world, my boy." he said. "Did you really expect them to listen to you when they don't listen to me?"

"Yes," I said. I had.

"Well this will make you even unhappier then. Did you know when a customer calls for sample pages we refer to the System 36? Larry was afraid to tell Harcourt it would take two weeks for ten pages. He wanted me to promise we could do it faster. How long do you think those pages take for my people in Baltimore?"

He always called the Baltimore staff "his people."

"That's right," he said without waiting for an answer. "A day. Just one fucking day. Manila could do it almost as fast."

"Maybe even faster," I said.

"Maybe even faster. You're probably right, David. Maybe even faster. We don't stand a chance against the Indians, or anyone else, with this System 36 ruling our lives."

"Why don't you just shut it off?"

"Don't think I don't want to. Just flip it off. Wouldn't that be nice?"

"Yes," I said.

"In time, my boy, in time. Now tell me how that person we hired down there is working out."

Dan had been right. Jackie hadn't given up on the idea of Clarinda putting someone in San Antonio. When no one would relocate from Iowa we had hired a woman Jackie had found.

"She's incompetent," I said.

"We already knew that, kiddo. She's hardly ever there."

"No, I mean she was out all last week because she had a car accident. She told me 'I was late to work because I couldn't find my glasses. I didn't want to upset you by being late again so I drove without them.' That's why she hit a parked car."

"She's OK?" he asked.

"Well, she's not hurt."

He laughed. "I'm sorry my boy, but that is funny. And at a time like this we need a laugh, right? What did your friend Jackie say?"

"She said, 'You really have to learn how to manage your employees.'"

My taxi had just pulled up to the gate. The guard carefully maneuvered a long pole with a mirror at the end under the rusted, pawnshop-advertising orange Chevy to make sure it wasn't rigged to explode.

ℓ

Back in Iowa, by two in the afternoon Dan hadn't made it into the office. He often called customers or checked in with Manila from the quiet of his room at the Super 8, and then would get stuck there as employees tracked him down, leaving message after message on his phone. The gap-toothed desk clerk brought him little packets of message slips with far more sympathy than the Clarinda receptionist. As I jammed another SubClub card of proof-of-purchase stickers in my desk, worrying when I would get to talk to him, the phone rang.

"Tell me what food poisoning is like, kiddo," Dan said, weakly.

"You don't know what food poisoning is?" Would he hear me if I unwrapped my sandwich?

"I've never had it my life. What does it do to you?"

The plastic crinkled too loudly and I reluctantly put it down. "The last time I had Korean food I was so sick I vomited kimchee out my nose."

"Kim-chee?"

"Pickled cabbage that they bury underground for a few months." I pushed the sandwich away.

"You and your fancy foreign food. Well, I think that's what I have.

First time. How about that?" He began to cough. "Just a second." He kept coughing. "Just a second, my boy." Another cough. "Jesus Christ. Well, I'm sitting here trying to get better and returning a few calls. I shouldn't be doing that, should I?"

"You should take it easy."

"Well, I am going to try and come in later. Can you do me a favor?"

"Anything."

"I knew you wouldn't fail me. Will you get Connie and Lorraine together out there to meet with me at <cough> say three, <cough> or maybe, four? Damnation this cough. It's Iowa, my boy. Every time I come here."

Of course it was the smoking, but rather than upset him with the obvious, I said what he always said, "You probably caught it on the plane."

"And ask Sally if she could come by at six, maybe for dinner? Could you tell them that I would like it if they could stay late to talk with me? You know how the Iowans are. Always running off to be with their families. As if we get to be with our families? Right? You'd much rather be with your friends in New York, wouldn't you? Those friends of yours, <cough> they're your <cough> family, aren't they?" He kept coughing.

"Maybe you'd like to go to a doctor?"

"You're a good man. You are too good to me, but I'll be all right. I've been through worse. <cough> You promise me you'll see if you can get them to come by my office and not have to skedaddle out of there at four thirty? Their families will survive without them for a couple of hours," he cleared his throat with a "kerragh." "In the meantime, I'm going to see if I can eat some of those crackers and cheese you dropped off for me the other night. Get something on my Goddamned stomach, right?"

ℓ

Connie and Lorraine sat in front of Dan's desk and I sat at the round conference table beside it, putting as much veneer and solid wood between them and me as possible. Connie was as unhappy looking as ever, like an un-watered carnation. Lorraine was the poster child for Iowa living. Despite being in her mid-fifties she appeared to be a younger version of Kathy from St. Paul: blond hair, blue jeans, and blue eyes. The only sign of her true age the thick layer of powder on her cheeks. My main interaction with Lorraine had been listening to her walk back-and-forth with the schedules: her loose sandals making a tha-fwick sound with every step.

A few minutes later Dan walked in slowly, holding on to the doorframe for support. He wore an un-tucked golf shirt instead of his usual crisp button-down and a Calloway Golf cap pulled down to the tops of his ears.

"I'm sorry," he said, "I've not been feeling well." He moved to his desk, lifting his feet carefully; balancing on the conference table, his desk, and at last his high-backed chair, which spun around when he put his weight onto the arm almost knocking him flat. He fell into the chair, took off his cap, and put it on top of the messages that formed the highest point of the pile on his desk.

"But down to business." He brushed his hair up with the palms of his hands and smiled, as well groomed as ever, but his skin color was month-old snow mixed with a flush of fever. "Lorraine," he said. "I understand from Beth that you turned away a job from Houghton Mifflin today."

Lorraine drew herself up in her chair and then bowed her head, as if she were both indignant and subservient. "The System 36 said—"

He slammed his hand down, knocking his messages and cap to the floor. The sound of his hand hit me in my stomach, like my father yelling at my mother—somehow my fault. I bent to pick the cap up. He continued without looking at me rummaging at his feet. "I never want to hear about that fucking System 36 ever again," he growled, his eyes locked on a spot near Lorraine's ear. "I said that I didn't want any projects turned down without my express approval. And that will never happen. We need that work to stay in business. To pay these people." He relaxed a little, his voice returned to a normal level, but hoarse from the coughing. "And today I heard that we decided to turn the work away because of the System 36. It will," he said, spacing each word, "never ... happen ... again."

It was the first time I'd seen him yell at an employee, although he didn't actually focus on either Lorraine or Connie. Lorraine, looked down, appeared to think of something to say, but didn't.

"Connie, I want to make sure you understand that. No work is ever turned down except by me."

"Dan," she said, wringing her hands, "Everything is so late already. We have no idea what to tell the customers."

"What do you think we should be telling them?"

"I feel like we should tell them when we are doing the books in Manila. They expect we are doing them here in Iowa with people they know. But when we do a job in Manila or Baltimore and it's one day late, two days, and then it still isn't done. The customers are upset when we aren't in control."

"Well, I do have control over Manila and Baltimore," he said, "And that's not the problem. There are only a few books being done in either of those plants, and that's the problem. Delays here are the symptom of not sending work out of Iowa."

Connie closed her eyes and said, "The books Manila is doing for Pearson are full of errors."

"Hyphens?" I ventured, remembering what I'd seen in Columbus.

"Yes, David," she said, opening her eyes. "Hyphens."

"I understand that Manila was sent the wrong style sheet," Dan said. "Fanta is beside herself over there. No one could be unhappier than she is that the customer is upset. But she didn't even know anything had gone wrong till I told her. The typesetters here in Iowa were taking it on themselves to fix the errors, rather than teaching or working with Manila.

You might even say," he raised his eyebrows and rubbed his tongue along his false teeth, "we're sabotaging ourselves."

"I know Dan, I know, I know—" Connie said, shaking her head in sharp little motions.

He continued as if she hadn't spoken, "And I don't know why we keep giving the customers new dates when we simply don't know when we are going to finish. If it's late, what can we tell them other than 'we're working as fast as we can'?" His voice returned to the good-old Dan again. "We don't seem to understand that we just need to get the books done when the customer wants them—"

"We have to give them a date!" Connie said, interrupting. "Dan! You don't understand what I'm up against." As Dan had regained his composure, Connie lost hers. Her voice shook and her hands trembled on the armrests.

Dan asked Lorraine and me to leave. Glad to be released, we hurried out—Lorraine's shoes rapidly slapping back to her office. I closed his main door and the one connecting his office to mine.

I couldn't hear anything from next door, so I loaded up *Age of Empires* as I did many nights. Just as I had amassed my Carthaginian elephant army to storm the Viking stronghold, Audrey, one of the shift supervisors, knocked on my door.

"I have that Pearson style guide you asked Shirley for," she said. Audrey reminded me of a Harley rider. It wasn't that she had tattoos or even a motorcycle, but she was originally from Texas, not Iowa, and had a rougher edge—there were rumors that she had come to Clarinda by running away from home with a trucker, or that she was currently having an affair with a trucker. Rumors tended to be undependable.

"Manila got the old style manual, right?" I asked.

Audrey sat down. "How did you know?"

"I heard from Dan."

"It was a real big mess," she said, "but we've got it under control."

"I'm glad."

She seemed in no hurry to go so I asked what else she was worried about.

"I'm glad you asked," she said, looking at me sternly. "Training is a failure. It doesn't work. You've got to stop it."

That was a surprise. I thought Sally's training program was going well.

"I went over to Sally's office one day to ask a question and the door was locked, but I could hear Sally in there," she said and scratched at her wrist.

How could I respond to that? What did a knock on a door have to do with a successful training program? I thought to ask, 'Is Sally's office the home of the Wizard of Oz? No one gets in to see the Wizard?' But what would be the point of that?

"Sally is always trying to get my production people off to do training," she continued. "There just isn't time for all that training. We're too busy."

"Too busy? How many people are in training?" I asked.

"I haven't sent anyone into training," Audrey responded.

"No one?"

"Why should I? Training is a failure."

Before I could come up with a response that could pry open that desperately-in-need-of-refutation tautology, Sally walked in. "Dan told me to stop by at six, but his door is closed."

"Are you finished with the Hopkins setup?" Audrey asked, not at all pleasantly.

"I left it on your desk on the production floor."

I had forgotten that Sally's new office used to be Audrey's. Apparently, training failed because Audrey and Sally hated each other.

Dan broke the awkward moment by opening the door into my office. I saw Connie's fleeting shape exiting through his other door.

"Well then," he said, "Just the people I wanted to see. Who wants to go to dinner with David and I?"

Audrey said she had some pages she had to finish checking. Sally had to pick up her handicapped son. Both of them dawdled seeing who would leave first. Ultimately, Audrey gave in with a shrug and after she was well gone Sally asked, "Could I meet you later, after I drop off my son?"

"Of course, dear," he said.

After Sally left, I asked Dan what had happened with Connie.

"What? Don't you want to be eating right now? It's late for you." He grabbed his jacket brusquely, his strength returned. "And seriously, we should get out of the office. You've been here too long today and I probably shouldn't have come in at all."

The Ice House was particularly quiet. A lone man watched us silently from the dimly lit end of the bar. Dan twirled a spoon in his beer cheese soup. He'd asked, as always, what kind of soup they had. The answer, as always, was "beer cheese." It looked like melted Velveeta. I tried to ignore the silent man.

"What are we going to do about getting rid of that System 36?" I asked.

"Connie is going through some hard times. Her grandmother's very sick and I hear that boyfriend of hers beats her. Did you see any bruises?"

"No," I said. She was in her fifties—her grandmother must have been in her nineties, at least, so wouldn't she be expected to have health problems? And why would a fifty-plus-year-old have picked a boyfriend who was abusive? And why would I be looking for welts?

"Well, she was crying in my office about it, my boy. I told her she could reduce her workload to just her customers. She feels like she's let me down, David. Remember when she was going to be our cheerleader?"

I grimaced.

"And she's sorry about the whole thing with Jo and TPC and she apologized for complaining about you." He took a puff of his cigarette; he had hardly touched the orange soup or his beer, but he'd eaten two crackers. "Do you believe her?"

I wasn't ready to forgive Connie just because she'd apologized to Dan. I hadn't seen her cry about her life or about defaming me. If she was really sorry, why hadn't she told me? Why did she run away at the end of the meeting?

Sally arrived and looked with apprehension at the booth. Dan made no motion to respond, so I moved over as far as I could, and she slid in with effort, taking up two-thirds of the seat.

"How's your son?" Dan asked.

"He's doing better." She was sweating a little and huffing when she talked. "But we're worried about that girl of his."

"Didn't you tell me he's marrying her?" Dan asked.

"I just don't know what to do if she gets pregnant. Oh, hi, Nancy." Sally knew the waitress. She knew everyone in town. "Is Bert working in the kitchen tonight? No? Well maybe just a little hamburger. Hey there, Ted." She waved at the silent man, who raised his glass to us.

Sally noticed we were confused. "That's Ted. Frank's son. Didn't you guys know he manages the Ice House?" I considered all the work conversations Dan and I had at these tables, and then understood that Ted was like his father. He didn't listen to what we said. He wouldn't listen without being asked to.

She continued, "There's no way my son or she is ready to take care of a baby."

"I don't understand," I said.

"The girl is also mentally handicapped," Dan said. "It's terribly sad. But isn't it better that they have found someone to love in each other?"

"I suppose," she said. "Although I swear, I wonder sometimes if they shouldn't be sterilized." She took a bite of her small hamburger, no cheese, no fries. If that's all she ate, how could she still weigh so much?

"I saw Audrey battling with you in front of David," Dan said, "Has she gone through the training program like I asked her to, Sally?"

"Audrey's supposed to go through training?" I asked.

"Yes," he said. "I talked to her about it at some length. Did you know that she's a typesetting supervisor but she doesn't know how to make a page, kiddo?"

Before I could say, *No, I don't know that Dan. I don't have all the sources that you have telling me stuff all day.* Sally said, "And every time she does, she screws it up and I have to fix it."

"Isn't that the point of training?" Dan asked. "How's the Superleaf coming along? Do you have most of the setup people trained?" Every project required one key typesetter, called a "setup person." Everyone else was a lowly "pagemaker." Without the setup person, nothing happened. Of over a hundred employees, a dozen did eighty percent of the work.

"That's the thing. I can't get any of the managers to let employees out for training."

Dan folded and refolded his paper napkin with the tips of his fingers. "So are we using Superleaf for anything other than Pearson books?"

"Technically, their FUN requirement doesn't go into effect until next season."

"So how much Superleaf are we doing?"

"Including the two books I'm working on?"

"Including those two precious books you are working on, my dear," he said, warmly emphasizing each word—making sure that she knew he respected what she was fighting against.

"Two."

Four men wearing flannel shirts and orange hunting jackets sat down heavily in the booth behind Sally and me. One of them swung his arm over the back—draping an oversized hand a hairy-finger's width away from my shoulder.

"Well that just confirms what I've been hearing," Dan said. "That's why I'm going to make a command. My first command ever in Clarinda and hopefully the only one. Are you two ready?" I had been distracted by the hand and the loud conversation of the men. They were bankers who'd spent the day golfing, not hunting. They had worn orange because of the proximity of the course to a gun club.

Dan kept talking without waiting, "Everyone has to go through an hour of training three days a week. Everyone. They can't say no to that."

Sally brightened, as if she were happy, but her voice sounded like Dan had just told her that she was a miserable failure. "I don't know. What about your staff in Baltimore? How about training for them? Francine doesn't know anything about typesetting."

"What she doesn't know," he said, slowly, "is how Clarinda does things. Francine has been making pages as long as you have. Maybe longer. She could probably teach you a thing or two."

Sally pushed a pickle slice around her plate.

l

"What are you doing?" I asked the typesetter working on a Red Bones' book.

"Fixing the math in Foid," she said, one hand on the mouse, the other holding her place on the manuscript that was covered in purple "PE" marks for Printer's Error. PE meant us.

"The equations aren't lined up," she said. I smelled her AquaNet.

"And how do you fix that?" I asked.

"I open each one with this control panel, change the coding for the math, save, reopen and then do the next one," she said.

"Can't you do them all at once?" *I should be able to fix these production problems*, I thought. *I had a god-damned mathematics degree.*

"Each one affects the others. I have to print it out and check after every fix."

"With a ruler?"

"With a ruler." Dan had been telling me for years, "The problem is they use the computer as if it were a light table." The mouse was an X-Acto knife cutting and pasting like they did a decade ago, but I hadn't understood till I watched the typesetter with her straightedge.

"How long does that take?" I asked.

"Oh, I can do at least five a day." Each page was only worth twenty dollars. To make any profit, we needed to be doing five an hour—without mistakes.

"Is there anything we can do to fix this?" I asked.

"Oh, you know," she said. "A lot of us have been talking—"

"Yes?"

"Well, we all think it's a real problem—" She looked around at the other typesetters for encouragement. "—that the carpet hasn't been fixed. I mean it's patched together with duct tape. Somebody could fall."

I went back to my office defeated. The workers weren't understanding the real problem and I couldn't fix anything because I couldn't make pages. I called Sally. "Do you have room in your next class for another student?"

"I can probably make room. Who is it?"

"Me."

ℓ

"It hasn't been a bad season, all in all," Dan said, looking at financial reports which mingled on his desk with five-year-old letters, cigarette ash and plush toys he got from the Manila employees every Christmas.

"What's that?" I had been checking e-mail. When I visited Baltimore I had nowhere to sit but in Dan's office.

"The report says we've got our nine million, my boy. One year of the David and Dan show and we have upped sales by 50%." He flipped through the pages. "And do you know how many books were late when all was said and done?"

"Half?"

"Guess again, my boy."

From his smile I decided to go down. "A third?"

"Ten. Ten, and you thought we were going down like an Irishman at a dog track."

I closed my computer. All that pain, all that customer complaining and teeth gnashing, and we had only been late on ten books? Did customers just enjoy complaining?

"Even I'm surprised those folks out in Iowa pulled it out. Determination. Whatever else anyone says, those Iowa folks are good workers. Their reputation for quality. That's what we bought and that's what they have. And Baltimore and Manila helped. Now we just need to get that revolver—" A typesetter knocked on the door. "What is it, my dear?"

"I'm heading out for my sister's." She had long greasy hair and an unfortunate mole half the size of her nose on her left cheek.

"Oh, that's right," Dan said and pulled out a roll of bills from his pocket. "Is five hundred going to be enough to get you through this?"

"I can get this back to you—" she said, brushing heavily past me to take it from his hand.

"Never you mind. Make sure to say hello to your sister."

She thanked him several times before leaving.

"What would you have me do, my boy? They need me." His phone rang. "Yes. No."

I flipped open my computer again—wondering if every year would be like this and if it was better to change the pattern of the industry or grow callused to it—while Dan confronted the caller with his best sales manager tone.

"I thought I told you … Yes, I know you know, Frank. It's not like I was unavailable … No, no, I don't want to act rashly. Don't do anything. I will call Hilda … Let me take care of this for you." He slammed down the phone.

"She did it again," he said, chewing his lower lip.

"Did what?" I asked, looking up from my e-mail.

"You know, if it had been her, I might have just fired her."

"Fired? Who? Hilda?" I said and closed my computer. He never fired anyone.

"No, Lorraine, that petty little scheduler. She told Mosby again that we couldn't take a job because the System 36 said 'no'. You know what her excuse was this time?"

I shook my head. Was it somehow my fault? It couldn't be, but his tone made me nervous.

"Her excuse was that she couldn't find me. It's not like I wasn't available by phone."

"Or she could have called me." I didn't want him thinking I wasn't doing everything I could to stop employees from screwing up.

He looked at me as if he had forgotten I was there. "Yes, she could have called you," he said, "And then you would have found me, am I right?" The "am I right" a sharp jab of anger—her insubordination getting to him more than usual.

"Yes," I said, nodding.

"You could have called me. She knows we talk every day," he muttered while dialing the phone. "Hello, Hilda, yes, it's Dan. About that book that just got turned down. I know, I know, I know. How can you sell to Mosby if we keep turning the books away? No, this isn't just like when David went to see McGraw. Hilda, we can take the book. No. No. Hilda, it's going to be OK. If you want I will call the Mosby people directly. I still have something of a name in there, don't I?" His voice rose to the crescendo of the barb of the rhetorical question and then descending when Hilda relented. "I thought so—"

ℓ

At five, the empty field outside the window was already starting to go dark. Fall came quickly in Iowa. One day there would be golden oceans of corn, and the next, dirt. GPS-navigated combines swept through the

Great Plains, their headlights deep in the fields, disorienting drivers in the moonless evenings.

I proudly presented my idea to Steve and Dan. I wanted to build SNAP to replace the System 36. A technical acronym, it stood for Steve's New Application. "I'm pinning it on you, Steve, in case it doesn't work."

He laughed, but looked concerned. Steve, the account manager for TPC, had been shunted out of the way much like Sally. He ended up making databases for TPC because it suited his tendency to work fervently through the night. Jackie Dee loved his three a.m. progress reports, and it had kept him out of the way of previous management.

"I'm joking Steve. I'm calling it SNAP because I want you to feel like it's yours as much as mine."

"Of course!" he said. It was autumn, but his skin was still a deep shade of marmalade from either golf or duck hunting every weekend and after I got to know his lazy eye, it creeped me out only occasionally.

Dan listened quietly while I laid out my goals for SNAP on the whiteboard. The problem with the System 36, I said, was that it was no more than a filing cabinet, an antiquated one. None of its components were linked. Pricing from estimating wasn't used to make invoices. Instead, the billing person literally went through finished books page by page. After she typed up an invoice, another clerk entered the data into the System 36. SNAP would fix that and many other problems.

Dan said, "Steve, you're our man. I know you can build this thing."

"Yeah, you guys are right. It does need an overhaul," Steve said. "I tried and tried to get Household to understand that, but they never listened. Still, kind of ironic that I'm the one who's doing it, isn't it?"

"Why is that?" Dan asked.

"Well, funny thing." He looked at Dan with his good eye and his lazy eye watched me as I sat down, or was it the other way around? "I was the guy who wrote the original System 36. I bet neither of you knew that."

Dan thumped the desk and snorted. "Well then, all the more reason you're the man to fix it," and turned to me, "But David, you and I both know what information this company needs and we could gather it in a week," and with that he got up and left.

I knew that he was trying to lead me somehow, but his statement was too Yoda-like for me to follow. How could the people understand without a system to give them data to understand from? Did he know his cryptic statement would just wind me up or did he want me to drop it? Was this his way of letting me learn? He wouldn't say and he didn't respond when I left screenshots of SNAP on his desk to review, so he must have wanted me to figure it out for myself.

ℓ

We held a Christmas party for the employees at the Ice House in the paneled backroom where the Rotary club met. I chose a table three down from Dan and sat next to employees I didn't know. They, of course, knew who I was, and after we'd covered their names, where they worked, and which towns they commuted from, dinner was spent in silence, but we smiled as we passed the salt or when someone accidentally dropped a fork.

Dan toasted the eight long tables of employees: "Our first full year has been difficult, but when all the results were in we got to our nine million. Thanks to the sales staff, we've added over thirty new customers and sold six million of new business, nearly as much as the company had done under Household. This is unprecedented growth for a typesetting company, or any service business, and we have a solid one million dollar profit to report."

He grasped the back of his chair with both hands and leaned forward. "Now you are probably wondering whether David and I should take our half million share in large or small bills." He winked at Frank who sat on his left. "Small ones. We've already spent that money on your raises, the biggest in the company's history I understand, and, of course, in paying

132   *Typo*

back all of our wonderful lenders." Minnie leaned over to whisper to Sally, who shook her head. Dan raised his voice. "In your Christmas card everyone has gotten an extra seventy-five dollars, that's our thanks and hopefully the start of an annual tradition." Minnie poked a bony finger on the table. She hadn't approved of Dan's gift. "Sets a bad example we might not be able to follow up," she had said that afternoon to try and dissuade him.

Another thing he had done over her objection was to keep the medical plan the same, despite a thirty percent increase. Rather than reduce the plan or have employees contribute more, he had signed the company up to swallow the cost, and he had decided not to make a point of it in his speech, which he finished with, "David said to me the other day that he wanted Clarinda to be the greatest typesetter on Earth. I told him then and I tell him now, that's not a dream. It's foolish." I felt my face turn red. "Because we already are."

After dinner baskets of fried chicken and soft rolls, a few employees stayed for drinks. I insisted on trying all the liquors that every bar has, but never uses—Galliano, Blue Curacao, Crème de Menthe. The waitress dusted off each bottle and we raised round after round of colorful room-temperature shots with a toast. "To Clarinda, the greatest city in Iowa." "To Sally, the best typesetter in the world!" "To Dan and David, the best bosses we've ever had!"

"Join me outside for a minute, my boy?" Dan asked. On the cold stoop, the crags in his face were illuminated by the Ice House sign that said simply, "Today's Specials."

"I've got a couple of little Christmas presents for you," he said, tapping his cigarette pack. "Since you're a New York Jew you don't mind I'm not doing it the day of, do you?"

I both hated his stereotypes and admired his determination to goad me.

"First of all, Luke called from Household and, as I expected, they are extending the revolver. He understood we were too busy fixing things to find another bank and besides, they've been getting those nice interest payments from us." He lit a cigarette in the curve of his hand to keep the wind from putting it out. "And those venture capital funds you contacted, kiddo, have been calling me up, all interested. So for now, my boy, our fortunes are safe."

Over the past year, he and I had often calculated how much we'd have if the company went public in a year or two—nearly four million each. As for cash, I was saving ten percent of my hundred thirty thousand a year like my dad taught me, but that still left plenty to indulge in hundred and fifty dollar dinners or three hundred dollar dress shirts. As for Dan, with his young son and alimony to his first wife, he wasn't putting much of his only slightly higher salary away, but it looked like he would finally be able to move out of his rented semi-attached two bedroom townhouse and buy a house.

"Yes sir," he continued, looking out at the parking lot and twirling the cigarette from finger to finger, "It's been hard, but only because we are trying to become something no one has ever achieved before in this industry. We just have to keep the employees opening up to change, like our favorite lady Sally."

The crème de menthe bubbled in my stomach as I reminded him he had promised me two gifts.

"That's right my boy. I just had to wait until now when all the buyers are out and no orders will be coming in till Spring." he stubbed out the cigarette and lit a second. "So you won't mind that I am going to wait until next week to fire Hilda?"

Fire? No one had ever gotten Dan so mad he would fire them.

"She'll never get another chance to try to come between us or sour another customer," he continued. "Unless you want to keep her?"

I shook my head—I didn't doubt he would keep her if I asked—but I would have fired her long ago. That is, if I had ever fired anyone myself, which I hadn't.

"Then you better get back to your toasts. You earned them, kiddo."

Typo

I left him puffing alone into the freezing air.

After hugs from Sally and the others, I drove at ten miles under the speed limit back to the Super 8. The streets were quiet and snow frosted while tiny flakes continued to fall. Because there was no traffic to hit an hour before midnight, my only concern was running aground on a snow-hidden curb. I cruised by the police car sitting in the Subway parking lot, and waved at it through a tunnel of happy inebriation. It was too dark to see if they waved back or were even inside. Then in bed at last, I dreamt of IPOs and having the best company in the world.

Revenue

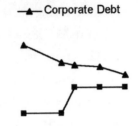
EBITDA
Corporate Debt

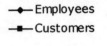
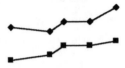
Employees
Customers

My Net Worth

Locations

Clarinda
Atlantic
Baltimore
St. Paul
New York
Syracuse
Manila

Revolver

Revenue	$9,000,000
EBITDA	$1,000,000
Corporate Debt	$1,500,000
Employees	150
Customers	80
My Net Worth	$3,750,000
Revolver Expires	18 Months

Commuting to Iowa

January 2001

I WAS TRAVELING EIGHTY PERCENT OF THE TIME—fifty percent in Iowa, twenty in Baltimore and ten out visiting customers. Since Dan had spent a couple of weeks in Iowa without me, in exchange I offered to spend an entire month there without him. I called the Super 8 for my extended stay:

"Hi, I'd like to reserve a room for January 2 to February 1."

"We're booked solid on the 23rd."

"What do you mean 'booked solid'?"

"We've got a wedding party coming in on the 23rd and they've had the whole place for months. They're really looking forward to it," the manager said. "Do you want me to go ahead and book the other nights?"

"Um, that's really not going to work for me. I'll be there for a month. What would I do the one night? Find another hotel? Sleep in my car?"

"That's entirely up to you, sir." I pictured her, behind the desk, looking at the breakfast nook with the Special K in the dispenser—they never cleaned it, but just kept topping it off—and the pool beyond seen through the steamed windows, the lone Exercycle parked at the shallow end. "If you could make a decision, sir."

"Did you know," I asked. "That I've spent over two hundred nights at your motel in the past two years? And that our company has been responsible for probably seven hundred nights for customers, employees, and ourselves?"

"Let me just double check, sir." That was more like it. "I can put you in the hot tub room."

"And on the 23rd?"

"Oh, we're booked solid on the 23rd."

I decided to call the only motel in town I had yet to try.

ℓ

It was an icy day when I slid my car up to the Clarinda Inn. I had stayed at every kind of hotel in my career: the Grand Hotel in Washington, DC that was so swanky it had an exact water selection temperature knob with a red control button if you wanted to override the safety of 106 degrees; the Beltway Inn near Dan's home in Baltimore, which featured a bullet-proof check-in counter, as in, "Why are they sliding the key to me under bullet-proof glass?"; and thousands of identity-less Marriotts, Holiday Inns, and Red Roofs. The Clarinda Inn was unlike any of these.

"The whole month of January," the owner said as I checked in. "Will you be paying for that all at once?"

"Um, OK," I said, and took out a credit card.

"Sorry, we don't take them things here. But you can write a personal check."

I searched through my bag for a checkbook.

"You know we had a Japanese fella from that ball bearing plant here for a couple months," he said, looking over his half moon glasses at me, "He just left so you can have his room." He handed me a key with a large green diamond-shaped plastic tag, but didn't let it go after putting it in my hand. "You'll like the room. It's got a stove. The Japanese fella cooked all his meals in there." He released the key. "A-yup."

The number on the tag led me to a small freestanding building between several other drive-up-to-the-door rooms that looked like they were auditioning for a role in a Stephen King film. Inside it smelled like the damp, spider-filled pine cabin I had spent one night in on a family trip to Maine. As promised, there was a small electric stove with three burners, but there were no utensils or pots in the plywood cabinets, only a half-full box of Domino sugar packets.

I laid out my clothes in the closet, which had a plastic sheet covering a hole in the wall where the winter wind snuck in. The twelve-inch television operated by knob—I hadn't seen that in twenty years—and got three broadcast channels. *Who Wants to Be a Millionaire?* was on. I climbed in the spring-less bed and pulled up the blanket, which was so thin I thought it might be a large piece of blue felt left behind by the mysterious Japanese man.

As I drifted off to sleep, my feet sticking out in the cold and unable to see the TV because the bed sagged so much—not that it mattered, the screen was so small the bottom two answers were clipped off the bottom of the image—I considered that poor "fella" on assignment from Tokyo. I supposed that in the case of ball bearings, Clarinda was cheap "offshore" labor. And I thought I felt forlorn.

ℓ

I woke up early and cold. I had to get to the plant by eight, which meant getting up at six. Iowa doesn't get much snow, but it does get blanketed in ice—thick ice that melts just enough in the afternoon to refreeze by the evening dark. With the sun also half awake, it took a solid thirty minutes of the defroster going full blast on the inside of the car and chipping at the ice on the outside to make a hole big enough to see through.

I bounced the car from curb to curb past the HyVee supermarket and down the back roads to the office—even the light traffic in Clarinda was too much demolition derby for me to face on January ice. I walked in ten minutes early and said hello to the receptionist.

"They haven't called yet," she said, adjusting her glasses with both hands. I took off my coat and gloves and sat down next to her at the front desk, which faced the wall three feet away. Anyone coming in or out of the plant by the main door had to walk through that little space. We both eyed it expectantly, like Red Army border guards waiting for the Americans, but since the employees used the side doors, no one disturbed our awkward closeness. She smelled like Bengay.

We were waiting for IPC to call. IPC printed scientific journals and we did their typesetting. Because journals keep the same layout month to month and are published on a regular schedule, it is the best typesetting work available—all we had to do was get the initial setup correct and then each individual article would be dropped into the template formatting the majority of it automatically. As our primary journal customer, IPC's million dollars in business represented as much as three hundred thousand dollars in net profit making them our most profitable account—and easily three times what we got for doing textbooks.

Clarinda had done journals in the past, but lost them all to India. The same facts that made journals profitable, made them easy to do in Asia. We planned to beat the Indians by matching their price and exceeding their service. IPC was our calling card to other journal publishers, so it would be hard to overstate how important IPC's business was, but Dan regularly tried to. "Our future lies in journals," he said. "We love journals! Let's all say it together."

The phone rang. The receptionist looked at me, wiping bobbed grey hair away from her face with both hands. I put down the textbook I'd been flipping through—*ah nice use of Garamond, beautiful sidebar placement*—and picked up the phone, "Hello?"

"Can I speak to Shirley," a woman's voice asked.

"Can I ask who's calling?"

"Oh, I'm sorry, Margaret, her cousin."

I put my hand over the receiver. "It's for Shirley," I whispered. The receptionist leaned over me to click the buttons to transfer the call. "Shirley, it's your cousin Margaret."

"Um, thank you, David," she said, recognizing my voice.

I returned to my book and the receptionist picked up a file folder from a big stack and began whiting out the label glued to it. Minnie had assigned her the task to save money on buying new folders. I watched her carefully cover each label in white, blow on it with pursed grey lips, and put it aside to dry.

IPC printed journals for Springer-Verlag. While we weren't exactly a secret in the relationship, the folks at Springer pretty much thought that IPC did both typesetting and printing. But, when a technology problem arose beyond what IPC's staff could resolve by passing messages back and forth, I needed a direct conference call with the client.

To avoid confusing—and possibly upsetting—the Springer people, I told IPC that we would answer the phone the day of the scheduled call by saying "hello" instead of "hello, Clarinda Company." It seemed a simple enough solution. When the call came in, it would be transferred to me and as far as Springer was concerned, I was just a production person at another IPC office being conferenced in. Only one difficulty: the receptionist didn't want to do it. She informed me that by answering "hello" instead of "hello, Clarinda Company" she would be violating her Christian ethics.

This wasn't the first time she had ethical concerns. A few months before, she had marched into my office and with her hands flat on my desk, leaned forward and said, "I will not tell people you are on the phone if you aren't." She leaned closer, her long face and helmet of grey hair three-quarters of the way across my workspace, staring intently at me through oversized glasses. "I will not tell people you are out if you are here. I will not put up with that kind of lying." Her tone was grim, like a movie scene where the hero confronts the morally corrupt boss. There was only one thing to say.

"I'm sorry, do I know you?"

"Minnie said she told you about my concerns."

I told her Minnie had neglected to tell me she had hired a new receptionist, but I would be sure not to compromise her morals.

She riled me, but I stuck with Dan's philosophy of treating everyone respectfully. Although he asked, jokingly, "So if I come in wearing a white robe with a hood, looking for this Jew in Iowa, would she tell me you're hiding under her desk?" I wasn't sure why he thought that was funny, and I didn't feel like posing the question to her.

So when she refused to say "Hello" instead of "Hello, Clarinda Company," I told her I would answer the phone. Whatever else I had to do—make a sale, call Manila, solve a production problem—would wait. She didn't appear to pick up on my attempted sarcasm.

The phone rang again. She paused in mid-Wite-Out blow-dry breath.

"Hello?" I said.

"Is that you, David?" the IPC service person asked.

"Yes, hold on a second."

The receptionist punched the buttons to transfer the call and I ran the twenty-five yards to my office, spinning around the corners like a cat on a polished floor. Connie jumped out of the way, spilling her coffee.

On Saturday I couldn't stay in the motel room. The moist cedar smell reminded me of the drunk old-man odor of my father's house—so I went to the office. I called Dan, but he was out with Helen and Ben visiting in-laws. I returned my handful of e-mails and after a couple games of *Age of Empires*, looked over at my bike leaning against the whiteboard. It was cold outside, just below freezing, but I had all the high-tech low-temp clothes the store manager in New York could think of and I had yet to use: lobster-claw gloves, a balaclava, winter pants, fog-resistant goggles, various thicknesses of thermal vests and a blue, waterproof windbreaker. The combined collection was an indication of the level of my disposable income and my lack of idle time to enjoy it.

I suited up in the empty parking lot. The cold wind felt good, and a few miles out of town snow covered the gravel just enough to make it smooth and fast. Southwest Iowa is awash in rolling hills a few hundred feet high. I would crest one, see seven more barren ones ahead, and roll downhill, pedaling to go faster before hitting the next.

I thought back to the day Dan had come to see my father. Around noon, I had waited inside the living room watching them through the window. Their heads bobbed and weaved from behind performing the motions of sharing a pack of cigarettes and talking old men.

"Shouldn't we go out there?" my sister had asked.

"No," I said. "Dad still thinks of us as his kids. Would you listen to what a two-year-old had to say about your life? Let Dan convince him. Man to man. Father to father."

When Dan came in alone—my father remained outside on the stoop— he said, "Your dad's a smart man. Not that I'm surprised, but he argued me pretty darn well."

"What? That it's OK to drink himself to death?" my sister asked.

"No," he said, "But he feels he's done all he can for you both and for your mother. After the two of you moved out and she died from the Alzheimer's he's free to do what he wants."

"Free to sit all day smoking and downing whiskey?" I asked.

"Yes," he said. "That's what he says is all he wants now."

My sister put her head in her hands and when my father appeared at the screen door, his hand on the handle, I pointed at him furiously and felt the rage boil up in me so fast I could barely speak a coherent sentence. "We're not done in here. Wait," I barked. Looking bemused, he dropped his hand.

"You told me before. He can't know if he wants this because the alcohol is twisting his mind," I said to Dan while watching my father through the window as he now walked slowly around the driveway picking up scattered leaves.

"No one would be happier to see him stop drinking than me," Dan said. "And if you want to try, I'm here to help."

We talked with and about my father until midnight when, at Dan's suggestion, my sister called the EMTs.

"You can't take me from my house if I don't want to go. I'm not a danger to myself," my father said, sounding perfectly lucid.

"That's correct, but I've got three other people in this house saying you might not be doing the best thing for yourself. So since I am no judge, I can either take you to the hospital with you getting in the ambulance or I can put you in there," the six-five three hundred pound medic responded.

My father, looking at me, relented. "I don't want to be any trouble."

At the hospital the doctor, a gastroenterologist who was on call filling in for the psychologist, talked to my father for two hours. At three in the morning he presented his verdict. "Your father is not clinically depressed. He wants to go home, so I'm releasing him."

No arguing from my sister or me changed his opinion. Dan sat nearby, wiping away tears. I walked outside and got the car, preparing to drive away without my father. "Let him find his own way home if he's doing so well," I said, the words hard in my mouth.

"You can do what you want. But I don't want you to regret doing this," Dan said.

I watched my father standing by the Emergency entrance, signing the last of the paperwork—barely able to stand he was so drunk—with a brown stain on the back of his hospital gown where he had soiled himself from the stress of the evening.

"Put a towel on the backseat," I said, but refused to look at him when he got in the car.

At home I had kicked in the screen door and punched the wall by the basement door so hard my hand had swelled to the size of a grapefruit.

My sister was scared at my unexpected violence. It scared me, too. I'd never lashed out like that. But Dan didn't question me. "There's no point trying to stop the emotion in the middle of it," he said. "Let it out. When it's over, then we can try do something."

He had known I had to let go of the father I remembered my own way. Dan was the only person I could trust.

Ten miles out from Clarinda, not near any other town, it started to snow. A mud-covered red pickup, the only car I'd seen all day, slowed beside me under the grey sky.

"You need a ride?" the flannel-shirted driver asked.

"No," I said, standing on the pedals to coast alongside the truck, "I'm enjoying being outside in the great State of Iowa."

"Where you from?"

"New York."

"New York! Well, you got a long way to get home!" he said, nodding with approval, "You keep up the good work!" and accelerated away.

For a moment I thought I should wave him down and say, "No, I didn't bike here all the way from New York!" Then again, why not let the farmer in the red truck tell his kids about the mad cyclist from New York City?

When I finally rolled into Stanton, twenty miles north, I was a toned biking machine. All those spinning classes at the gym had paid off. I stopped at the Kum and Go (how did they get away with the name?) convenience store, bought a pack of Fig Newtons, went outside, sat on the icy ground cross-legged and—was done. I couldn't get up. I was utterly exhausted. The longer I sat, the more stiff and unmoving my legs became. With effort I pulled my backpack around and fished for my cell phone.

"Clarinda Company."

"Sally?" I was lucky. Of all the people in Iowa, she was the only one I didn't feel embarrassed asking for help.

"David?"

I explained my predicament.

"You got all the way to Stanton before you figured out this was a bad idea?"

A half hour later, she arrived in her rusting Chevy Caprice.

"Why didn't you go inside?" she asked, moving jugs of antifreeze out of her trunk to make room for my disassembled bicycle.

"And just stand around in my bike gear with them looking at me?" I asked while trying to avoid stepping on the books piled on the floor mat.

"What do you do? Read while you're driving?"

"Sure!" she said. "It's a straight road. What else am I supposed to do? Watch a movie?"

We turned onto the main highway between Clarinda and Stanton: a two-lane blacktop without any lines. "We used to drag race down this way," she said. "You think reading a book is bad? See that telephone pole? I took that out when I was sixteen." Overweight, hands placed carefully on the wheel, pink sweatpants and matching sweater with pink and silver trim: a grandmother twice over, Sally didn't display the slightest sign of her wayward youth. "Before I got married, nobody beat me in a drag race."

At the office the two college kids, Tim and Tina, were in the training room learning Superleaf. I had hired them to, as Dan said, "inject some new blood in the Iowa culture." Tim stood up and shook my hand.

"Only been here a couple of weeks, and they already know Quark!" Sally said with pride. "Who wants to go out with David and me for a beer?"

The kids looked nervous. My God, I thought, it's their first job and I'm the big boss and I'm scaring them. "I'm buying," I said. "You're old enough to drink, aren't you?"

Tina smiled, and Tim continued to look like a preacher asked to go skinny-dipping. Then I remembered that Tim was not the kind of programmer I was used to. He arrived on time every morning and left on time to get to his Christian rock band practice. I noted the brown bag on his desk—even on Saturday his wife packed him a lunch.

Sally took us to the "Shid-le-e-dee" bar, which advertised its name on one of those light up marquees with the clip on letters like a gas station or garden store.

I remarked the last time I rode my bike down this way I got chased by a dog that managed to bark and bite at my ankle at the same time.

Sally pointed. "That's the Wilerson's. Bad part of town over here."

"A bad part of Clarinda?"

"Well, I wouldn't ride a bike through South Town."

"And you have a name for the bad area? Where does this South Town

Typo

end?"

"Right over there." Sally pointed at the parking lot in front of the Shid-le-e-dee.

Inside, the bar revealed itself as a converted doublewide trailer with a pool table and a video trivia machine. My metal-bottomed biking shoes clicked on the cement floor. The bartender looked up, eyed us sharply and shouted, "Sally! The regular?"

We played a couple games of pool—which Sally won, fair and square—beneath a NASCAR shaped light fixture. Tina watched, quietly peeling the label off a Budweiser.

"I heard about what happened with IPC," Sally said "She's telling everyone you're such a nice boss for not making her answer the phone."

"And wasn't I a nice boss for not firing her?" I asked, knowing Dan would never let me.

"They just don't understand what you and Dan are all about," she said and sunk the eight ball. "I really don't know if they are capable of what you want."

"Nobody's given them a chance before," I said, quoting Dan.

"Sally's right," Tina said. I was surprised Tina would disagree with me. She had just graduated college and had only been working a couple of weeks. But, that's what I'd been asking for, employees who thought on their own.

"Why do you say that?"

"I was in the Atlantic plant," she picked up Sally's beer to pull its label off too. "And there was a stapler lying on a keyboard. I took it off, but when I came back it was there again. An operator told me, 'The program needs me to keep pushing the enter key every now and then, so I put the stapler on it to, you know, automate it.'"

They both laughed, but I didn't see anything funny.

ℓ

At the Clarinda Inn, my bed had been sealed tight with sheets in flagrant violation of the "Do Not Disturb" sign still dangling from the doorknob. I had enough of motel rooms being made up against my will and stomped to the office-slash-owner's house. I heard a TV playing and knocked. The door swung open and the wife emerged wearing a floral print housecoat and brown shoes. The smell of roasted meat and pine-scented cleaner rolled through the frigid air. She had a wooden spoon in her hand.

"What'er ya want?"

I explained about the sign and the bed and that all I needed was maybe just some new towels once a week.

"But we pay her to clean the rooms."

"But I don't want her to."

"I can't pay her ta not clean your room. She needs that money." She put the hand with the spoon on her hip. "You want her ta not get paid?"

"No, no."

She moved her brown-shoed feet a couple inches apart. "She ca'n clean every other day. That OK?"

"That's great." It was a small victory and I didn't want to get hit with that spoon. I turned to go.

"We're heading out on vacation tomorrow," she continued. "Won't be back for a while." She moved the spoon to a forward position. "You gon'ta need anythin' else?"

ℓ

My month in exile concluded with a two-hour drive to the metropolis of Des Moines for a venture capital conference. The State of Iowa was eager to help us try and raise money and hire more Iowans and I was ready to try anything to continue Dan's plan for typesetting-based world domination.

I had been to venture capital conferences in New York and to the posh offices of VCs where they serve bowls of fresh popped popcorn and sandwiches with the crust cut off on rounded silver trays. Very nice, although none of those VCs had given us money.

As I drove past the burnt umber and sienna remains of cornfields, I thought about eating hamburgers off of red-and-white checked tablecloth last month with friends who had gotten that dreamt-of venture funding. Their dot-com had raised over fifty million and two years later it was beyond bankrupt.

Despite their implosion, they had advice for me. "It's as expensive to do a hundred million dollar deal as it is to do a ten million one so they want big money returns."

"Yeah," the second fellow chimed in. "They want to invest in sexy things. Whattaya got? A bunch of grandmothers in a cornfield, that's what. Most definitely not sexy."

I had heard it all before, but this time it made me especially angry. I had to borrow from Household and my father, and every day I worried about repaying all that money we had borrowed. We had been lucky enough to get the line of credit extended six months from December 2000 to June 2001, but the original acquisition loan was also coming due. If we didn't get all those debts repaid, we would go out of business—and my father, Dan, and I would all be destitute.

And we were in this perilous situation because a company like Clarinda, with a forty-year history, solid customers, experienced management, and a three times return on investment in one to two years, couldn't raise money because it wasn't sexy?

"Don't you see how dumb the VCs are?" I said. "They poured money into valueless dot-com companies, and even after they lost billions, they still somehow pretend like they are smarter than everyone else. We wouldn't waste money on Aeron chairs and sock puppet marketing campaigns."

Dan had made it so clear. If we'd had fifty million, things would have been different. If nothing else, we would have had fifty million. But we could have bought every typesetter in America without fear of the Indians.

I had faith the dour businessmen of Iowa I was driving across the State to meet with wouldn't be foolishly looking for sexy instead of substance. They would see the long-term value of Clarinda and benevolent capitalism.

I easily located the four-story high mini-skyscraper of the Iowa Department of Economic Development, the tallest building around. Being the first to arrive, I took a seat in the empty conference room.

"Do we just sit anywhere?" asked a man with a bad toupee, a lemon-colored shirt, and a red tie, and who smelled like cucumbers. The problem with arriving first was everyone assumed I knew what was going on.

"Sure," I said, and moved my stuff a few chairs down. "Pick any seat."

Another man entered. He had a briefcase that he popped open on the desk and began taking out PalmPilots, a dozen or more of them. "I can set up here, right?"

"Absolutely." I decided to step into the hall.

A short man ran out of the elevator. Out of breath and with a face like a raspberry Blow-Pop, he rasped, "Is this the room for the venture capital meeting?"

"That's what I'm guessing," I said, pointing at the sign. Twitching from worry, he leaned close to make out the words "Venture Conference, 11 a.m.," and grabbed his watch.

"It's OK," I said. "None of the Iowa people are here yet."

The meeting got underway and after the PalmPilot man—his idea was to sell insurance for the devices—and Blow-Pop face—who intended to build a fleet of carts to sell fried mushrooms—I broadcast my five-minute pitch to television screens set up at chambers of commerce across the State of Iowa.

Afterwards, outside in the cold beneath a modernist concrete veranda, I called Dan to tell him what a good job I'd done.

"I bet you wowed them," he said, "Did you talk to Joshua?"

"Who?"

"The banker Luke is working with—didn't I tell you the good news?"

"What good news?"

"Luke's agreed to come on as our CFO. He'll be taking on the money raising so you and I can focus on the company."

"He's not moving to Clarinda is he? I thought he hated Iowa."

"No, my boy, he's staying at home in Chicago, like you in that blasted city you love. Although, he's been talking about moving down here to be closer to me. It would be good for him don't you think, kiddo? My daughters do know a lot of single women."

"Baltimore?"

"Oh, that's him on the line now. You be safe driving back to Omaha, right."

"Uh."

"OK?"

"OK."

I knew Luke had been talking to Dan about coming to work with us, but didn't know he had been so close to accepting. As I pondered this, a man dressed like a cartoon spy, a dull-blue trench coat, fedora, pencil-thin moustache, and tightly clutched clasp-locked attaché, sidled up to me. "I was afraid I missed you."

"Joshua?"

"Luke told me you were sharp. I don't see why you'd be worried about your performance."

I asked if someone had said something negative.

"They just don't understand you city types like I do," he said. "But don't worry. Now that Luke and I are working together, you won't have to do anything like that again."

ℓ

On the flight out of Omaha I thought, *what did I know about Luke?* He had been the Household employee from Chicago who'd been appointed the last president of Clarinda. Rumor had it that he'd gotten the plum job commuting to Iowa by beating his boss at golf. He still lived in Chicago. He had a jeep. He had nine-and-a-half fingers. He'd lost the half finger in an accident that wasn't very interesting, which I knew because he'd told me several times and I couldn't remember it. He had an accounting background. Dan thought he was slightly overweight despite his frequent exercising, and also clearly liked how Luke agreed with everything he said. He probably had the right connections to raise money. He was responsible for approving our annually expiring set of loans from Household, and had given us that eighteen month extension. He liked basketball and he and Dan could spend all night talking about it.

Shortly before we bought Clarinda, he and I had gone on a 40-mile bike ride. On the way back, he kept falling behind. At one point, I had lost sight of him. Exhausted myself, I had collapsed on the side of the road. The sheriff had pulled over and asked if I needed help. "Did you see a rider a few miles back?" I asked. The sheriff nodded. "Ask him if he wants a ride." A few minutes later the sheriff came back.

"He says he's fine."

"Then I am too."

Arriving in Pittsburgh I ran to make my connection to New York at the far end of the airport terminal opposite my arrival. As I pushed past a slow moving family on the automatic walkway I thought: maybe I shouldn't be spending so much time away from Dan. Maybe I would be happier in Baltimore.

Dan tapped an unlit cigarette next to the half-eaten remains of his crab cake lunch on the small desk in my room at the Sheraton by the Baltimore-Washington Airport. There was a knock at the door. Dan stood, ran his hand lightly across his well-puffed thin hair, and straightened his tie.

"Smile, my boy."

The nervous, fat banker, who stood a foot shorter than Dan, popped open his thick Samsonite briefcase on the bed. "You must be David," he said, offering a warm, wet hand to me while continuing to empty documents with the other.

Dan and Luke—who had yet to join me in looking for Baltimore real estate—had decided to mortgage the Clarinda and Atlantic buildings. Just like in the game Monopoly, we would turn our property card facedown in exchange for cash—$650,000 that would go to pay off one of Household's loans that was coming due in less than a month.

The mortgage required a personal guarantee, which was why the banker had flown all the way from St. Louis just for this ceremony. The idea of forming a company is to avoid personal liability. That's the idea. In practice, banks are more comfortable ensuring personal liability.

The banker pointed us through the documents for my signature, Dan's and his—a pile of torn off sticky tabs growing on the desk. Signing a document that a banker thought it was important enough to fly halfway across the country for made me nervous. $650,000 was more money than I could ever hope to personally repay and it was on top of the couple million more of personally guaranteed loans plus my father's money, which had its own kind of personal guarantee. However, for the company the payments of $6,500 a month were less than our electric bill. Dan had told me: this was good debt. Then again, I thought, as I signed the last page and the banker offered to let me keep the pen, what choice did we have?

ℓ

A month later, asleep in the Super 8, I dreamt I was trying to open a big wooden door but constantly slipped on the highly polished floor. Why was I wearing socks? I woke confused and worried I was late. I had a meeting with the Indians. The Indians who were so determined to take our business.

I checked the clock—plenty of time. But when I got to the parking lot I remembered that important thing from the day before: the deflated tire on my rental car. I had driven from the office without noticing.

I'd seen my father fix a flat, so I understood the basic concept. However, my method of repair usually involved doing something terribly wrong. I have had shelves fall on my head (ah, the molly bolt goes in *that* way), caught my big toe with a pitchfork, and cooled a soldering iron with my hand. I had, by my estimation, an eighty percent chance of having the car fall on me, roll into a ditch, and explode. I called Hertz.

The helpful service person offered to call me back. Thirty minutes later she apologized for the delay and explained that her conversation with the authorized service company in Clarinda had gone something like this:

"This is Hertz calling. I have a car with a flat tire."

"Where is it?"

"At the Super 8 motel."

"That's just across town."

"So I can put you down for service in the next hour?"

"This is a body shop. We don't fix flats."

"You're the listed service agent, sir."

"Is it a woman?"

"No sir, it's a man."

"He can't fix it himself?"

"Sir, it's Hertz policy to help customers. If you won't do it, I have to warn you that your service contract may be revoked."

"We don't do that sort of thing."

The guy on the phone ran the body shop I could see from my office window and also happened to be Clarinda's mayor—a man who had been involved in approving the development loans we'd gotten to hire people in his community, although he couldn't have known it was me since he had refused to help. The Hertz person had to call two more places before she found someone willing to fix a flat for a man.

In the hour from when the man arrived, inflated the tire, had me drive it slowly to the shop around the block, patched the small hole, put it back on the car, and presented me the bill, he would neither speak to nor look at me.

I don't like being disliked, even if it's for as insubstantial a reason as not being able put on a spare tire. I gave him a twenty-dollar tip. He examined the bill as if I had just handed him a lace doily. I worried that I was even more of a pathetic city-boy. I had been told too much of a tip is considered insulting in Iowa, so I was relieved when he smiled, said, "If you ever need help again, call me!" and gave me his card.

Finally arriving at work, I began to perspire. The spring day had been unseasonably warm and the conference room, which had never been connected to the building's air conditioning, was too hot. The pendulum clock on the wall had long since stopped ticking. I asked Frank and he told me, a little sheepishly, that we were the first bosses not to insist on keeping it wound, and he had always hated its ticking. He showed me where he had hidden the key inside the mechanism.

The three men from Bangalore arrived with their hair uniformly slicked from left to right and all wearing double-breasted pinstripe suits, which they did not unbutton to sit down. Rather than spreading out, they arranged themselves directly next to me. Pradep, the manager, smiled and cocked his head. The other two scanned the room and inspected the mechanical action of their chairs. They didn't seem bothered by the heat at all.

"Did you have a good trip?" I asked while waiting for Dan.

"Oh, not bad, not bad at all," Pradep said.

"What is it? Nineteen hours?"

"Twenty-four hours. We had very long transfer in London, but there will only be twenty hours going back," he said, his head still cocked.

"You're going right back? You really came just to see us? All three of you?"

"Only to see this Clarinda."

"No other customers?"

"Only if we have to." The other two nodded. One of them pulled out a computer and began typing.

"So you have appointments with publishers in New York?"

Pradep smiled more broadly and pulled out a business card from his vest pocket. "I am sorry. This is your company." The other two also took out their cards and they queued up to place them carefully in my hand. I apologized for not having my cards and went to my office to get some.

I knew the men from India were frustrated. They saw opportunity in typesetting, but had had mixed luck selling directly to publishers in America. The low prices sometimes won, but at the same time buyers were leery of losing their jobs if schedules were missed, and usually preferred known suppliers like Clarinda. So, until they could get past this roadblock, the Indians reasoned, maybe they could sell to us.

We had our operation in Manila, but the six thousand a year we paid our Filipino staff was more than triple the average salary in India. Without the extremely low-cost production from India there was no way we would be able to compete once the publishers got over their fears.

I returned, chose a chair across the table, and asked if they had brought samples. The silent one without the computer produced a copy of the *Journal of the Royal Society of Veterinarian Medicine*. In much the same way we had ended up in Manila because of the American occupation of the Philippines, the Indians got their business from UK publishers because of the British Raj.

"Have you been typesetting for long?" I asked while leafing through the journal. I knew they had only been at their current company for a few months.

"I redacted for Reed Elsevier for many years," Pradep said.

"Redacted? You mean you copyedited science journals?" I put the journal upside down on the table open to a page that I thought Dan would find interesting. The two silent men frowned at the bent binding, and together reached out to right it. The first returned to his computer, and the second smoothed the cover before returning it to his case as if it was a hurt puppy.

Pradep beamed joyfully. "Science journals. We are all professional engineers from Chennai University."

"That's very impressive," I said "Is that why you all left Dataset together?"

Pradep's smile shrunk to a point. The silent man stopped typing. They had gone into business by the common Indian entrepreneur's practice of leaving their employer, forming their own company, and then targeting the former employer's customers. I received an e-mail every week from a new Indian company that had stolen a mailing list. Even the introductory e-mail they had sent was plagiarized. I knew because how likely was it that five different companies would all offer "99.99.5% accuracy"? I guess the extra decimal point meant they had already delivered 0.005 errors.

Dan appeared at the door wearing his blue blazer. In moments everyone was standing, smiling, shaking hands, handing out cards. "Thank you," Dan said and slid the cards into his pocket without examining them, causing Pradep and his men to knit their eyebrows in horror.

"So you fellows like the weather here?"

Pradep appeared to be still waiting for Dan's card. He clapped his hands lightly together several times.

"Ah, it is not as bad as we had worried."

"It's always the way," Dan said. "I bet you fine gentlemen were prepared anyway."

Pradep returned to smiling, which led his silent partners to return to computers and furniture adjustments.

"So, you fellows interested in doing a book with us?"

"We would be very honored and pleased to be considered—"

Dan tossed a manuscript on the table. "The customer needs us to use TeX. I understand you fellows are good at TeX."

Pradep grabbed the manuscript and began flipping through it. "And who is the customer?"

"I don't think—" I said.

"Oxford," Dan said. "Are you doing work for them in England? They haven't heard of you in the New York office."

"Oxford. We have done some things for them," Pradep said.

"Well, maybe we should find something else then."

Pradep was confused. He was so proud that he didn't perceive we were worried about him stealing our customers. Or maybe he just didn't care.

"Unless you promise to only do work for American publishers through us," Dan said.

Pradep understood that. "I...think we could make an arrangement for this book?"

Dan sighed and nodded a few times. "Alright, we'll discuss that later. What price would you give me?"

Pradep handed the manuscript to his men. They discussed in Hindi. There was much finger pointing at the manuscript and flipping of pages. I knew how much Dan hated people using foreign languages to hide their conversation in front of us—it went against everything he believed in about being straightforward with people.

"Maybe you need some more time to think this over? I was hoping to give you the manuscript to take with you."

"I am sorry," Pradep said. "This is a very generous offer. We suggest twelve per page."

"But," Dan said, and slid their cards out of his pocket to glance at them, "Pradep, that's what we would charge the customer ourselves." He pronounced it Pra-deep.

"Five dollars?" Labor was so cheap in India that he had to guess at the price because his cost, by my calculation, was only pennies.

I tried to bring the conversation around to the future beyond one book. Dan listened while I pointed out that prices were falling and that there would come a time when there would be no room for both Clarinda and an Indian company to make a profit on the same job. I told them I knew their labor costs and work process. I went to the whiteboard and showed them that one Clarinda employee (who wasn't that efficient in the first place) did the work of ten or twenty of their employees. They accepted inefficiency and manual work, I explained, because labor was cheaper than technology.

I didn't write on the whiteboard that when it came to people, India beat us hands down. Indian companies ran three shifts a day. Our third shift was one grandmother. Dan's proposals to run 24-7 got the response of "people have families, they can't work like that anymore." Racing to take away our business, the Indians didn't have such concerns.

Pradep nodded solemnly as I said, "What's more important to us is a partner we can trust in India. We know you have low costs, but we can teach you the most modern techniques. We'd like to help you. There is so much we can do together."

He continued nodding before realizing I had stopped talking. "Yes," he said, "We are very interested doing your work."

I squinted at him, not sure what to say.

"And—" Pradep looked from Dan to me and back again, opened up his palms and said, "We would be happy to teach you our management techniques."

"Pradep," Dan said, wearily. "How about four dollars a page?"

ℓ

"And where are we now, my boy?" Dan asked, wiping saliva from his cheek as he awoke in the passenger seat.

"Nearly there," I said.

After eight hours of driving and one hot dog—with a big hunk of bone embedded in it that clacked in my teeth—at an Amish truck stop, the sun gave one final, blinding glare in the rearview mirror before setting. Dan reached over to turn up the air conditioning even though he was wearing the same thin brown windbreaker he had worn through the entire winter. He liked the clean air from the vents, he said—it helped his coughing. He narrowed his eyes at the knob.

"I already turned it up for you," I said.

"Ah," he said, "Always looking out for old Dan," and fell back asleep.

We arrived after dark and Luke met us in the dining room of the Dubuque Holiday Inn—as far as you could get from Clarinda and still be in Iowa. Dan twirled a cigarette in his hand while sucking at his cheek where his dentures rubbed painfully against the soft inside of his mouth.

"You know those little brown fellas billed us seven dollars a page," Dan said.

"I don't think you're supposed to call them brown fellas, Dan," Luke said. He had driven down from Chicago, and seemed better for the trip than Dan and I. His thinning blond hair was neatly combed, and his baby face was flush from the forty minutes he'd spent on the hotel treadmill. It was the first time we'd seen each other since Dan hired him as CFO four months earlier.

"So what do you prefer I call someone who tries to rip us off?"

Luke shrugged as Rob Ranch shuffled up. Dan focused on Luke and said, "But nobody caught their scam until I saw the bill."

"Dan," Rob said, "I'm, ah, sorry I got held up at the office. I'm, ah, not interrupting anything, am I, ah?"

Rob shook Dan's hand, his arm crooked by his side.

"Not at all, my friend. We were just discussing how the business ethic of our little brown friends seems to be 'whatever you can get away with.'"

"Ah, yes, India. Ahh," Rob said. His voice trailed off after each word like an emptying balloon. Somewhere between forty-five and fifty-five with curly brown hair, he wore a faded button down blue shirt and freshly pressed khakis with several orange stains laundered in. Of the four competitors that we were trying to buy, his Ranch Compositors was number one on the list.

"You, ah, know," Rob said, "I just lost a, ah, couple of big books to that Indian, ah, company that bought, ah Lincoln, ah."

"Bookers?" I asked.

Rob smiled. "Ah, ahhh."

"Rob, I know all about them," Dan said, stubbing out his cigarette.

"We just hired another one of their top sales people away. But maybe you'd like to show us where we can get a nice steak in this town before we start telling you all our secrets."

ℓ

The next day we all met at Ranch's offices, which was the nicest typesetting plant I'd ever seen—maybe the nicest in history. They had recently moved across the Mississippi to a new building with two wings: one for the production folk and one for the executives. The "hall of executives" offices ran in rank order from the ones nearest the production department to the end of the corridor where Rob's corner quarters overlooked the river. They had very nice carpets.

In business for more than a dozen years, Rob Ranch had done well. He had about half the revenue of Clarinda, but less than half as many employees, which meant he should be quite profitable. The problem was he'd taken out loans over the years and the business wasn't generating enough cash to pay them off. He wanted to sell, and he wanted to sell to us because he liked the way Dan talked about the "glorious future."

We had a day of tours, meetings, and lunch in a small Illinois town littered with antique stores. We dreamt aloud of our new empire. "Eight facilities and growing," Dan said to Rob and his wife. "The question is— what are you going to do with your ill-gotten gains?" As always, Dan the salesman knew what the customer wanted to hear.

After leaving the Ranches, Dan asked Luke, "Do you really think Berry Capital is going to get us the money?" Berry was a firm in Philadelphia that I, not Luke, had found, but he had taken over the relationship regardless.

"If not them, someone will. We'll get the financing."

"Then the only real problem we have between us and all that money is management. Who is going to manage this place? David and I are already drawn too thin. And you heard Rob and his wife, they barely want to stay on selling, much less running production. We're going to be in locations all over the country."

"We could get a corporate jet," Luke said.

"And I suppose you would be the pilot?" Dan asked. He tented his fingers lightly. "Well, you know, that's actually not a bad idea. We used to have a corporate jet back in my days at Penta."

"Like a Cessna?" I asked.

"At Penta we used to ask the pilot for a swig of whatever he was drinking. If it was cola, all was well. If it was whiskey, well, at least there wouldn't be any pain."

A few weeks later I brought a torn advertisement for corporate jets from *Fast Company* magazine to Dan's office. He was perusing a document, his reading glasses on the tip of his nose. Luke sat in a chair, tapping his nine fingers.

"Clawback?" Dan asked.

"Only if we don't perform," Luke said.

"What's a clawback?" I asked.

"And it's not enough money to be sure we can run Ranch," Dan said.

"There's an option for more money," Luke said.

"For more equity," Dan said.

"Can I see that?" I asked, and Dan handed me the document. "Where does it say 'clawback'?"

"We build it—they get it for nothing," Dan said.

"It's an industry term for giving more stock if we don't meet the financing conditions," Luke said.

"And it's steep, my boy," Dan said. "Buying Ranch will cost us a third of our company. And if we don't hit their targets, they get a twelve percent clawback."

"Don't we also have to give some equity to Rob and his wife?" I asked.

"Not necessarily—" Luke said.

"Yes, we do. I made a promise and Rob is expecting it," Dan said. "So

Typo

right you are, kiddo. Tell them David and I say we need a better deal."

"They may not have one," Luke said.

"Well maybe you're ready to give up just because someone thinks we're desperate enough for a deal to take this one, Luke," Dan said, and picked up the airplane ad. "You'll just have to imagine flying into that empty lot they call an airport out here until we can get someone real financing. Now, on to other matters." Turning to me he said, "With friends like your boy Steve up in Atlantic we won't be able to hang on to even this lovely little company. He is still running up overtime up there—did you know that?"

As usual, Dan was privy to information I wasn't. Although I thought the problems had been solved, Atlantic had been running twenty percent overtime and missing schedules on Jackie Dee's TPC work for weeks.

"I can fix it," I said. I had had enough of dreams like acquiring Ranch being taken away from us again and again. I had had enough of processes running out of control. I didn't want to do any more apologizing to customers for delays or explaining to business friends our lack of rampant success.

"And how are you going to do that?"

"I'm going up there."

"Whatever you think, my boy. Whatever you think."

"Don't you think I can?" I'd also gotten fed up with Dan's doubting my ability.

"Kiddo, if anyone can you can," he said, "But I don't know if anyone can change them."

I packed up my bags at the Clarinda Super 8, drove an hour up the road to the Atlantic Super 8, where I began the next day meeting with the employees one by one.

Clara, a grandmother in her late fifties, came in to the conference room I'd had taken over with reports and whiteboard drawings of processes that I kept drawing and redrawing. She wasn't on my schedule, but I was glad to hear from an employee who wanted to talk.

"I hear there are some changes coming," she said, and took off her thick bifocals, which hung from a glass-beaded necklace. She reminded me of my first piano teacher, a grey haired woman in a twin-set who gave me a coconut macaroon if I managed "Spinning Wheel." But, I couldn't imagine which changes she meant. Training? Superleaf software? "I just wanted you to know that I used to work for Josie," she continued, "and she's a drunk."

"Josie?"

Clara smiled at me. "A terrible drunk."

"You mean Josie the job scheduler here?" I asked.

"I can't possibly work for her."

"Who's asking you to work for her?"

"She went crazy. You didn't know her then." Clara's voice became sharp.

"Aren't you in the proofreading department?"

"I'm telling you," she said, and put on her glasses, which made her eyes very small and dark. "You put her in charge of this place and she'll blow up like last time."

"Josie was in charge? Of the plant?" I had never heard that.

"She will be if you put her there like you're planning," she said, fully angry. "I saw the memo."

I tried to explain to Clara that no one was putting Josie in charge, and afterwards I called Frank.

"I don't know where that Josie thing came from. Do you want me to talk to her?"

"She's a proofreader, right?"

"No, she's a proofer," he said.

Proofreaders looked for typos. Proofers compared the file that was printed from the typesetter's desktop to the one that was printed from the file we put on CD-ROM to send the customer. The proofer ran the printer and then put the two versions of the document on a light table, page by page, looking for differences. Of course, they never found any. The practice originated when laser printers didn't always get all the fonts correct or color separations were faulty and printing out from the CD-ROM copy did sometimes differ—ten years ago. Now, proofing was a time wasting double check.

"I thought I'd asked you to stop the proofing unless somebody could prove that we'd had any errors. Can't we get Clara doing proofreading instead?"

"I had her doing just that," Frank said, his voice, as always, even—no anger, no worry. "But her eyesight's gotten too bad for that. Doctor says she'll probably be blind in six months."

That explained the memo confusion. We were employing a blind proofreader—an angry one.

The next day Clara delivered a piece of paper to me.

"What's this?"

"A proofing error as per your request."

I examined the page.

"But this is just a page that got stuck in the printer, isn't it? That's why it's slanted like that. There's no error with file."

Clara frowned at me.

"I was just told that this is what you wanted."

ℓ

As expected, Dan refused to even consider letting Clara go.

"There's two ways to go, up or down," he said, "and we have got to keep going up. Culture, my boy, that is what we are trying to change. All we can do is keep showing these people that we are bosses of a different kind. That, and hire some more new God-damned people who didn't grow up with a God-damned union shop mentality," he said.

However, other than our two college kids, bringing in new blood was not so easy—most locals were related to at least one employee, and not anxious to come work with their relatives that they couldn't avoid in the confines of the Pamida Discount Center. Therefore, when the young waitress at the Ice House approached our table and said, "I hear you guys run the printing company down the street. Any chance I could get a job as a graphic artist?" Dan hired her on the spot.

Her first week was spent learning proofreading. The class taught the basics: reading editorial marks and measuring the lengths of and distance between lines of text with a pica ruler. She passed—which was pretty good—four out of five didn't pass the test or dropped out in the first week.

However, at the start of her second week, she told her boss she was pregnant and therefore quitting. She was jobless, twenty-three with two children, and another coming, and it would still take her two months to come by the office and pick up her one paycheck. I was baffled. Didn't she need the money? What had happened to the person who had come up to us in the restaurant and bravely introduced herself? The only thing that was certain was that with this kind of attitude, we really needed Manila—not only for the labor cost, but just to find people willing to do the work.

Another, new hire we had more hope for was Missy, a twenty-year-old friend of Sally's. Also unmarried, she had, like the waitress, two children, although hers were with two different men. Unlike the waitress, she had put herself through most of a computer science degree from Northwest Missouri State College while surviving on state assistance and babysitting for four dollars an hour.

"What that girl—no child—she's just a child—deserves is a decent opportunity with a company that respects her," Dan told Sally. "Tell her we'll pay college costs and a salary. Not a big one, maybe twenty-five grand, but she's getting the schooling for free and we'll put her on the medical plan on day one. She's got two kids—she's going to need that. And tell her she's only got to work thirty hours a week."

"That's a lot of money for part-time work," Sally said. "There are plenty of typesetters don't make that much."

"Would you rather we offered her less than what the State pays her to not work? We've got to get with the times, or we'll never get good people in here."

"Don't you at least want to make her sign something to come work here after she gets her degree?"

"Why should I?" he asked, "In all seriousness, dear, those agreements are impossible to enforce, and why wouldn't she want to stay with us?"

The next day Minnie deposited Missy's application form on Dan's desk.

"You can't put someone in the medical plan without the waiting period," she said.

"Didn't Sally tell you that I wanted to do this?" he asked, picking up the pages to examine them. He didn't have his glasses on, so I knew he wasn't actually able to read them.

"Goes against our policy."

"I thought you got your friend at the front desk on without waiting." Dan said.

"That was a special circumstance. I was able to convert her COBRA. And you don't know the family that girl comes from. No good. All Southtown. Not a decent worker among them. Her uncle used to steal hubcaps, you know—"

"Are we hiring her uncle?"

"No."

"Is this David's and my company?"

She frowned. "Well, there are the loans. If you don't pay, the company reverts to Household."

Dan remained calm. I'd heard him argue with her about this a thousand times, and he never got angry—not until we got to dinner and would say, "Who does that crow think she is? Doesn't she understand this is *our* company? Yours and mine."

"Well until they come to collect, it's our company, yes?"

She crossed her arms.

"As much yours," he said, "As your house is yours and not the mortgage company's?"

"That Missy's no good," she said.

"It's not just about Missy," he said, "I want this to be the start of a college tuition program for the whole company."

Minnie headed for the door.

"You need to submit these, don't you?" He held up the forms. "Oh, and Minnie, I had almost forgotten," he said as she reluctantly took them, "I thought we were going to start putting David's signature on the paychecks. It's still yours on there, right?"

Her mouth turned further down at the edges.

"He needs to make a stamp with his signature," she said flatly.

"Next payroll?"

"If that's what you want, sir," she said coldly. "We will have to try to do it."

With a staff of five, I knew her resistance wasn't about the time it would take to order a rubber stamp.

Missy passed the training course in record time and began working on projects for Sally. Dan remarked "See, people aren't always a product of their environment. They can change."

ℓ

At one point, I asked to see Missy's course schedule—as a former computer science major I was curious what she would be studying—data structures, discrete math, all exciting stuff. The next day she had forgotten to bring it, and I asked again. When she handed over the printout two days later, I saw why she had been avoiding me. She had planned a more-than-full load of five classes.

I asked Sally, "How is she going to work thirty hours a week for us?"

"I guess," she said, "This would be a bad time to tell you that she's pregnant again and getting married." Going to school, planning a marriage, taking care of two children, and going through the pregnancy of the third was possible—if she didn't come into work. "I'll talk to her," she said.

A few days later we met in Dan's office. He talked about his childhood and how he'd put himself through school with a full-time job. Then he stopped to let Missy respond.

"I have to finish my degree by the end of the year," she said looking at her feet.

She was thin, less than a hundred pounds, and pale. Hunched in the chair next to Sally with waist length hair the color of dried cornhusks she looked like a doll, but her words contained the suppressed rage of a person three times her size.

"Why?" Dan asked in his most grandfatherly-ish voice and waited calmly, his fingers interlocked under his chin.

"Next year they're switching to Java. I'd have to take everything all over again. I won't graduate for years."

Dan pointed a finger out of the interlock at me. "I called the college," I said, sadly, looking at Sally and then at my own shoes. "They said the courses you need will be offered in the spring. You'll be able to finish by the end of next year." Didn't she need a job? Didn't she want us to pay for her school?

"You're not paying me enough. You pay Tony and Tina more," she said, her anger bubbling like over-microwaved soup.

"Tony and Tina both have degrees," Dan said, more slowly, his hands still touching lightly. "We aren't paying for their schooling. You also have a flexible schedule we don't give any other employee."

Missy gave the floor the evil eye.

"Missy, this is your choice," Dan said. "You can stay. We like you and we like your work, but these past four months you were here as little as twenty hours a week. Sally covered for you, and I overlooked it, but we cannot overlook what you are planning for the fall. I will stick to our original deal if you will."

Missy said nothing. He repeated himself a few times. The floor began to wither under her stare.

"You'll get back to us?" Dan suggested.

The next day, Missy quit. Then she applied for unemployment. Unfortunately, there's no unemployment if you quit. A week later Minnie got a letter from the State of Iowa indicating that Missy had been in a tuition reimbursement program for unemployed mothers, and her unemployment application had revealed her scam. She had been double-dipping.

"I told you she couldn't be trusted," Minnie said so happily, she forgot to frown.

ℓ

"Sally said you wanted me to come down today," Laura, a typesetter from the Atlantic plant, said sitting in Dan's office.

"I hear you're a legend in the world of typesetting, even won an award or two," he said. "We could use someone with your skills. How would you like to be moved into the training department?"

"I was told I could keep my job." As she spoke, she clenched her left hand through her locks and dropped the split-end strands that came out on the floor. Dan sucked at his cheek, and she pulled out some more hair. "I need my job."

"No one is talking about taking away your job, my child," he said. "You would be the new trainer in Atlantic, and you'd be reporting to Sally here in Clarinda."

She pulled faster through her hair, which was more grey than blond. "Donna has been letting me set my own hours so I can see my husband."

Ninety percent of the employees at Clarinda were women, and although most were the primary breadwinners in their households, they were still the ones picking up the kids and making sure dinner was on the table. A lot of the husbands described themselves as "handymen," which meant unemployed with no plans to change.

"He works second shift?" I asked.

"He's in jail."

"I'm very sorry, my dear," Dan said. He curled his fingers against his cheek. "Would it help to know we'll be giving you a raise?"

"Will people be expecting me to teach them?"

"Not until you're ready."

She took her hands out of her hair, and placed them, shaking, in her lap.

$$\mathscr{e}$$

In short order, Donna, the Atlantic plant manager, complained about Laura. She apparently liked to work a sort of third shift, and it was hard for the first-shift person to hand over projects.

"The others are complaining that because we let her come and go whenever she wants that we're giving her special treatment," Dan said.

"But she gets her work done, right?" I asked.

"Remember what we're dealing with, my boy. It's not what you do—it's what others think you're getting. They think because I gave her a raise that she's my favorite," he said while adjusting his glasses with one hand and dialing the phone with the other, pushing the buttons down with a tentative click.

"Nevertheless, Donna's right." He slammed the phone down and started over. "Damn this phone system? Do you have this problem with it?"

"It gets confused if you dial too slowly," I said. He looked at me sadly. "Or too fast."

"Nevertheless, she's got to come in when other's are expecting her. Damn."

"Would you like me to dial for you?"

"Would you, my boy?" he asked, turning the phone towards me. "It's these god damned Kmart glasses. Go ahead and put her on speakerphone, kiddo." I pushed the button. "You've got Laura there with you Donna?"

"Yes," Donna said.

"Laura, I understand you've not been sticking to your promise with Donna." He folded his glasses in his hand and closed his eyes. "A promise to her is like a promise to me. You don't want to break your promise to me, do you?"

"No, Dan," Donna responded. "She doesn't."

Dan talked for forty minutes. It was Laura's penance, and at the end she promised to come in on time. But, within a week, she had reverted to her old ways. Dan talked to her again, and she came in again on time for a few days and then she didn't.

"How's it going with her husband's case?" he asked Donna.

"Word up here is that he sold drugs to the police. It's his third felony."

"Wouldn't you think that child would be pretty upset by the fact that she's going to be living without a husband for the rest of her life?"

"Yes, Dan."

"Then maybe we should give her a little time to adjust."

"Did she tell you that she's been indicted with him?"

He paused. Could a piece of information not have made it to him before it got to me as well? "Do you think she's done something?" He said slowly.

"I don't know, Dan"

A few days later the police came to the plant. We didn't get many details, it was late at night, but we did know her pocketbook was searched and the next day she was arrested.

Dan decided to stand by her. "We need Laura to work on those Mosby books, my boy. If we don't get them done, Mosby will toss us out. And she's too far along for someone else to pick them up."

He fidgeted with the end of his yellow and blue tie, rolling it up and down in his hands.

"It's also the right thing to do for any employee—innocent until proven guilty—you agree with me my boy, don't you?"

I nodded. Of course I did. He had helped me through my own personal difficulties so many times. He had been there for me when I broke up with my girlfriends, when my father started drinking, when my mother died.

He did it for everyone in his life. It was what I had always admired about him.

"Still, I need to know you are comfortable with this," he said. "Do you want us to loan her money for bail? She'll have to pay us back, of course. But it's your money just as much as mine."

"Why shouldn't we support her?" I asked.

"That's my boy," he said.

I drafted a letter to setup a bail loan to Laura and delivered it to Minnie in her fortress of an office in the back of the accounting area and behind the fireproof vault.

"You know what the employees are saying," she said while stamping the form. She looked much smaller sitting behind her desk. "They think Dan is helping her for other reasons."

"He'd do the same thing for you or any other employee."

"I don't get arrested for drug dealing," she said, putting the form and my letter in an envelope.

"What?" I asked, "Do people think he's having an affair with her?"

She patted the envelope on a little red sponge in a plastic container that sat next to photos of her grandchildren and sealed it. "People talk, David. You can't just go around bailing out criminals."

"There's no proof the police are doing anything other than trying to get the husband to tell more information. With his third felony, he has no reason to and maybe by arresting Laura he will. That's the rumor I heard," I said.

She handed the envelope to me. "Will you be putting postage on it or using the company meter?"

Laura was working only a few hours a night or not at all, and she began to fall further behind schedule on the Mosby books. We were supposed to be converting from the old Xyvision typesetting system to Quark, and Laura was taking two hours to complete a page. At that rate, we would never finish. Dan sent me to Atlantic to help. "You know these conversion jobs as well as anyone," he said.

"Did Laura come in on time?" I asked. Donna nodded. "See, we were right to have faith in her after all." She said nothing as she took me to Laura's small office where I watched her laboriously convert a page. Her skin was almost translucent and I could see the thin blue veins in her hands as she typed.

"Why don't we send the rest of the pages to Manila?" I suggested. "They do data conversion jobs all the time. Then you can focus on checking the final pages and take the time you need."

She curled her fingers on the keyboard. "You're so wrong."

"Wrong about what Manila can do?" I could practically see the deoxygenated blood circulate in her cheeks.

"I told you that it was wrong to convert the files from Xyvision."

"But that's what the customer is paying us to do."

"They're wrong. We'll never make schedule now," she yelled at me.

"Laura, the customer may be wrong; I don't disagree with you," I channeled Dan's calm, managerial style. "Xyvision is a great system, you're right about that, but if we don't do it, they will find someone else."

"Then we should send the book back," she said and turned away from me.

Over her objections, I sent the book to Manila, but the situation did not improve—the customer found dozens of errors. Not little hyphens, but whole sections missing, and it wasn't Manila's fault, although Laura hadn't obviously done anything malicious.

Dan would not budge on his loyalty to her. "That would be giving in to the mob," he said. "We have to see this thing we started through. Besides, now she owes us thousands of dollars in loans. How is she going to pay that back if she isn't working?" His logic was irrefutable, and I also didn't want to let Laura go down if the reason was because we were responding to the sniping of the other employees. She needed help, and we were giving it to her. It's what my father's IBM would have done.

Dan gave her a new job with less pressure. She would go back into Xyvision work, be taken off the fancy training job we'd given her, and she would have to show up on time.

"If you ask me," Minnie said handing me my expense account to sign, "That kind of treatment only tells the employees that they can walk all over you."

Laura showed up on time for two days. Donna called Dan when she walked in late the third day.

Without another word, he fired her.

Other than Hilda it was only the second time I'd seen him fire someone, and the first time it was someone he liked.

"I am sorry, my boy, but we couldn't help her," he said after hanging up the phone. "We went above and beyond and that was the right thing to do, you would agree, wouldn't you?" He was on the verge of tears.

I nodded.

"She simply couldn't be helped," he repeated, cupping his fingers around his mouth.

She was arrested the following day on drug charges. The rumors were confirmed. I was surprised that Dan, the master reader of people, had not figured her out as an addict and a liar, and not some poor waif who wanted to do the right thing. On the other hand, maybe he did, but still wanted to help her. I didn't care what Minnie thought—there was no person in the world as good as Dan.

ℓ

Even with the employee challenges in Iowa, by the June of our second year not only had sales gone up again from our champions like Red Bones and Jackie Dee as well as the new accounts like IPC and Academic Press that Dan and I had brought in, but Luke had managed to help out both us and his old bosses at Household. Via a complex swap we bought defunct companies from their defaulted loan pool, and they took a tax write-off. In exchange, Household forgave the rest of our term loan. It was a nice if slightly shady deal. Better yet, he was also close to getting an alternate loan to get rid of Household's other debt, the revolving line of credit.

On the first of July, Dan did a line-by-line review of our sales projections. "Maybe we haven't managed to buy Ranch or our friends with the editorial services in Ohio, but do you think they will be more interested when they see this?" he said, and lifted the sheet with his scrawled totals by a corner—waving it in the air like a flag. "Twelve million this year. And mark my words, if we don't do fifteen next year I will personally come over to that little apartment of yours and wash your toilet by hand—not that I think you're the kind of person with a dirty toilet, my boy."

A week later in Columbus, I was riding in a taxi back to the airport after a positive meeting with Red Bones, when Dan called.

"I've got good news and some maybe not good, which do you want first, kiddo?"

"The good news, of course."

"Well then, your buddy Rich has agreed to come work with us," he said. Rich was a high school friend of mine who'd been out of work since the dot-com company he had worked for went out of business. He was a 'bean man's bean man,' as Dan liked to say. He had passed the CPA exam, which eighty percent fail, on the first attempt. And he had been intrigued by coming to work for the benevolent capitalist, although he had been unsure if another entrepreneurial company would be a good choice.

"I told him," Dan said, "that I thought he would be happier at a big company and you know what he said? He said if I really wanted him to take another job because it would be better for him that I was everything you said I was, boyo."

"And you are," I said, happy that Rich liked Dan as much as I did.

"So, he'll be starting with us January one, after he finishes up his severance."

"And the bad news?" I asked.

"Well, that's for you to judge, kiddo. We have another loan offer from Berry Capital. It's better, but we still have to give up almost a twenty percent of the company and pay a big chunk of the money to them as a commission. I think we can get a better deal, and I want to turn it down, but I wanted to call you first. If you want to do this deal, I will sign it."

"Dan," I said, "whatever you think. You know I trust you."

 —■—Revenue

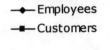 —■— EBITDA
—▲— Corporate Debt

 —◆— Employees
—■— Customers

My Net Worth	Locations	Revolver
	Clarinda Atlantic Baltimore St. Paul New York Syracuse Manila	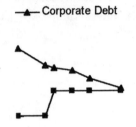

Revenue	$12,000,000
EBITDA	$1,000,000
Corporate Debt	$1,100,000
Employees	200
Customers	120
My Net Worth	$4,500,000
Revolver Expires	10 Months

Maalox Leaves A Chalky Residue

We are dealing with a conflict of feeling and intelligence, a form of willful self-deception whereby a part of the mind knows full well that its overall belief is false or wicked, but the emotional need to believe is so strong that that knowledge remains, as it were, encysted, isolated, powerless to influence word or deed.

—Why Lucky Jim Turned Right *by Kingsley Amis*

August 2001

WE TURNED A CORNER BY THE FIREHOUSE into a small square lined on three sides by trendy restaurants, which called themselves 'bistros.' "Canton?" Dan asked, his arm hanging out the window, but in deference to me, no cigarette between his angular tan fingers.

"That's what I'm told," I said. It was my fourth weekend of house hunting in Baltimore—I had finally given in to Dan's suggestion Luke and I move, although Luke had yet to even call a realtor—and Dan had advised me to check out wherever the "young people" were living now.

"Slicker than a hound's penis, that real estate man of yours," he said.

"What on Earth does that mean?" I asked.

"It means when I was growing up, this was Highlandtown, and you, my boy, would not want to be caught down here if you weren't poor, Irish, and white." He pointed at a California-style pizza restaurant where a man in a tuxedo and woman in an evening gown were walking out. "My mother rented that very house for fifteen dollars a month." He'd told me before that his mother had been a prostitute and that he'd had to support his two sisters with whatever he could earn as a laborer at Bromo Seltzer.

"You really grew up right there?" I asked, examining the house for clues to his life. It was four stories high and adorned with green shuttered windows. Workmen wearing protective jumpsuits were removing the dull grey formstone that covered most houses in this part of Baltimore. Officially intended to beautify brick buildings in the 1940s, it was the most depressing architectural feature I'd ever seen. It made the grey sky, road, and houses blend into one patina of economic weariness. The real estate agent told me dissolving the lumpy fake stone to expose the brick beneath cost a couple thousand dollars per floor. "Did you have formstone?"

"Formstone! When I was growing up you would have given your grandmother for formstone." He paused to pick a bit of lunch out of his teeth with a fingernail. "We lived in a house until they figured out my mother wasn't paying rent and then moved on to the next one. You know, I can't even remember how many houses we lived in."

I turned onto a leafy street where half the row houses had been renovated with bright red or purple doors and half still had battered screen ones with old women in padded housecoats and curlers sitting on the stoops or bent over tiny gardens with three blades of grass and a cement Madonna. It was one of the nicer streets—most had no trees at all.

"You'll be happier here," he said, squinting at the buildings. "You'll make some new friends, get out of that little hole you're living in up there in New York, it'll be good for you."

"Left or right?" I asked.

"You know, I don't remember, my boy. It's been too long since I've been down here. Look at that, St. Anne's. I went to school right there," he said, sounding like anyone seeing his old school for the first time in decades.

I turned right at the bar on the corner. Every corner in Baltimore had a bar or a liquor store, or both.

"We'd have done anything to get out of here when I was growing up and now you're going to spend a fortune to move in. Times change, my boy. Times change." He pulled a cigarette out of his pocket and lit it. "Where are we going now?"

"There was a condo on a pier in the Harbor I wanted to show you."

"Well, let's see it!"

"It's too expensive." The next traffic light featured two bars, a liquor store, and an empty storefront that advertised "Imported Mexican Items." I rolled down my window, but that caused the smoke to be sucked in front of me instead of bringing in more air.

"What are you worried about? You're a wealthy man. Every year from now on you'll be making more and more money."

"Half a million for a condo? You think that's reasonable in Highlandtown?"

"What I think is, you need to do whatever makes you happy," he flicked his cigarette towards the window, but the wind blew it backwards. He fumbled between his cowboy boots to get at the still smoldering butt.

"And there's the church where they buried my father," he said after retrieving it. "Did I ever tell you what I felt when I saw him?"

"Nothing," I said.

"That's right, nothing. He was a drunk and when he managed to find his way home he'd beat my mother—but seeing him lying in that casket I felt absolutely nothing."

"Is the way back to your house left or straight ahead?"

"I'm sorry, David. How is your father?" He lit another cigarette.

I turned the fan to full speed. "Drunk."

"Don't be so hard on him, my boy. He did all right by you growing up, didn't he?"

"This is Baltimore Street," I said. "Is that right?"

"Baltimore Street! Look for a sign with a naked neon girl."

There were lots of signs with naked girls, some neon, some painted, and many fronted by Middle Eastern men handing out fliers.

"That's where I used to play guitar with my uncle's band, and, my boy, the ladies took quite a shine to me. Turn up there and we'll be at the tower."

The bottom two-thirds of the Bromo Seltzer tower were a plain office building finished in concrete and without any ornamentation. The top third featured a Big Ben style clock topped with castle battlements under a giant lamp ringed with more battlements. It looked like a lighthouse designed for Medieval Times.

"I used to have sex in the stairways at night in that building."

"What?"

"I was a young man back then, athletic. I almost got recruited out of college to the Philly's farm team, did I ever tell you that?" Without turning my head I could see the outline of his thin legs and the balls of his kneecaps etched in yellow khakis. "Loyola, my boy, the Jesuits. If they can't teach you, no one can because they've smacked you so hard your brains have fallen out." He carefully let the second cigarette drop outside the car. "Made fizzies. You know what a fizzy is?"

"Not a clue."

"Looks like a Bromo Seltzer, but makes your glass of water into a soda pop."

"95 South to your house, right?"

"Very, very unpopular," he said, looking in the review mirror at the receding Bromo beacon. "Tasted like dirt."

On the way to his house, we passed Camden Yards, which was both a stadium for the Baltimore Orioles and the home of Waverly Publishing. He didn't look over as we stopped beside the renovated brick massif for the last few traffic lights before getting on I-95, but I knew he must be thinking about it.

They weren't a customer, in spite of several attempts and the fact that Dan had once been their number two man. He'd started out as a copyeditor and worked his way up to ultimately becoming president. His mentor had been the company's owner and CEO, "Old Man Pasano," a descendent of the original founder of Waverly. As Dan had put it, "He was that rare kind of blue blood who could spot talent in a wrong-side-of-the-tracks Irishman like me."

Everyone who had known Dan from back then told me how lucky I was to be working with the best boss they'd ever had—how he'd transformed Waverly from setting hot lead type to computer typesetting without firing anyone, and how he'd been the only president to play on the company's basketball team.

But Dan had been forced to train the Old Man's son, Junior, to take over as CEO. Not only was Junior not very good at business, he didn't care about people the way his father did. When Dan told me about those days, which was rare, he would tell me a story of talking to Junior in the boardroom.

"Dan, would you answer a question a few of us have?" Junior had asked. "You play basketball with the negroes. You see them in the locker rooms. Is it true about the size of their penises?"

"I don't know," he had answered. "I'm not much for looking at other men's dangle."

I turned off the highway near the airport and took the back way to Dan's house in a freshly divided subdivision on the edge of an older Baltimore suburb.

"Did you see that big church downtown?" he asked as I slowed for speed bumps beside rows of identical houses all flying either American or Disney character flags. "That was where they buried Old Man Pasano. You know, at his funeral, the line of mourners stretched out the door and down the street." I spotted Dan's salmon pink Ford Contour, and drove into the neighbor's too-close driveway by mistake. "I'll tell you, when I saw him in the casket, I did *not* feel nothing. There was a great man." He put his hand on the seatbelt clasp. "My funeral won't be downtown, but you'll come, won't you, my boy?"

I frowned. "Dan, we're going to see your family."

"You're right, my boy. We should be thinking about the wonderful mashed potatoes and gravy awaiting us."

He had bought the house a few months after we took over Clarinda. "I promised my bride a house, and I am going to get her one," he'd said. It hadn't been easy. He had to pay double the down payment because the bank felt that as an owner, he was at greater risk of losing the company than one of our employees was of losing their job.

The house, therefore, was modest. Two bedrooms and an office upstairs, a kitchen separated from a small living room by a wood post railing, an unfinished basement, and a two-car garage that only held one car because of a ping-pong table occupying half—but it was much larger than the townhouse he'd rented for the eight years I'd known him and it was "fully detached."

He'd been close to becoming wealthy many times, but never collected. At Waverly, he had been part of taking the company public, but he decided to leave rather than work for Junior and so his stock had never vested.

He became president of Penta Systems—the company that made the typesetting software he'd bought for Waverly. As Penta was going public, a Concorde had been held so that Dan and the owner could make a promotional event in London. "But," he told me, "it didn't matter. Every share had already been sold."

What should have been his second fortune disappeared when Dan ported the software to UNIX. The owner thought the company should stick with Data General, and, to make sure everyone understood his position, one night he threw the completed UNIX tapes into a trashcan, poured whiskey over them, and set them ablaze.

Dan lost his job and his Penta stock sank, as his marriage to his high school sweetheart fell apart. Clinically depressed, she lived either in institutions or simply vanished, leaving him to raise four children and put them through college. Technically married, but practically alone, he found another woman, Helen.

Maryland divorce law went against a man who cheated, no matter the circumstances. The court forced him to sell his homes, one in Baltimore and one in Ocean City. Worse, the IRS decided that the taxes on the sales should be paid by Dan, not his ex-wife, to whom the proceeds had gone. Thus, as Dan said, "I'd never earned less than a hundred grand a year since 1970, yet I was destitute with a decade-long lien on my income by the government."

The injustices became almost comical. His first wife got re-married to the CFO from Waverly, who had made a fortune on the company's stock. When the CFO died, she was cheated by a devious broker, and Dan found himself both paying alimony and giving her extra to help with rent and doctor's bills. "She's not a bad person, and I do what I can for her," he would say.

He married Helen, who had his fifth child, Ben, and he found a job at Datadata, which was looking for help with their IPO. He built a typesetting unit in Baltimore that did much of its production in Manila—the model for Clarinda—but Datadata management was not interested in typesetting, and he found himself again with worthless stock. "The only things I don't regret about my career," he liked to say, "were meeting Helen, having Ben, and meeting you, my boy."

ℓ

Helen came out of the house—a middle aged woman with black shoulder-length hair and a face taller than wide, she reminded me of my elementary school art teacher. She wore a light green windbreaker and jingled keys in her hand.

"I've got to go see my father," she said from the doorway.

Dan had made it to the first of the three front steps. He held the railing with both hands while lifting his left leg from the knee and keeping his foot horizontal. The leather of his brown boots was cracked with a network of grey lines. He kept telling me he intended to go get a new pair, something actually orthopedic.

He gazed up at Helen—although she was ten years younger than him, being in her early fifties, it was her brisk movement and not her looks that set them apart. "But David here was looking forward to your Sauerbraten. Maybe some nice mashed potatoes."

"Then you should have called me and told me you were bringing him."

She said, the flat tone of repeated aggravation in her voice. Looking at me, standing on the lawn, holding Dan's briefcase, she added a note of sympathy as best she could. "Nice to see you, David. Dan can call for a pizza, if that's OK with you."

Inside we sat at the kitchen table while Ben, who had turned thirteen that year, called Pizza Hut.

"Do you like pepperoni, Mr. David?" he asked, keeping the Pizza Hut man waiting. He'd starting calling me Mr. David when he was nine and the habit stuck.

"Sure," I said.

Ben had spiky blond hair and stood with the kind of slackness that comes from growing two feet in one year. "Do they let leprechauns eat pepperoni?" He referred to my half boots with the silver buckle I'd bought in Soho.

"Leprechauns love pepperoni," I said.

"Make that green pepperoni," Ben said in the phone. "Yes, you heard me. Green. I am certain that, if you have the desire for green pepperoni, it will happen. I have complete confidence in you, Mr. Pizza Hut."

"My son has been listening to his old man for too long," Dan said. "Now give me that phone, kiddo. Yes, give it to me. Hello, yes, that was just my son. He's a little rambunctious, but a good kid. Smart as a whip."

"Have you seen one of these?" Ben asked, pulling a large scientific calculator from his school bag and pushing it into my hand.

"Takes after his old man," Dan said on the phone. "I bet you know the type. And yes, I understand that phone of yours is ringing off the hook with other people calling their orders in."

"It's the best one on the market," Ben said. "Everyone at school is allowed to have a calculator and Mom bought me this one. It's the top of the line."

"Yes, I'm sure if you put some peppers on there he'd be just as happy. Wouldn't you Ben? Is that what you wanted? Peppers?"

"Can you help me with my homework?" Ben slid his math workbook

Typo

beneath the calculator. "I bet you can. I bet you're going to be happy to help."

"Ben, here, hang up this phone. And leave Mr. David alone. We've got business to discuss. Finish your homework and then maybe Mr. David will play ping-pong with you on that table your mom bought."

"But what about his apartment? You said Mr. David is moving to Baltimore."

"After homework."

Ben ran upstairs, thumping each landing with both feet for effect.

"Did you know his coach said he'll probably get a tennis scholarship into whatever school he wants? The boy's that good." He took the bottle of Maalox from his leather case. "Someday you'll understand, my boy." He took a sip. "There is no greater joy in this world than seeing your children grow up. He's my fifth, but he's more important to me than any of them." He took another sip. "Not that I don't love the girls and the two boys, but Ben is number one." He took one more sip and wiped his thin lips with the edge of his blazer.

ℓ

On the first of August, I drove down to Baltimore with my belongings jammed into a minivan. I had settled on a condo in a renovated warehouse on the water. In the evening the fourteen-foot aluminum-framed windows lit with reflections of the harbor. Four bedrooms, a breakfast nook, laundry, a "powder room." My single, green Pottery Barn couch floated in the middle of nearly three thousand square feet of blue-grey carpeting, like a child lost in a shopping mall. It was a fabulous New York loft apartment, but in Baltimore. I looked up at the railings of the duplex-ed bedrooms. Nobody, not Jose Bembo, not my friends who complained I was always busy with work, not my father, could think I hadn't made it. In the morning, I left for Iowa.

This trip, to resolve production problems on Jackie Dee's work, had come at a terrible time. The night before, Dan's mother-in-law—who had been in and out of the hospital for months—had a stroke, and between our getting on the plane and arriving at Clarinda, she'd gone into a coma.

"They put her on a respirator too late," Dan said, his voice weak over the phone from the Super 8. "And I'm just a bastard. I'm not there for my Helen, my lovely bride, when she needs me."

Minnie walked into my office. "Is Dan coming in?" she asked, paying no attention to the phone at my ear. "He said we would go over my concerns with the Household deal."

"Is that Minnie, my boy?" Dan asked.

"Yes," I said into the phone, and then to Minnie, "I mean. I don't know when he's coming in."

"I've got to go get my mother this afternoon," she said.

"Can you tell her I am probably going to miss our meeting today?"

She had already dropped a stack of expense reports on my desk and left.

"And, can you see to the meeting with 'fuzzy hair' today? You know what I'm up to with that, don't you, my boy?"

I assured him I knew.

"You know the terrible part, David?" I heard him puff slowly on a cigarette. "That damn father of hers, the poor woman's husband, refuses to go into the hospital. Can you believe that?"

"Helen's father won't help?"

"He just waits at home down on Eastern Shore there and waits for her to come and make him dinner. Can't face hospitals, he says. Excuse me for saying this my boy, but what a filthy cocksucker."

"Can her son make it out from Chicago?"

"Oh that's another one, kiddo. That's another one." He began coughing and I heard him take a sip of either Maalox or cough syrup. He had been downing a bottle of Robitussin every trip and his case was now more red and white than leather inside.

"That bastard won't even come to Baltimore and he's not even working. Did you know that?"

"Do you want to head back?" I asked.

"That's my door," he said. "It's probably another urgent message from Helen. I've got to go. Will you mind the shop for us?"

"Fuzzy hair" didn't show up for her meeting so I went to her office located at the nexus of the front hall, the lunchroom, and the handicapped bathroom.

"Do you have the material for Dan?" I asked.

She did indeed have fuzzy hair and her face was an order of magnitude too wide. Her cheeks connected flatly on both sides to her ears, and her eyebrows rose far into the curls. It gave her the appearance of being amazed, and while I spoke she nodded rhythmically—raising and lowering her head from the back and intoning, 'un-hunn.'

"The status report on Manila keying?" Despite our having made an arrangement with M&T nearly a year and a half ago to send our keyboarding to them, virtually nothing was being sent other than keyboarding for the work being done by Fanta's typesetting group, and there wasn't much of that being sent either. "If I don't personally ask to have a job sent to Fanta or Mai," he complained to me nearly every day, "nothing goes over there."

She blinked very slowly, which drew attention to the fact that she hadn't been blinking until then.

"Dan's not coming in today," she said.

"I know. I'm here to see if we're making progress on sending more keying to Mai at M&T."

Typesetters needed keyboarders to type in manuscripts and copyedits. Before the Internet made it possible to send the work to Asia, farm wives had done it. It was easy and the farming and typesetting seasons didn't overlap.

"Un-hunn," she said and began laboriously searching through the piles of marked up manuscript on her desk.

Keyboarding—per 1,000 keystrokes—cost $2.50 in Iowa versus $0.65 from Mai. The difference wasn't just lower salaries overseas. In one of those government actions intended to help that ultimately caused harm, the IRS had decided part-time keyers deserved to have taxes withheld and receive compensation for their mileage to and from the plant.

The economic reality had driven every one of our competitors to Manila, India, or even China for keyboarding. I knew because Dan and I had sold most of them their keyboarding when we worked at Datadata. For every keystroke we didn't do with Mai, our net cost exceed the Indians price for a complete page—keying, typesetting, *and* corrections. Fuzzy-hair located the report and handed it to me.

"We're sending two jobs to Manila?" I asked.

"That's what Dan, unhun, asked me to do."

I had overhead Dan's conversation with her months earlier. I had heard him coaxing her, seen her hair nodding, and heard him pause for her extended blinking.

"He asked you to send these two jobs?"

"He said, 'Find a couple of jobs, unhun, to let Manila try?"

Two books. Small ones. "And how did they do?"

"Lots of, unhun, errors."

"But they do good work for our competitors."

"Unhun." Without a pause in her nodding, Fuzzy Hair had single-handedly ruined our plan. From Dan's complaints I knew that she had sent projects without instructions. She had argued that we shouldn't be hurting the homeworkers by using Manila. She had come in late and on weekends to personally do keyboarding—doubling her pay with overtime—despite the fact that Mai had contracted with us to do corrections for free.

"Are those corrections to M&T keying on your screen right now?"

"Un. Unhun."

I called Dan to tell him what I'd uncovered.

"Is that you, my boy?" his voice was hoarse, completely devoid of strength.

I had had enough of people working against him. I didn't want to have to hear him complain about them fighting him anymore. "I can fix the keyboarding problem for you."

"Maybe I care too much," he said. "You don't think I care too much, do you?"

"Of course not," I said, "So you'll let me take care of the keyboarding? I can tell Frank to let the homeworkers go, unless you're planning to come in."

"She'll never forgive me."

"Fuzzy hair? Why can't we train her to be a typesetter like you said?" I asked.

"You don't understand, she won't forgive me for killing her mother."

"Whose mother? Helen's?"

"Yes, David. Helen's mother. Her mind is dead and since her rat of a husband is sitting on his fat ass at home, the doctors insisted Helen make the choice to keep her mother alive or not. And she couldn't do it, bless her, she just couldn't do it. She needed me. Needed me and I'm here in this fucking motel in Iowa. So I did it. I was the one who told the doctors what had to be done and now she won't forgive me. She won't forgive me for killing her mother."

"I don't understand. You said Helen had to tell the doctors."

"But I told her," his voice was angry and tearful, "I killed her mother."

ℓ

Back in Baltimore in the middle of September, I moved into my new office that was no more than an anteroom of Dan's. My little window that looked out on the Hampton Inn was cut in half by a column. I arranged the stapler, telephone, and penholder on my desk while waiting for Dan to arrive. Ralph, who'd worked for Dan since Waverly, knocked on the door mere inches from my head. He had grey hair and his belly stretched a stained polo shirt over his waist.

"Did you see what's happening in New York?" he asked. "Some kind of plane crash."

ℓ

My only connection to events and friends in New York that day was the reload button on the *New York Times* webpage that showed brief glimpses of the towers on fire one minute and "page not found" the next.

That night, a friend sent pictures—fire trucks crushed like soda cans, the single skeletal piece that remained of the buildings. Personal images of history e-mailed like someone's baby photos. My old apartment had been less than a mile away, the towers visible from the window.

Baltimore was quiet, and the sense of disaster remote in the aisles of the grocery store. Instead of dinner, I bought a bag of chocolate chips. As I watched the news alone in my waterfront condo, I stirred sugar and butter into cookie dough.

In the morning, I rode my bike to the light rail by Camden Yards and then on a path to the office. The trail rose on a hill near the airport and from there I could see the planes from every airline motionless on the tarmac, like toys abandoned by a giant.

"I'm sorry your books won't get to you tomorrow," I explained to the angry Florida customer who had complained to customer service so much they gave her my number. "No planes are flying anywhere in the country. That means no overnight delivery. Yes, we will do everything we can. No, I can't promise when it will get there. I am sorry. I suppose it is a shame what happens in New York has affected your book."

Dan arrived around ten. He leaned into the doorjamb—holding it with his left hand—while severely clutching a briefcase with his right.

"Well, the bastards have come for us," he said. "Are those friends of yours OK?"

I told him one friend's in-law escaped from the fiftieth floor of the first tower, and everyone else I knew hadn't been harmed.

"Good." He stumbled towards his office. He grabbed at my desk with his free hand while still rigidly gripping his case with the other. "I'm sorry, my boy," he said, "I've been up all night. I don't think I closed my eyes once."

I overhead him call Minnie in Iowa.

"Yes, we're all OK here. And you? It's come to this, hasn't it? Oh this is just the start, mark my words. But they've won. You don't think so? Look at us. The whole country brought to a stop. They've got what they wanted. It'll take years for the economy to recover, if it ever does. Really? Well let me ask you if you're still going to want to fly anywhere. I see, you didn't fly much to begin with. Well, what about all those New Yorkers, like David? He nearly could have been there. You do feel sorry for them, don't you? Yes, no, you're right Iowa's not New York. No, I don't think New Yorkers should have expected it." He lit a cigarette. "But Iowa's safe, you think? Nobody coming after your drinking water or hiring one of those little crop duster planes and dumping something on you? I see, you wouldn't have thought New York was safe in the first place."

He hung up the phone, puffed a few times, and then called out to me, "Are you ready for lunch yet, my boy?"

For the next week Dan came in later and later. He spent a few minutes making calls and then went to his car to smoke and listen to the latest radio report. Our lunches across the road at the Holiday Inn stretched to two and a half hours. He wouldn't eat the crab cakes he ordered, but didn't want to go back to the office either.

He fell behind at work and I began making decisions without going over them with him—something I'd never done, and I felt both confident and nervous about it. I told Frank to get rid of the homeworkers and move the keying to M&T. When I told Dan of my accomplishment at lunch, he said simply, "I know, my boy, you know best." I couldn't tell if there was sarcasm in his voice.

ℓ

We sat in Dan's salmon-pink Ford looking at the golf course. The keys lay in his jacket pocket and he still wore his red Marlboro cap, 70s style sunglasses, and one mesh cotton glove that he rested lightly on the steering wheel. The day had not gone well. Wanting to give him some relief from work and the 24-hour news channels, I'd offered to go golfing with him. However, aside from the version of the game with windmills, scale-model elephants, and clown faces, I didn't have much aptitude for it.

"Go down after the ball," he had said over and over. "Down after it."

I had no idea what he meant, and after four holes of missing or hitting the ground so hard that my chest hurt, I walked behind him the rest of the day.

"I'll get over this, you just have to give me a little time," he said.

"I know you will."

He looked straight ahead. It had started to rain lightly. "Can you really buy that Viagra stuff on the Internet?" Seeing my expression, he said, "You're the only one I trust now, boyo."

I told him I probably could figure it out, although I'd rather not.

"The thing is," he said, "Helen hasn't forgiven me for killing her mother, and now she wants Jake to move in." Jake was Helen's adult son who lived in Chicago.

"Isn't his wife pregnant?"

"Yes, that little commie," he said. I frowned. "Forgive me, David, but you didn't have to read her book. She may have gotten her university degree from here and a life she could never have had in China, but she's a commie."

Ignoring his political baiting, I asked, "Where would they live? Would you give up the home office?"

"And her father. Helen's always going off to visit him and, I knew it would happen, she wants him to move in too. I told you, I knew this would happen, didn't I, my boy?"

"But I thought she hated him after he refused to come to the hospital when her mother died?" Somehow Dan's home life had become more confusing and stressful than work.

"And you know where she wants us to live?" I had no idea. There weren't enough rooms in the house. "In the basement. The fucking basement," he said, loudly, and tightened his grip on the wheel. I thought of the keys locked away in his jacket. "In the basement, my boy. I bought that house for us and now there won't be room for me."

I asked if there was anything I could do to help.

"You know I haven't dismissed the idea of asking you if there's room for me in that new condo of yours."

"Downtown?" I couldn't believe Dan would be forced to move into his basement, much less move in with me.

"You would let your old pal in, wouldn't you? I'd pay you whatever's fair." He had stopped looking at me.

"Of course, Dan," I said. I imagined him in one of the upstairs bedrooms, walking to the shower in his jockey shorts.

"But I'm a smoker, that probably wouldn't work," he said. The rain was coming down hard, pinging on the metal roof. "It was just a pretty dream, kiddo." He pulled the keys from his pocket. "That's why I was thinking the Viagra might help. Maybe if I could make Helen happy again. My lovely bride. I killed her mother and she won't forgive me." He started the car. "You'd do that for me, my boy, wouldn't you?"

ℓ

The day before another trip to Iowa, I heard a sucking sound from Dan's office. I detest the sound of chewing—especially when I haven't had lunch. I jumped up, took the one quick step to his door, and watched him stuff a bottle of Absolut vodka into a drawer—the blue typeface as clear as a page full of mis-sized hyphens.

I stepped back. He had seen me. In one-half a second a dozen thoughts spun through my head: *drinking in the office? But, didn't Dan have every reason to drink a little? He'd suffered for months with illness, his home life was a mess, business was as hard as ever, and September 11th had shaken him terribly*—and then they were gone. Like a gridlocked intersection, I could not pull them apart. The thoughts fused into a non-specific dread. The only person I trusted to ask for help was Dan, and I couldn't ask him.

An hour later we went to lunch, and I sat quietly while he ignored his crab cake and beer and told me that next year would be the time to start thinking about going public.

The following morning Dan pulled into the office parking lot. We had planned to meet there so I could drive to the airport to save on parking fees. It was a chilly November morning and he was an hour and a half late. He pushed with both hands on his car door, which flung open and then rebounded back at him.

He tried a second time with the same result and then turned around and lit a cigarette inside the car. I walked over, but he didn't acknowledge me. I knocked on the window until he lowered it.

"Sorry I'm late, my boy," he said and coughed on his hand that held the cigarette. "But I had a few problems at home this morning." He spoke slowly, growling each syllable.

"We're running late," I said, thinking about that bottle. I just needed an opening to ask him.

He coughed again and wiped his hand down the front of his brown windbreaker—scattering ashes over himself.

"I'd have been here sooner, but I had two flat tires this morning."

"Our flight's in an hour," I said, and looked around the parking lot. It was Saturday so there would be no employees coming in to see us like this.

"Slashed. Slashed, my boy. Do you think one of the neighbor kids would have done that as a prank?"

"I don't know." His face was darkened by several days of brown-grey beard.

"Last night Jake tried to kill me." He glanced up at me. "Oh I don't think he meant it, but he hates me. Especially when he's been drinking." He stubbed out the cigarette on the dash and pulled another from the pack—his fingers pressed together like a claw. "He's been here all week, scoping out the place for him and his wife. Measuring shit." He lit the cigarette and nodded to himself. "Came by with a case of beer. Do you know how many beers there are in a case, my boy? Not a six pack."

"Dan, can I help you to my car?"

He put an arm on the door as if to open it, and I heard the click of the latch.

"Twenty-four. Twenty-four beers. And he wasn't offering me any. He drank the whole thing."

I reached in the window, feeling the wet polyester of his jacket, pushed the lock and opened the door. He looked at the mechanism—realizing that he'd pushed it the wrong way.

"He's gotta be six four, more than two hundred fifty pounds. That's a big kid, but twenty-four beers?"

I picked up Dan's case, which had been wedged between him and the door.

"I tried to defend myself, my house. You know he said I was a terrible father. A terrible father. Right in front of Ben. You don't think that, my boy," he said, and looked up at me again. I saw the wetness of tears in his eyes, and put out my hand to help him stand.

"Then he pushed me. Shoved me. Right here." He put his forearm in my palm, and with his cigarette hand balled in a fist, gestured at his chest. "So when I saw those slashed tires this morning. I knew it was him. Or Helen. You don't think it was Helen?"

"Maybe it was someone from the neighborhood." The thought of him faced with a violent son-in-law twice his size terrified me, and it also began to justify more what I had seen the day before. I would still ask him later—when he was feeling a little better.

"I had to wait for AAA to come. In the rain. An hour, I waited, and I didn't dare go inside. I called them from that cell phone you got me. Helen standing on the front porch, just watching me. And that Jake, asleep, drunk, in my house."

It was our first trip since September 11th, and he didn't hear the security guards ask him to take off his hat or understand the commotion about his cigarette lighter. "It's for smoking," he said. "I understand I can't smoke in here."

He slept on the flight, and when we arrived in St. Louis for the connection, he walked with such enormous effort that I asked for the cart to drive us to the gate.

He leaned on me as he grasped the pole topped with a revolving warning light. "Look at me," he said, sadly, "an invalid." When he pushed against me to get onto the vinyl seat, I felt how much weight he had lost.

At the airport lounge, he ordered a beer and nachos. I thought this would be my chance to confront him, but he didn't touch either. He didn't even look at the beer. I ate the nachos.

The first day back in Iowa he had stomach problems, and didn't come in until everyone else had left. The next day he called me around noon, his voice thick with phlegm. "Not well, my boy, not well at all."

I began fielding the calls from the salespeople and responding to the production issues. "Dan's very ill," I said to everyone who asked, which was everyone I spoke to. "Yes, that cough of his is pretty bad. No, I don't think it's the smoking. He's probably got some kind of ulcer—you should see the amount of Maalox he drinks! No, I know that's no cure. Yes, he should see a doctor. But about the book we were discussing—"

By night I hadn't got through half of the calls, so I collected the pile of pink memo slips, bought some soup from Subway, and knocked on Dan's motel door. He thanked me for the broth, but let it go cold on the table while telling me about the troubles at home—ESPN playing silently on the

TV. I looked around for alcohol, but all I saw was my friend and mentor, his shirt un-tucked and his hair uncombed.

"Make me a promise, kiddo," he said, sitting on the edge of the bed, his head slumped forward.

"Anything, Dan."

"Promise me you'll make sure Ben gets to go to college." He rubbed his legs with his hands—even his hands were thin. "I'm serious, David. I may not make it through this. I just realized that today. I don't know if I can survive what's going on at home and the only thing that matters to me is you and Ben."

"Dan, I—"

"Promise me, my boy. Promise me, that you'll take care of Ben," he said, his blue eyes lit by the Maryland Terrapin's game.

"I promise."

The next day I received an e-mail from Helen. I had never gotten an e-mail from her. I closed my door before reading it. She wrote that Dan had been so sick, and he refused to go to a doctor. He was being difficult at home, and she needed my help. Did I notice anything unusual in his behavior? Would I help her get him to listen? Would I write back and not tell him?

I deleted it instantly.

How could she ask me to betray his confidence? She was much, if not the majority, of his suffering, and I really needed him back. If I could get his health restored we could sort out his personal problems. I told him he had to get treatment.

"I guess you're probably right," Dan said. "I should see a doctor. Go ahead and make an appointment and see if you can get me in."

"I already did," I said. "We're on for tomorrow."

The drive to Omaha was exactly an hour and a half and Dan talked the entire time—his head lolled to the side, nearly asleep but not sleeping, his lips barely parted and his voice a fingernail-on-chalkboard, mucousy ramble. He talked about Helen, about Jake, about Ben, about Minnie,

Luke, Frank, Old Man Pasano, Jose Bembo. He talked and talked. I wanted to be supportive, but he didn't pause long enough for me to interject even a "Dan."

While the sun set in tangerines and reds behind the Loess hills, he rambled. I could not stop from focusing on every word as if it were one of his lessons in business. Despite my desire to feel sympathy, I felt my anger rising. I wanted him to shut up. I wanted to scream. "Dan," I said over his mumbling. He ignored me. "Dan." He kept talking. I wanted to punch him. As I drove into the growing darkness of the Iowa night I wanted to rip his head off and throw it out the window.

"The doctor's appointment is in an hour."

He nodded. The suite I had gotten him had a sleeping loft, kitchen, and the stucco and wood beamed architecture of a Swiss ski lodge, but guessing from the crumpled boxes of Newports by the phone, he had spent every minute since I left him the night before calling Helen.

"He's going to charge us whether you go or not." It was the only reason I could think of that didn't sound like I was desperate for him to go.

He nodded again. On the coffee table were two open bottles of Excedrin, cigarette ashes, and a tray of untouched drinks, the glasses overflowing slightly as the ice melted.

"You haven't eaten in days. You haven't slept."

He pursed his lips.

"If you're afraid of the doctor, I understand." Maybe he was drinking, but maybe that was only the symptom. He could be dreading a diagnosis of cancer or emphysema. His weakness, the coughing, and the lack of medical care—he would know better than I how bad it might be.

He picked up the phone. "Let me just call Helen. Let me just talk to her. You haven't heard anything from her, have you?"

I shook my head. I worried Helen would tell him she had emailed me, but there was no answer at home and he relented. "I've never had a physical. Can you believe that? I'm afraid, my boy. What if it is cancer or emphysema? I didn't want to admit it, but I'm afraid."

When the exam was over, he showed me the prescriptions: antidepressants, pills for insomnia, and vitamins. "He says I'm just an old man who isn't sleeping or eating enough."

"I could have told you that."

"I'm actually in pretty good shape he said. You know what it is? Isometrics." He pressed one palm into the other. "He said I had the muscle tone of a thirty-year-old."

I drove us around Omaha for a little tour—it was his first trip there in all the years we'd been coming out. It was turning into a much better day than the one before.

"That's where my friend Jane lives," I said. I would come up on the weekends to spend time with her, her five-year-old son, and her ex-husband who liked to tell stories of his days cutting cattle in half at the meat packing plant.

"You know Helen asked me for oral sex before I left this time," he said.

I decided I hadn't heard that. "Um, and around here somewhere is Warren Buffet's house. Did you know he lived in Omaha?"

"You take my word for it, she may not forgive me for killing her mother, but she still wants the sex. Women, my boy, women."

I knew he was trying to tell me she still loved him, although their relationship was in desperately strained, but instead I got the feeling that maybe all would not be well.

The next day we went to the Omaha airport to begin our trip back to Baltimore At the connection in St. Louis, I again provided a shoulder to keep him vertical. He called home repeatedly, but no one answered. He began to cry. "She won't even take my call."

Finally, he got an answer. "Hello? Ben? What do you mean Ben doesn't want to talk to me? I'm his father. Put Ben on." He held the phone at arms length to try to read the display. "He hung up on me!"

I offered to call. I pressed redial and a teenager answered. He told me that Ben wasn't there, and then laughed. I demanded that the boy put Ben on immediately. I told him this was no joke. Dan's life depended on it, but the boy kept laughing. I said that when I got back to Baltimore I would personally track him down for hurting Dan this way, and the boy hung up. When Dan stumbled off to the bathroom I checked the phone. He'd dialed the wrong number.

$$\ell$$

At Thanksgiving I visited my father. Nothing had changed. He still drank all day and the aides still came to clean up the house and him. I had gone on a drive through the Catskills when Dan called. He'd moved into the Holiday Inn by the office. I told him I would be there as soon as I could.

The room was in the Baltimore Washington Airport Holiday Inn, second floor. The date was Saturday, December 1, 2001. I arrived at two in the afternoon. Dan had peed on the floor. He'd peed in his pants. He lay back on the bed, unable to sit up. The room was decorated with full glasses of drinks and unopened beer bottles—like the birds on the telephone wires in the Hitchcock movie. I told him he had to go to the hospital.

"Helen. If Helen wants me to. I will go if she wants me," he said. "And Ben. Promise me Ben will come."

I called Helen. "I'll be right there," she said. After everything Dan had told me about her mistreatment of him, I didn't believe her.

I couldn't take being in the room with him and went down to the bar where we had so many lunches. Our regular bartender—who Dan liked to tip with twenty dollar bills—said, "He's been up there ordering whole bottles of vodka. Now I know what to do with him. I put a lot of water in there before I send 'em up, but the night guy. He just cares about the tips and sends 'em up." He wiped the bar with a cloth. "I'm just letting you know."

But I had seen the full glasses. There weren't any bottles in the room. How could it be true?

Helen did come. She wore a sweatshirt and jogging pants, and Ben had on a wrestling t-shirt. Dan, who still wore his rumpled yellow shirt, waxed in and out of consciousness. At midnight, he agreed to go to the hospital, but his legs were too shaky to stand. I wrapped my arms around his chest from behind, pulled up, and dragged him off the bed, his feet scraping the floor. He swung an arm under a bed pillow and raised a small bottle of vodka over his head in triumph. He looked at me, his eyes turned to glass. "Here's one you didn't find!"

At the University of Maryland Hospital I pushed his back towards the sliding glass emergency room door. He stretched his arms out like a cat trying to keep from going into a box. It was comical. I laughed. He laughed. "I must really not want to go in, my boy," he said. It took three pushes.

Dan was wheeled into the examining room with Helen at his side. Left on our own, I took Ben out to dinner—he didn't need to sit there, watching the drunks and homeless watch us. Over hamburgers, I tried to explain that his father still loved him—that he'd told me so many times.

Ben opened a packet of sugar and poured the contents in his mouth. "Gives me energy," he said.

I thought about my pledge to Dan—to make sure Ben was taken care of. Speaking with my most adult voice, I told him his father had just gone through a hard time with Ben's grandmother's death and 9/11.

"You only get to see us when you come to visit, Mr. David," he said, toying with pouring sugar on his half eaten burger. "You don't know what he's really like."

ℓ

An IV drip had been connected to Dan's arm to re-hydrate him, and although he was wearing a hospital gown, he still had his boots on. "They let me keep them after I refused to take them off," he said. He smiled and took a spoonful of applesauce. It was a private room with a solid, purple plastic couch without any seams or cracks—you could wash it with a hose.

"Food's better here than in Iowa?" I asked.

He considered the applesauce. "I could get used to this," he said. I removed some reports from my backpack. "What have you been telling people about all this, my boy?"

I put the pages on the rounded-edges coffee table. "I tell them that you've got a bad case of pneumonia."

"Well, that's truer than you think. True true true. I actually had a case of that."

I nodded. I wanted to go through the pile of clothes by the bed searching for vodka bottles.

"Doctor took away my Robitussin, can you believe that? Just little cough syrup."

"Doctor knows best," I said.

He clicked the spoon around the empty applesauce container and I looked out in the hall.

"How's the sales numbers?" he asked.

"Great," I said, picking up the report with relief. "Looks like about 8.5 million."

"That's what I thought," he said. "Is that work for your girlfriend down in San Antonio almost done?"

"She's a customer." His half-rude comment bothered me differently than usual. I didn't feel like he was playing around to get me to rethink my own stereotypes—he seemed genuinely spiteful—but I tried to ignore it because he was here to recover. "But I don't think we'll be able to bill until January, if that's what you're asking."

"Then I need your help, my boy. I can make phone calls from here, but people get suspicious if they see the number of a hospital come up. I need you to move those invoices back into this year. We've got to get sales over nine million and show an increase from 2000. The investors won't be interested if we don't show an increase. You understand, don't you?"

"We can do that?"

"You're starting to sound like Minnie, kiddo." There was an edge of anger in his voice. "The only people who care about when we close a month are investors and the *federales*. The IRS won't care if we show more profit—hell, the bastards will love us. And when the investors see we do fifteen million next year, they'll be too busy creaming themselves."

He leaned up to look out in the hall, "This damned buzzer. Would you give me a hand to the," he gestured at the bathroom, and I saw that he was confined to the bed, his legs too weak to walk, "or would you go out and find one of those nurses?"

I went to get a nurse.

ℓ

Although it was a sunny day, the room was half-dark with the closed curtains and the swirl of cigarette smoke. "I know it's not the Holiday Inn, but it's better than the Super 8," Dan said. He'd been in the hospital for a week, and when he left he checked himself into the Comfort Inn, where the staff hadn't seen him being hauled out like a sack of Iowa corn. "And this way Minnie won't be as upset about the bill," he said.

"Minnie?" I asked. "Are you charging this on the company card?"

I stood because there was nowhere to sit except the bed, which was covered with papers from his open briefcase. "Helen threw me out of the house again," he said. Helen had gotten him that briefcase the Christmas after we bought Clarinda. It looked now like it had been dipped in Robitussin and Maalox. "Either I let Jake move in or I move out, well, what choice did I have?" He asked. "Did you bring the new sales reports?"

"I asked Luke to move the TPC invoices to December like you said." He put the papers on the bed without looking at them. His eyes were wet and unfocused. "He was reluctant. It took me almost an hour to convince him."

"Reluctant," he said, not quite a question. "What's his number?"

"He's out on vacation this week."

"You're not pulling a fast one on me, are you, my boy?"

"What?"

"You're not trying to take the company away from me, while your old pal Dan's out sick with pneumonia and locked out of his house?"

"No, Dan, of course not. I told you I don't want the company without you. I want you back."

"Oh," he said, rubbing the tips of his fingers on his head. "I know, I know. You are one of the few left. Stay with me a little while. Won't you, my boy?"

Later, after listening to him repeatedly try to get Helen to talk to him on the phone, I hesitated in the parking lot. Would he be able to see me from his room? Would he suddenly decide he needed to go shopping for Tums? What did it matter if he did? Was Dan still the kind of ornery old man who insisted on not locking his car door? He was.

Ten seconds after I began rummaging, I found the bottle of cognac.

Having nowhere else to turn, I called Helen. We met for lunch. She brought along a copy of Dan's phone bill—a single night's calls occupied three pages.

"I don't know what to do," she said. "I try answering, not answering, but he won't stop." The dark circles under her eyes were thinly covered with makeup.

"I know it's not my place to say anything about this, but Dan really is a good guy and he just, well, he just thinks you haven't forgiven him for what happened with your mother."

"That? I forgave him months ago," she pushed a cherry tomato into the depths of her enormous chef's salad. "Although now that you mention it, I should probably have been more upset."

"About him killing your mother?" I asked. Dan had said the phrase so many thousands of times it had become ingrained.

"Killing my mother? Is that what he says?"

I told her about the drive to the doctor in Iowa and his worries about Jake moving in. I tried to leave out anything negative he'd said about her, I certainly left out the part about the oral sex, but her deepening frown made me say more than I wanted.

"He's a liar," she said.

"What do you mean? He didn't decide about your mother's life support?"

"She had a living will. Do you want to know what our conversation really was about that night?"

I nodded, relieved to stop talking.

"Sure he was on the phone all night with me, but it wasn't about my mother. I couldn't change her living will. No, he was on the phone yelling at me, 'Is this what you're going to do to me when I get old and decrepit? Are you going to let me die like that?'"

If that was a lie, what about her father and Jake moving in with them?

"Nobody's moving to Baltimore. When Jake comes here he's trying to stop Dan's drinking." She lit a cigarette. "I'm sorry, I just started again." She inhaled the smoke deeply, but did not relax. "He's a liar. He's always been one."

A very different Dan emerged as I began to compulsively question her. What about being born in Canton, the Philly's farm team?

"He didn't grow up downtown, he grew up in one of the suburbs. And a farm team? For the Phillies? That's a new one."

"He told me that years ago," I said.

"Yeah, well, did he tell you he was at the Battle of Bulge?"

The Dan I knew was unraveling like a cartoon sweater pulled by one strand. I thought he had just turned sixty. She said he was around seventy, but nobody knew for certain. His mother had never been a prostitute. Of his four adult children, that he spoke about so proudly to me, his two daughters were in contact with him, but of his two adult sons, one would not talk to him at all and the other, well, no one knew where he was. He had a problem with alcohol when he was in his thirties and checked himself into an institution. Although Dan never admitted he was an alcoholic, he had stopped drinking for years.

"That's why when I saw him have a beer after September 11th, I was stunned. I told him I just couldn't believe it and he told me to mind my own business."

"But seemed like he was hardly drinking," I said. "All those full glasses."

"One of the neighbor's girls found three bottles stashed in the bushes behind our porch. Didn't you notice?" she asked, lighting another cigarette. "Maalox leaves a chalky residue." She looked at me knowingly. "When he wipes his lips, there's no white. He fills the bottles with whiskey."

I continued to tell everyone that Dan's health was declining. What could I do? This was *our* business. For nearly two weeks I slept four hours a night. Work, which had already been non-stop, found previously hidden pockets of time to replace: brushing my teeth, pumping gas, folding laundry. I thought I was doing a pretty good job holding the company together and covering for him.

At the office in Baltimore, Francine came in my little anteroom and closed the door. Although she had worked with Dan since his days in the 70s at Waverly Press, she was one of the most difficult employees. I knew all about her twenty-year troubled relationship with a married man, her weight

Typo

problems, her constant screwing up of customer accounts, her sometime collaboration with the difficult Minnie in Iowa, and her dislike of me. He had been clear that she didn't like me or my "young punk from New York" ways, so he had always dealt with her, and in his absence I had limited our interactions to going over messages and status reports from Manila.

"I need to talk to you." Her voice grated like a stepped-on cat's yelp. Even the way she sat in the chair, her arms crossed in defiance, bothered me. She was just another problem employee that had contributed to Dan's decline.

"I don't have much time," I said. "What do you need?"

"It's Dan. You know, I think you should know that we've all been talking here in the office."

"Yes?"

"It's just that, we think you should know," She looked into his empty office. "You know how much he means to us. And I know he's important to you."

"Yes. It's sad how sick he's been. But I hope he gets better soon." The lie tasted like metal on my tongue.

"Well, that's the thing. I know you don't like me much." Her? I didn't dislike her, she disliked me. "We want to help you."

"Me?"

"Oh, I should just come out and say it," she said and put her hand on mine. I wanted to pull away, but her wrinkled palm was insistent. "David, Dan's been drinking."

Francine told me that she had been there when Dan had been a drunk thirty years before. She'd seen his first marriage fall apart and Helen threaten to leave. There were drunks in her family as well, so when he started spending hours in the car after 9/11, she knew he was drinking. She had kept it from me because Dan had told her I didn't trust her and that she was his favorite. His ranking system—his number one favorite person or child or whatever, his number two and so on—drew the lines that separated us. It felt endearing to be high on his constantly changing list, but the logic was: number one would not confide in number two.

The grey man squinted in the afternoon sunlight reflected from the harbor. "There are two ways of doing an intervention," he said. "There is the classical approach, type one approach, where you surprise the person, like a birthday party." The way he said birthday party made me never want to eat cake again. "I do not recommend that."

Ben, Helen and the grey man had come to my apartment to prepare for a type two intervention—let the person know you were thinking of doing a type one. Although the phone was against my ear, Dan wept loudly enough from his hotel room for everyone in my kitchen to hear. Helen held Ben's head to her shoulder.

The grey man motioned for me to hand him the phone. "Daniel, you have a lot of people here who love you." Sitting on one of my blue plastic folding chairs and still wearing his floor length raincoat, he looked like the Grim Reaper in a nightmarish IKEA ad. "I understand you know something about this process, which is why we are letting you know what we are planning." He nodded slowly. "But this is more truthful, isn't it Daniel? Yes? Ben is here also. Yes, he is crying." He clicked the phone off with a sharp, nail-chewed forefinger.

"Why did you hang up?" Helen asked.

The grey man smiled widely—two enormous bent lips hiding his teeth. "Daniel has agreed to go."

Dan went into rehab as 2002 began. I was overjoyed. My fear of every new day had been erased. In twenty-one days he would be back and retake command of Clarinda, his personal problems under control. In the meantime, I could easily keep the company going for another month.

He would be allowed three visits at Father Martin's Ashley, which overlooked the Chesapeake Bay from a panoramic bluff. The visits were, I felt, for his family. Besides, I had a lot to do. In those three weeks I traveled to Orlando for a conference, Philadelphia to meet with Reed Elsevier, the dentist for a long overdue appointment, San Antonio to recap the year with TPC, the dentist again, Iowa, the dentist yet again, a weekend eating a bottle of Advil to keep the swelling down, one more time at the dentist, and then back to Iowa.

Rich, my old high school friend, was supposed to have started in January helping Luke raise capital. I called to tell him everything that happened in the two months since he'd been offered the job. I told him Dan had gone willingly into rehab, but I understood if he didn't want the job anymore.

"Do you think Dan still wants me?" he asked.

I assured him he did, and reminded him Dan was not trying to hurt anyone.

"Do you still need my help?"

I assured him I needed that too.

"Well, it can't be worse than stupidity dot com," he said, "Book me on that trip to Iowa."

ℓ

The day before Dan was to get out of rehab, I had planned a meeting in Clarinda to buy new equipment for the year: five new servers, fifty super-fast workstations, an equal number of LCD monitors that reduced eye strain, a test install of gigabit networking—a nice budget of eighty thousand dollars.

"Gigabit isn't really going to make much difference," Penny said.

I could never understand why Penny, an alleged technology person, resisted buying technology. I suggested that she could give it a chance.

"I'd be ready to give it a go in Atlantic," Jim said.

"What about fonts? You've got people just buying fonts now that you've given them credit cards," she said, rocking forward in her chair.

"Nobody has a card except Sally, and she OK'd that one font with me."

"Well, it's getting out of hand."

While she continued to resist and I continued to try and change her, the receptionist delivered an overnight envelope from Reed Elsevier. I'd recently attended two meetings with the new chief of production and all the buyers: one in Philadelphia for books and one in New York for journals. Reed had bought most of Harcourt, including three of our customers, Saunders, Mosby, and Academic Press. I had received encouraging rumors that we'd be getting more, but the letter—signed by a Herr Doctor Achen—said it all in one paragraph: they were dropping us, immediately.

"What about the keyboards?" Penny asked. "A lot of people don't like the new keyboards."

"Can we finish this later?" I asked. Jim and Penny left, still arguing about the new equipment I now acknowledged we probably wouldn't be buying. I closed the door. We'd lost a third of our business in a sentence.

ℓ

"I know, I know. It was a shock to me too," said Geri, one of the buyers who had misled me into thinking we were doing well with Reed. "I really don't know more than the rumors I'm getting now. Only three American vendors are left, and we're supposed to be sending everything else to India."

I asked if there was any way we could get back on the vendor list.

"They told me I have to cut three people. Three editors, David. I really don't know what we are going to do."

More calling brought more rumors: it was the book Laura had messed up that ruined our name, it was bad blood over the Mosby services person we'd not hired when we first took over Clarinda, it was because we'd fired the salesperson Hilda, it was because we hadn't fired Hilda fast enough. It didn't matter, the decision was India, and we were out. I didn't open my door for a long time.

The next day—Dan's last at Father Martin's Ashley—Rich and I met with the company lawyer in Omaha. There were several items on the agenda: getting Rich his promised five percent share of the company, a review of our incorporation in the Philippines, and Dan. Other than Rich and the employees who had come to me in Baltimore, only the lawyer knew Dan was at rehab for something other than pneumonia.

When my cell phone rang showing the number of the Baltimore office, I stepped into the hallway. Why were all Midwestern offices wallpapered in the drab brown?

"David, this is Dan. You remember old Dan, don't you?" His voice had a hardness I hadn't heard since my father scolded me as a child, and it reached deep into my irrational fear that I had betrayed him by speaking to Helen, Francine, and the grey man. "I understand you're with our lawyer up there in Omaha. What have you been up to in old Dan's absence?"

I had made no secret of my meeting, yet I felt as if I had done wrong. I recapped the past month, but he kept questioning.

"This Reed letter, it came yesterday?"

"Yes," I said.

"And this was the first you heard of them cutting us off the list?"

"Yes."

"No inkling from Geri?"

"None, Dan."

"And you called her right after you got the letter?"

"Yes."

Rich came out of the lawyer's office. They had run out of small talk while waiting for me. I motioned to him to come outside with me. While Dan continued to talk, we got in the car and Rich began driving to the motel.

"But you're feeling better, right Dan?" I asked.

"And why wouldn't I be?" he responded. His icy voice was not apologetic. Rich pulled up to the electronic gate of the Sheraton and motioned for me to give him the code.

"I've got to go, Dan, my cell phone is running low. I'll see you when I get back on Monday, OK?"

"Whatever you say, David."

We rolled in silence into the mostly empty lot. "That was an odd conversation," Rich said, and went to the trunk to retrieve the boxes of accounting papers Minnie had reluctantly allowed him to take for examining.

"Isn't one of the recovery steps to apologize to people you've hurt?" I asked. Dan hadn't said anything about what I'd done to get his family together, to get him to hospitals, or to hold the company together while he was away. He hadn't mentioned the drinking once.

Rich slammed the trunk shut. "I believe it's number nine."

On Monday I was back in Baltimore. Although Dan was only a dozen feet away in his adjoining office, and had to walk through mine to come and go, we barely spoke. He spent his first two days talking with other people, and several hours with Rich going over plans for buying competitors. He was dodging me and I didn't mind.

On Wednesday, we all went to the pizza shop (there was no mention of Holiday Inn crab cakes). Dan was pale and had trouble holding a slice even with both hands. I got him a fork and a knife, but he ignored them. "We'll have to fire people. A lot of people," he said.

"I thought next year was going to be fifteen million. Without Reed, that's maybe twelve million, right?" I watched his hands tremble. "Here, use my napkins."

"A lot of people, David. I don't know, but it's going to be a lot." His voice was hard, as he dabbed at the grease puddle edging towards his jacket.

"What about Minnie? She's always been trouble for you."

He'd let the pizza fall to the plate, and began yelling. "If you want to start breaking my promises, you do that! But I'm a man of my word!" Dan had never yelled at me. People looked at us.

He'd already said we had to lay off people. If not Minnie, who?

"Do whatever you want," he growled. "Maybe you know better than me. Maybe you'd like to decide."

Heading back to the office, he slumped in the passenger seat, his hand

Typo

limply holding the seat belt without plugging it in, his eyes focused in the distance, pizza on his shirt.

On Friday he didn't come in. Ralph told me he'd seen him drinking in the parking lot the previous night.

Saturday I talked with Rich, Francine, Ralph, my girlfriend, my sister, Helen, I even called my father. "You have no choice," they each said, except my father, who asked when Dan would be coming to visit again.

Sunday I drove to Dan's house. Helen let me in and waited by the kitchen table ten feet away. Ben had been sent to stay with one of his older sisters.

Dan sat crumpled on the couch, his fly undone, his legs splayed. His hair, which he'd always been so careful to comb into a puffy blob, was matted down in every direction. He told me he'd spent the night sleeping on the couch. He smelled like disease. His body molded to every lump of the cushion and his eyes stared crazily at me like a madman picking a fight in the bar—except this was his home and I had been his closest friend.

"You want something?" he asked.

"You need to stop drinking," I said. "Or resign." I felt no anger or hurry, like I was filling out forms at the DMV.

"Oh, so that's it, you want me to resign? You want the business! You've betrayed me!" he said with a snarl, but not shouting, not seeming to mean it. The words were like the reflex of a threatened animal, and the untruth and his lack of emotion bit at the emptiness I was feeling. "I'm not drinking," he said, slurring the words, "and I'm not going anywhere." He kept his gaze on me as his head rolled, unable to stay vertical, and his upturned hands—no longer tented—were heavy weights on his legs. He was a robot version of Dan soaked in gin.

I repeated myself.

He repeated himself and threatened me with more overused filibusters. Then he pleaded with me to forgive him. Then he cried a little. Then he got angry again. I repeated myself for the third time and told him I was done. I would not do the round-and-round discussion of a drunk anymore. I left him muttering to himself. At the door, Helen said the only words she'd spoken since I'd arrived, "I'm so sorry, David."

The next day was the BookTech trade show in New York, and I needed to be there to manage the salespeople and meet with customers. As I shook hands with a buyer from McGraw-Hill's school division, my phone rang. It was Mai from M&T keying in Manila.

"I hear Dan is sick," she said, over the static-y connection. I wished I hadn't picked up—this was no time to try and explain his drinking and rehab and our teetering relationship. They were close, so there was no telling how she would react and what it would do to the business.

"Yes, yes, he's been unwell. But it will be OK. Can you hear me?" At least she was in Manila, thousands of miles away from finding out. I walked through the trade show looking for a quiet corner to stand and figure out what I could tell her. Perhaps I could just hang up and pretend it was the bad connection?

"I am coming to see him," she said. "I have a plane ticket for tomorrow."

"Um, that's not going to work. He's in the hospital right now."

"I will visit him in the hospital. Tell me which one it is. I will call there to talk to him. I miss my talks with Dan."

Someone tapped me on the shoulder from behind. "David, haven't seen you in a while!" It was the chief engineer from a company I used to work for—a tall man with a tiny yarmulke who was holding a thick packet of glossy tradeshow handouts. I pointed to the phone and dug in my pocket for a card to hand him. "Clarinda? And look at that, President! You must be doing well."

"What is going on, David? Is there something about Dan? Is it cancer?"

I pointed at the phone again and covered the mouthpiece. "Why don't you stop by the booth?" I said.

"If it's not a good time," she said. "I can talk to you when I get to Baltimore."

"No, no, Mai, I've, I've got to tell you something about Dan." The engineer nodded and moved on. I took a breath and told her about his drinking, the rehab, how it hadn't worked and that I didn't know what would be next with him.

Her sympathetic reaction surprised me. "It isn't unusual in the Philippines to spend a year or more in rehab," she said. "I will wait to come until next month."

At the end of the day I took the salespeople out for dinner. I stood at the table in the Hilton and told them about my continued hope and plans for the future, that Dan was still very sick, but would be back with us soon, and that they were doing a great job, but would have to work harder.

Larry spoke up, "We're all glad to hear Dan will be OK. I do have a question, though."

"What's that?"

"That fellow who came by the booth for a lunch appointment with you, was he from India?"

"Yes, with all this overseas stuff going on, we've been using him for a couple of projects, and more in the future."

"I thought that was him," the salesman said, "I just left McGraw-Hill and he was walking in to sell them typesetting as I was leaving."

e

On Tuesday, I waited in the office in Baltimore for Dan. When he came in, he was drunk.

"You have to do it," Francine said. "You have to do it for the company."

I went in his office, closed the door, and offered to buy him out.

"And what would I be?"

"You could be chairman emeritus," I said.

"How much?" He sucked his cheeks in tightly.

"Seven hundred thousand. We'd pay you seventy thousand a year for ten years." It was less than half his pay, but, I thought, a fair deal for his half of the company. I would have been happy if someone had offered it to me.

"Not enough," he said. "Two million."

"Seven hundred thousand. And you have to sign this before I can draw it up." I presented him with documents to transfer voting of his shares of stock to me. He said no. I told him again to sign.

He got up to leave and I put my open palm on his chest. Aside from when I'd hauled him off that bed, it was the most we'd ever touched. I tensed, resisted his weight, my arm straight. He pressed his cowboy boots to the floor and put his hand with its long yellow fingernails around my wrist. I prepared to put his skull through the thin office wall.

He released me, turned and collapsed in the chair.

"Is this what you want? Is this it?"

"Sign," I said. He signed, stabbing at the page, and then put his head in his hands and cried. I left him to tell the employees. When I came back five minutes later, he'd snuck away. I had fired Dan.

I hired the grey man to serve as a support counselor for the employees—Dan had been a friend to many more people than just me. Sitting in the airport in San Antonio waiting to go home after a bad meeting with Jackie Dee at TPC, I decided that I needed help, too.

"It took him years to get where he ended up with alcohol," the grey man said. "No twenty-one day program was going to solve that. It might have turned him in the right direction, but it didn't. If he stopped drinking today it would take more than six months for him to be anything like the Dan you knew and, more likely, years to become his old self. By then he would be almost eighty.

Typo

"Unfortunately for you, none of this matters. What I tell you next is a fact. You will never be able to work with Dan again. That relationship is over. If he recovers, he will be too ashamed of what he's done, and as for you," I rolled the strap of my Tumi garment bag in my palm waiting for his verdict on me, "You will never be able to forgive him."

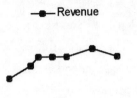
Revenue

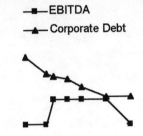
EBITDA
Corporate Debt

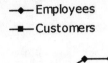
Employees

Customers

My Net Worth

Locations

Clarinda
Atlantic
Baltimore
St. Paul
Syracuse
Manila

Revolver

Revenue	$9,000,000
EBITDA	$0
Corporate Debt	$1,080,000
Employees	200
Customers	120
My Net Worth	$4,000,000
Revolver Expires	3 Months

We Can't Do It For That

> *Moreover, it's far from clear whether 'good intentions plus stupidity'*
> *or 'evil intentions plus intelligence' have wrought more harm in the*
> *world. People with 'good intentions' usually have few qualms about*
> *pursuing their goals. As a result, incompetence that would otherwise*
> *have remained harmless often becomes dangerous… The conviction*
> *that our intentions are good may sanctify the most questionable means.*
> —*The Logic of Failure* by Dietrich Dörner

March 2002

"YOU'RE GOING TO HAVE TO FIRE MORE PEOPLE," Rich said.

He had taken over the table in Dan's office and much of the floor with dozens of accounting file boxes. The desk, like Miss Havisham's apartment, had been left intact complete with cigarette butts. I pulled on the unlocked drawers.

"I'm trying," I said. In the bottom drawer I found a half-drunk six-pack of Budweiser still entangled in its plastic netting. "Look at that."

"It's a bag of shit, David." Half Irish and half Chinese, he had let his wavy black hair grow out to his shoulders since leaving Ernst and Young. He looked like Johnny Depp in his *21 Jump Street* days. "You've got to fire a lot more."

"Thirty?"

"When I say, 'bag of shit,' I mean I don't know how big. Dan did things with these numbers and the costs are out of control."

"Forty? You can't mean forty," I said. "That's more than one in five. You're asking me to go from good old Dan, who never fired anyone, to chainsaw murderer."

"It is what it is," he said. "If you don't we'll be out of business in a month."

I had Dan's playbook of formulas memorized: we needed to earn three to four times labor; labor was eighty percent of the cost of a typesetting business; we wanted a forty percent gross margin; we wanted a ten percent EBITDA.

But the more I looked at what Dan had taught me, the less it made sense. Three to four times what labor? Total labor cost? Cost of just the typesetters? Cost including benefits? The harder I stared, the fuzzier the playbook became. Lines and circles and scribbles with no useful meaning.

I had a miniature robot of Dan that crawled around in my skull telling me "the publishing industry works like this." I could channel him perfectly. The question I couldn't answer on my way to meeting with the executive committee was whether the robot was the brilliant business mind that had managed three public companies or a drunk.

"How do you want to handle it," Frank asked, "Everyone at once or one at a time?"

"We could get everyone in the cafeteria in Atlantic," Steve suggested, "Maybe rent a bus."

"Wouldn't individual be best?" I asked, "A little privacy and respect? So they can ask questions?"

"A half hour each is—" Frank said, and began calculating with his pencil in the air.

"There won't be any questions," Rich said. He'd stopped sorting accounting records to join the meeting, "There's only five questions people ask when they get fired, some people will ask two or three of them, but most won't ask anything. Five minutes each, tops."

"Twenty years and no questions?" I asked.

"When do I get my last paycheck, what about my health insurance, what about my 401K," he said in rapid succession, "and, and, oh yeah, is there anything I did wrong?"

"What about questions about the layoff, the company?" I asked.

"Only about themselves."

"That's only four," Steve said, checking his fingers.

Rich shrugged. "I've never heard the fifth."

ℓ

I flew back to Baltimore to make preparations before coming back to Iowa for the layoff.

"I knew it, David," Luke said on the phone, "When I saw nothing was coming in November and December, I knew we were in bad shape."

"How did you know that?"

"Dan didn't tell you? It's all he could talk about with me. That and your crazy scheme to move the invoices to cover up the lack of business coming in. What were you thinking?"

He'd been telling Luke business was bad, and me that we would do fifteen million. "Dan told me to ask you to move the invoices."

"He said it was all your idea." I could tell from his tone that he didn't fully believe me. Dan must have called from the hotel room the night I brought him to the hospital. "But I see where you're coming from," he continued. "The company can't really afford me anymore."

"I can get you four weeks pay, maybe six," I said.

"On the upside, I think I can get Household to give you another extension, given everything. I won't tell 'em why Dan left, but they will appreciate cost cutting. Get me a report after you have the layoff and I'll see what I can do."

"I'd appreciate that," I said.

"Least I can do." One down, thirty-nine to go.

"Mai's here," Francine announced. I had forgotten Mai's planned trip, and there she stood, as bejeweled as ever and bearing a palm-sized stuffed dog.

"For you," she said and sat next to my desk in the cramped anteroom that still was my office. Francine and other employees crowded in to welcome her and each received a small stuffed animal or lacquered picture frame in return.

When we were alone, I told her I had fired Dan and had no idea what had happened to him—if he was at home or in another hotel. She nodded. I told her I hoped that our business relationship would continue. She nodded again, her manicured hands in her lap. I asked if she had any plans beyond visiting us. "I have cousins in Virginia," she said and smiled showing her polished teeth. I waited for more, but she said nothing.

Rich leaned in from Dan's old, now his, office and introduced himself. After some small talk about how hot the Philippines were and how cold it was in March in Baltimore, he said, "I've been going through the books and I noticed a thirty thousand dollar loan Dan gave you. Just wondering if you established a payment scheme on that with him."

Her smile faded. "Dan had given that as a gift."

"What loan?" I asked.

"It is customary in Manila for customers to send money in advance to help build up staff and purchase necessary equipment," she said, ignoring me.

"Well, that's great. So since it's been a couple of years of us doing business with you, maybe this would be a good time to establish a payment schedule?"

She shifted in her chair.

"You've got a lot to do on your trip, so how about I send you something after you get back? No hurry."

Her lips moved into a scowl held back from completion by an apprehensive smile.

"Hey, did you bring this for David?" he asked, picking up the dog. "Nice."

After she was gone, he asked, "What are you going to do about Minnie?"

I didn't know. Despite my bravado at the pizza place, I wasn't ready to fire Minnie. Manager after manager had left her in place, including Dan and Luke both as president of the company under Household and when we hired him as CFO. I preferred to let Dan's promise—to slowly move her into

Typo

retirement over the next six months—stand. More than that, I didn't want to have to deal with her.

"You've got to do something," he said. "She's been fighting me with everything. You know what she asked me to do?"

I shook my head again.

"She asked me to upgrade the System 36."

"What? Now? But we're having a layoff. Why would she be asking you to do that?"

"Exactly," Rich said. He went on to explain what he'd uncovered despite her resistance, and how Dan's indulgence of her had cost the company. At the start of 2002, the accounting department payroll was half a million. We ran our own paychecks, which required two full-time staff and were nevertheless riddled with errors. She paid vendors on time, but never called customers who were late. He also found double payments to vendors and jobs that hadn't been billed. We were overpaying on payroll taxes and for the health care plan. "I don't think it's malice, just incompetence," he said, waving report after report in the air. "Although she did complain about your giving money to the Boy Scouts."

"I only gave ninety bucks. The fundraiser is the ninety-five-year-old woman who irons my shirts at the Spin-n-Dry."

"Well Minnie told me she's a bad lady, whatever that means, and what about this?" He showed me a receipt.

"The Clarinda A's," I said. "Dan gave them money, and I already know Minnie wanted to cancel the gift because they bring kids in from all over the country to learn baseball. She said they weren't local boys."

"That must be why she took it on herself to ask for the money back as soon as she found out Dan was gone. Did you know that?" He showed me she had doled out plenty of gifts I didn't know about: hundreds of dollars to the local high school wrestling team (where her grandson was a team member), to her friends' charities, and wherever she wanted to. When Dan was around I would have considered it another small insult. "Small or not," he said, "it's not her money to spend. You're going to have to call her. If you're not ready to fire her, you at least need her onboard with the layoff. While we're out here, she's complaining that the layoff is going to kill the company."

I nodded sadly. I closed the doors and sat up straight. This call required good posture.

"Minnie," I said. "I know you're uncomfortable with the layoff. If you can find a way for us not to do this, I would be happy to hear it."

"I've known these people for a lot of years," she said. "A lot longer than you and Dan."

"I understand, but as an executive of the company and as a friend to these people, what do you suggest I do? We are spending nine to ten million a year and with Reed's work going to the Indians we have to cut costs."

"I don't know why you were surprised about Dan. People saw him buying beer at the Hy-vee and drinking at the Indi-Clar. I could have told you he was drinking."

My shoulders slumped towards the desk. "Then why didn't you?" There was an extended silence.

"Kathy is spending a lot on travel," she said.

Kathy had to travel for customers, especially Red Bones, but I said, "Well that's a start. How much is that?"

"I don't know, David," she said, her voice nasal, "But it's at least ten thousand."

"We've got to cut a million out of the budget. We've got to cut everywhere. I'm going to have to ask you to think about your own retirement deal. I may have to ask you to shorten the number of days a week."

"Dan made me a promise," she said, icily.

"He made me promises, too."

ℓ

I came back to Iowa on the Saturday before the Tuesday layoff. "Never fire people on Friday," Rich said. "There's nothing they can do except go out drinking. Monday's almost as bad, smacking 'em when they walk in. Tuesday, first thing. Everybody's going to know as soon as it starts, get it over with early. The important thing is that management is together—all working from the same playbook."

I couldn't sleep that night and went into the office and thinking about what I would say to the remaining employees and found an e-mail from Minnie.

I am asking at this point to be relieved from my duties on the executive committee and do not plan to be present on Monday. I don't wish to be the witness for the termination process on Tuesday in the Clarinda plant. I realize this puts you at a disadvantage with your planning process, but I feel I can better represent the company's decision without being drawn into the specific termination process.

The storm postponing our planned trip for state wrestling team duels until Monday helped me to make my choice of family over my loyalty to the company at this time. I had planned to be able to do various things this spring with my family and have experienced the same sleepless nights that you've had with making this reduction decision. Some of these people have been there as long or longer than I have and given their best in total to the work commitment during these years. So I guess I am taking the easier road by asking for your respect in my decision. I've weighed it in great detail and feel it is time to spoil myself a little as I enjoy more free time with my family while I am capable.

If this decision causes you to be unhappy with my performance or wishing to discontinue the agreement I had with Dan and Luke, please feel free to put my name on the list. I am due 3 weeks paid and earned vacation at my full time rate. Otherwise, I will be at work on Tuesday a.m. and continue to represent the employee and the company to the best of my ability.

Her sinecure promised by Dan and Luke, I thought, *unfortunately, for her, they weren't here anymore.* Dan used to say that she behaved as if "it's her company and she's protecting it from the bad men sent in from the outside world." She had been the truest embodiment of the "Clarinda culture," and by his basic nature, he'd insisted on trying to win her allegiance to his plan and person. It hadn't worked. Now, I needed her help letting go some of those people she'd known all those years, and then to keeping the business going with the rest of them; but it wasn't about them, like her letter said, it was about her. While they were being fired, she would be hiding.

At least she offered to resign, if I didn't want an HR director who didn't do HR. Maybe her letter would make it easier for me to accelerate her retiring, or at least cut her down to one day a week.

On Tuesday, I woke up coughing and couldn't stop. The cough came from the top of my throat, which had constricted so much I couldn't eat or drink. I came in at six and sat in my office with the door open. At eight, I watched as Ron went and got the employees one by one. He walked them into the conference room next door where they met with Frank and Shirley. The same scene, I knew, was playing out up the road in Atlantic with Steve and Jo.

If they had any questions, they would trust Frank or Shirley much more than me, but I still felt like an outsider as the employees went by, and then reappeared, shoulders bowed, eyes watching Ron's feet take them to the door. Some should have been let go long ago—like Penny, the network engineer who refused to give people Internet access, Fuzzy Hair, the saboteur of overseas keyboarding, and the blind proofreader—but how could I feel good about firing people? The fifteen minutes we allotted was far too long. No one asked any questions. Not one turned to look at me as they came or went.

By ten, it was done. Frank, Shirley, and Ron accompanied me to the lunchroom where the remaining employees had assembled. Frank's standard non-expression matched his yellow short-sleeved shirt; Shirley's cheeks were flushed, and she smiled with the hope that someone else might smile also; and Ron rested a hand in his thin brown hair while pale light filtered through the trees outside onto the white linoleum floor. The tables had been pushed aside and chairs found for most people, while a handful stood against the back wall or leaned on the soda machine or the little table with the microwave and two coffeepots.

I made my speech. I wrote new numbers on the whiteboard. I told them the truth. I told them everything. We had to succeed. We couldn't do anything else. I would accelerate the programs for productivity improvement, in the spirit of the old Dan, the man who I'd begun working with who had done wonders back at Datadata, not the one I had pushed out of the company. I still believed he was right, and that what my father had believed in at IBM was true: respect people, be honest, and all will be rewarded.

I told them about Dan, unable to prevent tears when I said, "I had to let him go." I told them we were already the greatest company on Earth. No customer could take this from us. No competitor in India could take it either. With fear, I looked away from the whiteboard and into the eyes of each employee, but instead of rebuke or anger, I saw resignation. I wanted to will them to motion. I wanted to inspire in them the drive that rekindled in me as I spoke. I had to keep moving, running forward. They had to come with me.

I finished. Silence. Some shuffled off to their desks. Some looked at the floor. Sally and two others came up to me and, also teary eyed, talked about Dan.

"I didn't know," said a typesetter, who babysat Ben when Dan brought him to Iowa.

"I'm so sorry, he was such a good man," said another he had let borrow from the company.

"I will do everything I can," Sally said.

For Baltimore, Syracuse, St. Paul, and Manila a conference call had to suffice—my scratchy voice explaining the fall off in sales, the predictions for the year, the reasons why some people were chosen and others weren't—we had to cut staff and the managers selected the best to keep—why I was still hopeful about the future, why they must be hopeful about the future as well, and why—because we were committed to Dan and my father's ideas about treating people with respect and being honest with employees and customers—Clarinda was still the greatest company on Earth, and of course, about Dan.

Then I was off to Atlantic, with Rich driving. I sat silently in the car for an hour and then walked into another lunchroom where I repeated the message. I felt the same pain I had in the morning.

Rich and I headed to Omaha. On the way we were pulled over by the police—our Virginia-plated rental car excited the junior deputy's hopes of finding drugs. I watched him in the rearview mirror as he rummaged disappointedly through a trunk full of textbooks. The layoff felt like it had happened months ago.

Instead of my usual Sheraton suite, we booked a budget motel not even as nice as the Super 8. Life was going to be different until the company recovered. I sat on the thin bedspread and as I closed my eyes, my cell phone rang. Jackie Dee needed me in San Antonio, Monday. I was on hold with the airline when Rich knocked on my door. "I need to talk to you about Minnie," he said.

Her spies had told her we left for Omaha and it was safe to come in. Rich's spy—I was surprised he'd already gotten one—let him know she was there complaining about Dan, the layoff, Rich, and most especially, me.

There was a long wait for her to get to the phone. "David," she said. I felt the anger in her voice.

Maybe it was time to let go of another piece of Dan. "OK, I accept your letter," I said. I hung up the phone, laid down, and fell asleep on the floral bedspread in moments.

Five minutes later Rich woke me up. I sat up too quickly and spots rolled in my vision. "I know you thought Minnie understood, so I called her back to make sure," he said. "She told me that you had accepted she could continue with Dan's plan."

I was angry, not because she wanted to hang on to her job, of course she did. I was angry because I didn't want to come to Iowa and fire twenty percent of the staff. Where did she get off blaming me? Where did she get off jeopardizing the company and her friends' jobs for her own "promise"?

I pushed the remnants of Dan out one by one. "Could we let her work one day a month?" I asked. "Could we just pay her for two months severance? What about if she decides to sue? Dan said—"

"How many times does Minnie have to abuse the company and undermine your management before you fire her?"

I nodded, resigned.

"I will take care of it for you," he said.

For the rest of that day and the morning of the next, Rich talked to her. As we sat in the airport terminal waiting for our flight, he was still on the phone with her.

"David was willing to consider a month's severance for you or maybe one day a week of work." He shook his head and held the phone to my ear. She was sobbing.

What had I done?

"What would you like us to do, Minnie?" he said. "We can't have you in there complaining about David." He nodded and held the phone out again, his fingers over the microphone.

"I am not complaining about David! How dare you accuse me!" She yelled. "I've worked for the company for thirty-five years and this is what I get? I deserve better," she said, no longer screaming, but speaking in a stern and furious monotone.

"Well, Minnie," he said, "this company has only existed for two years."

"For all my years of service? Nothing?"

"Didn't you get a paycheck?"

"Well, *sir*," she said, biting the word into a hiss, "if that's how you feel, *sir*. I will go. When do you want my two weeks?"

"Oh," he said, calmly, "I think you deserve the same package everyone else got. Why don't you finish up today?"

We boarded the plane and I thought, at last, she is gone, but when we arrived in Baltimore, he had another message from his informer. Minnie had calculated how much she felt was owed and had the clerk cut her a check. "Call the bank," he said, "stop payment."

The next day in Baltimore, I heard a "wham!" from his office. I found him sitting in one corner and his chair in the other.

I picked up the chair—Dan's old high-backed leather one.

"Do you still feel bad about firing Minnie?" he asked.

I shrugged. I still felt bad about any firing.

"Well, don't. I got through some more of the accounting records, which, by the way, they didn't want to send me."

"Who didn't want to send you?"

"I'm sorry," he said and leaned his head back until he was looking at the ceiling. "I mean they didn't want to go into Minnie's office. Even Frank was afraid. Must be some wicked bad mojo. Anyway—" he stood and picked up some receipts. "Did you know that we offered blood screenings in Iowa?"

I shook my head.

"Apparently, the doctors came by and gave free tests. You and Dan were left off that list, and a bunch of the other programs our medical plan offers. Did you know she paid full medical coverage for Eddy in accounting, but a lot of the St. Paul people had their coverage underpaid? Although, honestly, it's a little hard to tell with these records."

I looked at the stack of boxes that filled one wall.

"And whenever you or Dan tried to change something, she would call the lawyer to verify the two of you weren't getting away with something." Dan's stories of winning her over even the slightest amount were another lie to throw on the pile. "We paid more than twenty thousand dollars for her to try to sabotage you."

"Is that why you threw the chair?"

"No," he said. "I threw the chair because that accounting genius that

Dan hired to supplement the partially-retired Minnie decided to send a $35,000 check to the IRS while we were away in Iowa firing people."

"$35,000?"

"For a period where we actually lost money."

"He shouldn't have done that, right?" I asked, the question sounding more foolish spoken aloud.

"We lost money. Why would we be paying a tax bill?"

I didn't feel bad about Minnie anymore. "I'll take care of it," I said. By the time Rich came back to Baltimore on Monday, I had fired the accountant. It took four minutes.

The biggest surprise about the layoff was that there weren't any surprises. Business continued. Books came in and went out. Customers said nothing. We were more on schedule than before. Employee complaints about the carpet disappeared.

In fact, there had been just one complaint. Shirley told Rich that a typesetter was commenting that we had ended the 401K.

He said, "We didn't end the 401K. We didn't take anyone's money. We ended the 401K matching contribution to keep five jobs. A company this small had no business matching anyway, it was a holdover from Household, who was okay with losing money."

Shirley nodded and held her hands clasped around her belly.

"Just tell her if she has any more questions, to come by my office. I'd be happy to explain it to her." Then he turned to me, "I don't suspect we'll be having any more comments about the 401K either."

A week later Rich and I were in Chicago to seek another extension for the revolving line of credit. A few miles from O'Hare airport we met with Luke, who Household had kept on retainer. He flipped through our financials.

"I don't see a problem getting you another six months, but it's up to Matthew. And he hasn't had a lot of time to talk to me about Clarinda," Luke said.

Matthew, a senior VP, was responsible for hundreds of millions of dollars in mortgages. We were one of the few remaining loans in the commercial division. On the one hand, the relatively tiny size of our line of credit in Matthew's empire gave me hope it would be an easy meeting. On the other, I had never met him. His only communication had been with Luke and Dan and now both were out of the company. And, there was one more consideration. Matthew had been the first president of Clarinda that Household had appointed. Back before Luke and the crazy guy before him, Matthew had been going down to Iowa himself to fix the financial troubles of the company. His fondness, or lack thereof, for the people who made his life difficult all these years was an unknown quantity.

Matthew arrived late and apologized. He looked like a banker—a solid jaw line that had gone perceptibly soft with age and dark hair with specks of ash. He ran a finger over the reports.

"These financials look different."

"Rich built them in Excel now that Minnie is gone," I said.

Matthew raised an eyebrow. "So how are things now at Clarinda?" he asked looking at me.

I wished Rich had been able to talk to Matthew beforehand, but it was up to me, the least financially trained person in the room to report on the numbers.

"I think we will hit six million this year, maybe a little more. That's almost as much as we did our first year, but with fewer people."

Matthew nodded and said, "No." He put a hand on the table. "I mean, how are you doing with all those trips to Iowa? God, that must be the most boring place on Earth. I will never get over that Bed and Breakfast I had to stay in, and you Luke, you lived in that woman's basement for what? Three months at a stretch?"

The conversation rapidly devolved into each of us relating our worst days in Clarinda.

"So do you think we can get another twelve months on the line?" I asked.

"Boys," Matthew said, folding up the financial reports he had hardly glanced at. "Tell you what. For keeping the place going all this time, having the layoff you really needed and most of all, for getting rid of that Minnie—God she used to drive me crazy—how about another eighteen months?"

ℓ

After my mother died, and before he started drinking, my father went through the thousands of newspaper clippings, paper bags and tchotchkes she had accumulated. She had been an amateur ceramicist and he smashed several dozen already broken artworks on the side of the house—he claimed it would help the drainage. My sister and I found over a hundred old notebooks she kept after pulling out the used pages because the rest were "still good." My mother had saved a lot of junk, and it was cathartic to throw it away.

After the layoff, Rich spurred me to embark on nighttime cleaning expeditions with him. There was stuff that had to be gotten rid of, but there was also a need for us to sever our relationship with the past, with Dan. We did it by filling dumpsters at two in the morning.

There were the obvious things: calendars from 1970, cases of Wite-Out (cases!), time cards from 1980, and just like my mother, deep reservoirs of slightly used paper clips, notebooks, and rubber bands.

A side effect of sending stacks of manuscripts back and forth was the endless trade in rubber bands. Enterprising workers made personal stashes, but they needn't have, since there was a four-foot high bucket of them on the loading dock. It had been someone's winter project after one of Household's consultants passed through, utterly forgotten until rediscovered by me, the Dr. Livingstone of rubber bands.

Rich issued a stop on any new supplies being bought until we'd gone through what we had, which he estimated at three years. Tina, the computer science graduate, came by my office shortly after, "I hear we aren't supposed to order any rubber bands, but I need some." At night, during my rounds, I deposited fistfuls of them on her chair. After the third day she left a note on my desk, "OK, I get it, we have lots of rubber bands."

There were several dozen banker boxes wrapped with two layers of tape I found stuffed in the attic space. They contained bids the company had made—and lost. Those boxes were carefully labeled: "BIDS: LOST." Why were we keeping them? No one knew. It's just what we did.

We found useless equipment: SyQuest drives a decade old and media that the world stopped using in 1992, SCSI cables that attached to nothing we owned, five boxes of mice that didn't work, keyboards missing keys, printers labeled "does not work, do not use," twenty boxes of old software labeled "not installed," old manuals, and odd-shaped toner cartridges for devices that no longer existed. We found an entire filing cabinet of microfiche of the company's payroll dating back to 1959—and a microfiche reader in its original box if you wanted to read them. The reader and the fiche were in Minnie's fireproof vault. We found a cache of backup tapes hidden in the calm chill of steel-lined walls in the back of the plant. Inside Penny's ultimate fireproof archive room lay a 5-drawer fireproof filing cabinet that contained—nothing, save a single key that did not fit the cabinet. The south wall of the room was filled with neatly labeled 9-track tapes; the kind featured in 70s TV for that "computer look" with big wheels of tapes spinning back and forth. We didn't own a 9-track reader, which was OK, because the tapes were so fragile that they would disintegrate if disturbed. The north wall contained 8mm backup tapes. These were wrapped with plastic tape and a stern warning: "8mm backups, DO NOT USE! USE 4mm BACKUPS." I searched for the 4mm tapes—the one thing in the room we really used—and found them in the only available space: piled two deep on the floor.

If the plant burned down, payroll from 1972 and all of the software were safe so we could start anew like Sanctuary in *Logan's Run*. But although we could verify withholding from the bicentennial, where we would start up without computers to load the software onto was a mystery no one could answer.

An empty fireproof cabinet in a fireproof room filled with junk wasn't what was really upsetting. It was the cost—a million dollars worth of the stuff and we were still buying—a monthly consignment of 4mm tapes at twelve dollars each. We were adding to the pile to the tune of a hundred thousand dollars a year. It had been bad, but overlookable, when Dan was hoping to grow the company—there hadn't been time to fix sales, production, and catch waste—but in cut back mode, it was unforgivable.

Rich and I filled our two dumpsters. When the dumpsters were full, we put the garbage on the loading dock. When there was no room on the loading dock, we built a wall fifteen feet long by six feet wide and deep made of printers, cables, and software in the back of the production room. A grandmotherly typesetter asked, "Are you throwing all this out?"

"If you want it, you're welcome to it," I said, watching her cautiously lift the cover off a dot matrix printer.

The next day, as I continued to build my Penny memorial, I asked the typesetter, "Did you find anything?" She shook her head, having picked through the valueless remains of a decade of corporate hoarding with dawning comprehension.

Something I couldn't throw out, but wanted to, was the old job folders. A third of the building was dedicated to every project we'd ever done because publishers expected us to keep copies of their books going back to the beginning of time. The folders contained the paper files. The electronic files, which is what the publisher needed, might be in there, or might be on one of those tapes on the floor in the fireproof vault.

We could charge for the archive only when the publisher needed a file. And if they did, which was rarely, we recouped a fraction of our storage cost—partially because of our own difficulty with the thrown-on-the-floor filing system.

The publishers also kept their own archive, but they could never find anything. Maybe they had a fireproof cabinet.

l

"They're not fucking getting it," Rich said.

I had just come back from a short bike ride over the hard packed dirt roads of Page County and was examining the back gears for mashed locusts caught between the chain and teeth. "Not getting what?" I asked.

"Twenty five dollars every week for new mops, fifty a week for floor mat cleaning, fifty a week for coffee, fifteen for a potted plant, ten for plant food, four-fifty for donuts, ten for a screwdriver. Don't we already have a screwdriver?" he asked, gesturing with both hands.

I said we probably had a room of them somewhere as I checked my messages.

"I told her to stop buying things in Atlantic, but they can't help themselves."

There were a couple of calls from Red Bones. He was upset that I didn't tell him about the layoff before we had it, although I had been leaving him messages to call me for two weeks beforehand.

"And coffee. They spend a hundred bucks a month on coffee in Atlantic. In Maryland there's a little tin you put money in if you drink coffee. And plant food?" He picked up a hand-blown glass paperweight I had gotten in Omaha. "They don't seem to understand that's your potted plant."

"And yours," I said. There was a call back from Jackie Dee, she was upset about the new person we had hired to be a Clarinda company employee in San Antonio. The woman was frequently late and had made the serious mistake of showing that TPC, and not us, was at fault on a recent Florida project.

I nodded. On the bottom of the Jackie Dee's telephone memo was a note that Jack had called. He was the attorney Rich had hired to deal with Dan.

"What do you think Jack wants?" I asked.

Rich put down the glass and punched his number in the speakerphone. Jack recapped the letter Dan's lawyer had sent and our preferred reaction—tell him to get lost.

"What about my offer to give him some money?" I asked.

"We can't afford it," Rich said.

"I know, but something. The man used to be my friend. Can't we get him something?"

"He's a loser," Jack said. Physically, he could be easily confused for Wilford Brimley minus the moustache; on the phone, his voice had the resounding toughness of a New York mayor. "And he's always been a loser." The word 'loser' sunk to the bottom of my stomach like a swallowed block of lead type.

"Only when he started drinking," I said in his defense. "He was a great man before that. I wish you'd known him."

"I don't," he said. "I repeat—he's a loser and he's always been a loser. So tell me again why you are trying to get him money?"

"I promised him—"

"First of all, as Richard pointed out, all bets are off now that you are in save-the-ship mode. Next point."

I still hadn't recovered from the 'loser' comments. "I promised I would see that Ben would get into college."

"You promised him that his son would get into college. David, I promise you that if you don't accept this guy is a loser you're going to have a lot more to worry about than getting his fucked-up kid into college. And that's what he is. Your non-friend Dan has done this to him."

"But you don't understand. He taught me everything I know about business—about being good to people. I wouldn't feel right that Clarinda becomes the success he always dreamed about and he gets nothing."

"OK, so he'll get an earn-out. If you make it, he makes it. But David, I want you to understand, this guy is fucking you in the ass. And he's not done. He's going to be pounding away at you whether you pay him or not."

ℓ

Rich's focus on cost reminded me to see how we were doing with alterations, our original 'gold mine.' I still believed in Dan's philosophy about convincing people rather than forcing them, so I asked Shirley if we ever switched to having the typesetters count the alts.

Shirley shook her head, "We decided that they would have too hard a time."

"It's how they do things in Baltimore."

"Oh," she said. "I guess we can try again."

"What about the billing? Did we switch back to billing by the line instead of the alt?" Clarinda had changed from the standard practice in 1995 when one customer made a deal with the then general manager, and it was costing us ten percent of our overall revenue.

"I don't think so," she said. "Do you want me to change that too?"

The next day she said, "The billing manager wanted to know if you're sure you want to charge to by the line."

"It's industry practice, isn't it?"

"Oh, yes, I think so." She nodded, but wasn't happy with my question. "But what if the customers complain? How do you want to handle that? Do you want to talk to them?"

"How many times a year do customers call with comments on our alteration counts? More than three?"

"No, not that many," she said.

"Then we'll worry about it when we get our first call."

The next day, she came back again. "The typesetters say that we're going to fall behind schedule if they have to keep counting the alts."

"It's only been two days," I said.

"Well, yes, but they say it's taking all day."

I didn't understand. According to Dan, it should have only taken about a half hour, but she was telling me it took as long to count the alterations as to make them.

"Maybe they just need time to get used to it," I said.

She came back the next day and the next, trying to get me to relent and let the process go back to the old way.

"Why don't you show me?" I asked. When I saw the form, I understood. We counted twelve different kinds of alterations, AAs, EAs, MAs, and variations thereof—most of which meant nothing to the production operator, the customer, or me. "What's that?" I asked, pointing at the MA.

"It's a Mosby alt."

"For Mosby?"

"Yes."

"The one Reed bought?"

"Yes, I think so."

"But they dropped us for India two months ago."

Because "we always did it this way" we kept counting them, even if the person doing the counting wasn't sure what they meant. I made new forms. And, unlike Dan, I dictated a new process.

1. The typesetter makes the alterations and at the bottom of each page tallies the total lines changed.

2. The typesetter flips through the pages, totals the number of alts, and writes it on the new form, which had just one big box for the number. (One determined typesetter could not be swayed from the old ways and squeezed all the individual page numbers into the box in tiny tiny handwriting.)

3. The pages go to QC. Error pages are rotated ninety degrees and the whole pile, with the bad pages sticking out the sides, is sent back to production. Not only was the job not uselessly separated and recombined, but the supervisor could spot check quality at a glance. A job that looked like it had a bad hair day had a lot of errors.

In a month the new system had been implemented. Two years and counting for Dan's method of change. One month for my mine. Score one for me.

ℓ

Thuckita-Thuckita-Thuckita. T-ah. Thuckita-Thukita-Thukita-Thukita—a capital "T" and then a small "huckita." On the way to Sally's training room, to ship a package to a customer, or to rummage through the endless pile of technological junk in Penny's office, the T-ah-thuckita was always there.

"What is that?" I asked Sally.

"Ruthie's stamping the pages," she said as she drew a shaded box in a world history textbook.

"Doesn't it bother you?" The "Ta" part I could ignore, but the "huckita" reverberated through the adjoining walls and went after the soft parts of my brain as if she was stamping the back of my skull.

"Doesn't what?"

"The stamping?"

"What about it?"

I made Sally take me to the source—the windowless room beside the shipping area that was filled with aluminum flat-files, except for a wide grey spot on the carpet where the Dylux used to be. Ruthie, the proofer, a brown-haired grandmother wearing a lavender and pink striped sweatshirt and matching pink pants, slapped a silver Bates numerical stamper on the corner of page after page—flipping them expertly with her thumb. Next to her was a Glenn Miller festival coffee mug chock full of nubbly rubber fingertips that she wore through on a continual basis. Up the road in Atlantic, another proofer was doing the same.

"Why do we stamp every page?" I asked, speaking loudly to be heard over the full-bore Ta-thuckitas. "Don't they already have numbers?"

"They're not as reliable as ours," Sally said, shouting also, despite standing directly next to me.

Ruthie looked up, smiled, and said while continuing to stamp, "It's a real problem if someone drops a job on the floor. Got to put 'em back together tha' right way."

"Could you stop for a moment?" I asked.

"And when we separate the jobs for QC," Sally said, her voice too loud for the silence.

"But since I changed the alt process, we don't need to separate jobs, right?" Breaking the job apart for QC had been our own institutionalized version of tripping and dropping the job on the floor.

Sally shrugged and Ruthie started stamping again.

Back in my office, I thought about what I'd seen. For any page to enter production it had to get stamped—the very definition of a bottleneck. The two proofers cost a hundred thousand a year in pay and benefits. What if a job was dropped and had to be resorted? How long would that take? An hour? Four hours? A day?

I called Sally, "When was the last time a job was dropped on the floor?"

"A couple of years ago, I think, wait, maybe it was four."

"Well let's say we dropped two a year, for the sake of argument," I said. "Do you realize that to fix those two would cost—" I typed the numbers into my Page County Savings Bank calculator, "around five hundred dollars in labor—versus one hundred thousand to ensure we never have to spend five hundred. Do you still think we need the stamping?"

"Why would you want to change what works, David?"

Sally and Ruthie thought about their own jobs, pagemaking and proofing, as separate and tried to be as fast as they could in that job. Two years of Dan, but still nobody thought about the total cost of a page from the moment it entered the plant till it went out.

"What happens when Ruthie is out sick?" I asked.

"Well we fill in for her, but I'm not anywhere near as fast as she is."

Our number one typesetter and trainer, filling in for the stamper.

Ta-thuckita.

ℓ

In April, SNAP had gotten to the point where I could tell which projects had been done in which plants, how much money they were worth, and how many pages they had. Rich had wrested control of the payroll from the System 36, so I decided to go after the number that Dan had always wanted, but never been able to get, the number that tied together costs with sales, the source of the Nile of all other statistics about the company—dollars per page.

I gathered three months of data—a two-foot-thick stack of payroll and billing records, and began calculating hours versus dollars—cross checking from one printout to the other and then against SNAP. Three days later, at one in the morning, I had my first financial analysis of production:

Plant	Dollars Per Hour Revenue	Dollars Per Hour Labor Cost
Clarinda	$17	$25
Atlantic (TPC customer)	$40	$40
Atlantic (all other customers)	$12	$25
Maryland	$60	$25
Manila	$30	$3
St. Paul	$30	$30

The numbers didn't include fixed costs like rent, heat and light, much less sales expenses and other important costs, like my salary. Even so, we were losing money everywhere except Maryland and Manila—and they only accounted for fifteen and two percent of revenue respectively. Despite the layoff, there were too many people and, especially for TPC, too much overtime.

I walked back to the shipping area, located the shiny Bates stamper, and put it in my pocket. I wandered the halls, surprising the lone third-shift typesetter, locating more stampers—master, first proof, second proof, billing copy, original manuscript—clutching them like a shopper who neglected to get a basket.

I returned to my office and organized them in rows on my credenza—a tiny multicolored Napoleonic army. If anyone wanted to keep stamping, they could come get them from me.

ℓ

I wrote the profit, or lack thereof, numbers on the big whiteboard in the conference room. Frank, Shirley, Sally, Steve and the rest of the executive committee sat there as they had always sat through Dan's long lectures, but this wasn't a Dan lecture.

I wanted a reaction. I wanted them to see what I'd just seen—what Dan had been hiding away in his head. I slapped my hand against the numbers, smearing my palm with orange dry-erase ink, and said, "if we don't fix this now, we are done in less than three months. We are in this together. And you are the experts." I paused between sentences, hoping someone would speak. "We have to cut costs and become more efficient. We have to complete the training we've been putting off. We have to send work to Manila." No one so much as nodded. "You, the managers of the company, the executive committee, you know the process better than I do. You need to come up with a plan that can fix this profit problem."

"Is that why you took the stampers?" Frank asked.

"No," I said. "I mean 'yes.' I mean that was just one cost. There are so many others. What about the daily run? Every day George drives the company van from here and someone else drives from Atlantic. They meet at that church parking lot in Morton Mills, right?"

Frank and Ron nodded.

"But the Clarinda van has almost completely fallen apart," I continued, "So George has been using his own truck, and we pay him mileage. Did you notice that our part-time janitor has just bought himself a new truck with what we've been paying him?"

"Do you want me to talk to George?" Frank asked.

"No," I shook my head. "I want you to think about what to do. Rich tells me the run costs two hundred dollars a day. That's," I went to the whiteboard to work it out, "Forty thousand a year. The cost of a typesetter."

"So we should get a new van?" Ron asked.

"I'm not saying that," I said. "We need to keep operating and cut costs which are either expenses or people. My question is, our work is electronic. What are we sending back and forth between two plants in Iowa everyday?"

I left them to come up with a plan that was their own and went for a walk. On my way out, I heard a surreptitious small "t", small "hukita" coming from Connie's office, and another from behind stacks of boxes by the proofreaders. It reminded me of a man gone blind still turning on the lights.

Three hours later Rich worried that we weren't hearing anything from the conference room, and went to try to help them. He came back an hour later.

"How did it go?"

"Not well."

"What does 'not well' mean?"

"Well, Sally said, 'It's the prices. They're too low."

"I know," I said. "But that's the Indians' doing. Not us."

Rich nodded, annoyed by my interruption, "But that's not what she said. She said the customers don't understand. That the prices they want are too low. That they, the publishers, don't understand, we can't do it for that."

"We can't do it for that?" I repeated. "What did you say?"

"I said someone is, and if we can't, we should close up shop right now."

That night I put together my own plan. It was the agenda Dan had been talking and talking about since the beginning, but now it had to happen. I would be trying to cram a literal decade of change into three months. In between drafts, I walked the halls seeking out by morning the remaining personal caches of stampers—massing an army fifty strong.

ℓ

"You know Frank and Steve are doing pretty good with the agenda, we're on track to have more work going to Manila," I said, while considering the rice pudding. We had come to the all-you-can-eat Chinese buffet for a dinner of bright red sweet and sour chicken because I wanted Rich to like Sally as much as I did and also to help me figure out how Clarinda, Iowa, could support two Chinese restaurants.

Sally nodded. "They're really trying to get things working for you," she said.

"Well so are you," I said. "That's what I keep telling Rich, isn't it? The best typesetter in the world."

Rich smiled slightly. "He's been telling me since you picked him up from the cold ground last winter. How far did he get before he called? Twenty miles?"

"He'd've made it," she said, and lightly slapped me on the arm.

"I bet he would if he'd had some of these," he said and held up a fried object with his chopsticks. "What is this again?"

"You never had a Crab Rangoon?" she asked.

He pried it apart on the plate like a lab experiment. "Nope. And what's this in here? Bean curd?"

"Cream cheese," I said. "You mean your father never made cream cheese wontons? I thought he was from Taiwan."

He closed one eye and looked at me from under his brow with the other.

"Moving on," I said. "So how's it going getting the regular typesetters into job setup? I haven't heard from you about the agenda items."

"I've been meaning to talk to you about that," she said, frowning. "I'm not sure they're smart enough to do it."

I'd heard her make that comment before, but Dan had said she tended to overstate her worries. "Well, how about Superleaf. How many people have the trainers got able to set up a Superleaf job? Can anyone in Manila do it?"

Cross training was crucial to my plan. Skills were so specialized that a production person who used Quark to make pages was unable to use Photoshop to change the size of a piece of art. The art department ran overtime while the typesetters were surfing the Internet—and vice versa.

She dipped her egg roll. "You know, Superleaf is very difficult, I'm not sure Manila can learn it, and I'm still having trouble getting the managers to let me have people for training."

"But what are you doing all day?" I asked, "How about the new keyboarding scheme? Is that done?"

"David," she said, putting down her napkin. "We're in the middle of the season—is this really the right time to be trying to spend so much time training?"

"Of course it is!" I said, "We need to get ahead of costs or we're going to go out of business. We need to become more efficient to compete with India. Manila, training, that's how we will keep ahead of the competition. Don't you believe in the new coding scheme?"

"I don't know, what about the search and replace?"

We spent the next hour discussing how the new keyboarding scheme would save money and improve efficiency. When Rich and I got in the rental car to drive back to the Super 8, I felt like I'd done a good job. Tomorrow, she would push the agenda ahead.

"If they're so stupid, why do we have them working for us?" he asked me, pulling on his seatbelt for the three minute ride to the motel.

"What?"

"If Sally thinks the people can't do the job, why are they working for us?"

"She was just worried."

"She wants to argue with you," he said, looking out the window at the dark buildings of the local fairground and cattle market—the sound and smell

Typo

of lowing cows all around us. "She wants to be right. She doesn't understand that the time for comment went with Dan. Whether she admits it to herself or not, she wants training to fail."

It was true that she was fond of pointing out how she'd found a way to make a typesetter's job easy, but neglected to realize that she had become the bottleneck on Anderson and the two other projects waiting for her. And the rest of production was slower because she hadn't done the training. Had she been sabotaging her own training department to prove her point that the people were too stupid to learn?

I trotted out the line that Dan had taught me when I had been pressing him to get rid of Francine in Baltimore, "If we get rid of Sally, who will do the work?"

"I don't know," he said, "But she is fighting you every step of the way. How is that better?"

The next day I called Sally into my office. I had spent the night admitting to myself I'd been asking her to implement the new keyboarding scheme for months and she had done nothing except ask me continuously to explain why. "I'd like you to take your vacation," I said.

"I'm plenty busy, I don't need to take any right now," she said, not sitting, leaning on a table.

"Look, you've got ten weeks in the system and everybody should be taking their vacation if they can. It will help with the balance sheet. That vacation time is a huge liability."

"I'll see what I can do," she said.

"How about taking some now. Just take the time. Take it and focus on something other than here. I need you to do that."

"And what do I do when it's over?" she asked, standing up.

"I don't know. We'll have to talk then," I said, and when she left without comment, I closed the door, pulled the shades, and turned off the computer. I sat in the dark holding my hands still on my lap. I hadn't exactly fired her—I could always ask her back after her vacation was up—but I hadn't exactly not. She had been fighting me. Why did Rich have to be right?

I went to meet Jim. In the cramped computer network room surrounded by the buzzing sounds of cooling fans we stood shoulder-to-shoulder.

"How did the luncheon go?" I asked. Jim, who had taken over technology maintenance in both plants after my nemesis Penny had been let go with the layoff, was also a volunteer fireman in Cumberland, Iowa—and he had just come from his first trip to the annual barbeque where the police, as a gesture of goodwill, served the firemen hog testicles. "Takes three men and a lot of very angry hogs," he had told me.

He paused in his examination of the thousands of wires snaking around the room. "I thought maybe they would serve something other than just the testicle-in-tomato-sauce sandwiches."

"Did they?"

He shook his head, and pulled out a little plastic clip from one of the network boxes. "No."

"And?" I asked.

He yanked the connecting wire free, "Kinda tasted just like you think hog testicles in tomato sauce would taste."

I asked if he would be going back next year.

"Likely not," he said, and held out the connector, "Thought you should see this." He pointed at a blue wire connected to a green clip. "See, you're supposed to plug the wires red to red, blue to blue, but Penny did something else. I'm not even sure how she got it to work, and looking at it, I don't think she knew either."

"Why's that?"

"Well, when you told us to upgrade to 100-megabit, that takes all eight wires, when the old 10-megabit only took four."

"So how did she connect the additional wires?"

"See, that's the thing," he said, showing me the mangled end of the cable. "She cut 'em off."

ℓ

Typo

After returning to Baltimore, I continued to use the tiny anteroom of Dan's old office as my workplace in Baltimore. The thought of sitting at that desk with the image of him on the phone, a cigarette in his hand, was unbearable. I let Rich have it—he had no fear of bad mojo.

So that's where we both were when Helen came in and shut the outer door behind her. Not even a thin piece of desk separated us—she standing, me sitting.

"Where's the money you promised?" she demanded.

"Steve, can I call you back?—What money?" Her angry inquisition reminded me of my mother scolding me. I was both ashamed I hadn't helped her and angry that she felt she could treat me like a child.

"You know very well. And why aren't you answering Dan's phone calls?"

Rich must have gotten up because I saw the inner door to his office quietly close. I was trapped.

"What? I—" I held the side of my tongue between my teeth to keep from being overwhelmed by the anger that rushed at me on hearing Dan's name spoken. "I told you that he has to sign an agreement. And I can't give any checks to you, only to him. He was the employee."

"That's not what he said. He tells me he's ready to come to work if you would just talk to him!"

I bit harder. "I don't want to talk to him." What new lies was he telling her?

"What would it take to get Dan back in here?"

"In here?" *Dan, back in here? Dan in the office instead of Rich?* Customers and salespeople managed again. Back to the technology for me. A living nightmare, but one without all these sales and employee pressures on me. It was impossible to imagine, but maybe the grey man was wrong. Maybe Dan could do something to help me forgive him. "How about an apology?"

She looked me up and down, surveyed the papers on my desk, glanced at my computer screen. "Fine," she said and left.

"Can't we send her a check for something," I asked Rich, pacing back and forth.

"For what?" he asked, writing notes on invoices.

"For her, for Ben, I don't know. Something."

He put down his pen. "I know you want to help. It's your company and your decision, but think about me." I stopped pacing. "Why would I want to help someone who just yelled at my friend?"

ℓ

Rich had arranged a birthday party for his wife at a trendy Lower East Side bar.

I got there early and ordered a Cosmopolitan at the front bar while Rich and I waited for the back room to be setup for the two-dozen guests. That afternoon I had met with the manager of our Syracuse plant and told him we would have to let him and his five people go. He had reminded me of how many years back Dan and he had gone in the industry and how much there was still a need for skilled typesetters in America. I had offered that if he thought there was work, he and his staff could keep their computers, but I couldn't afford to pay them anymore.

"I just want out," I said, and sipped my drink. It tasted like an unwashed hand, but I drank it anyway.

"You've got the personal guarantees," Rich said.

"I know. I know. I mean, I want Dan back."

Rich turned to greet his wife's mother. She looked expectantly towards me and I smiled wanly, but couldn't bring myself to step away from the bar and hug her. She went to the back room to lay out gifts.

"You heard what Jack said. Dan's a loser."

"Jack wasn't there when things were going well, or all the years we spent together."

Another couple arrived and Rich shook hands with them. I avoided their stares and finished my drink.

"I don't think I can stay," I said.

"Aren't you going to wait for the birthday girl?"

"I just have to go."

"You're not going to do anything foolish, are you?" Rich said, looking at me to see if I had changed imperceptibly like Dan must have when he stopped caring about work and started drinking in earnest.

"No," I said. "I know I have to keep going. I have to pay off my debts. Get my father's money back." I put on my coat. "I just can't go back there tonight and pretend to be a happy person."

Revenue

EBITDA
Corporate Debt

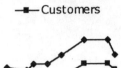
Employees
Customers

My Net Worth

Locations

Clarinda
Atlantic
Baltimore
St. Paul
Manila

Revolver

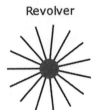

Revenue	$9,000,000
EBITDA	$0
Corporate Debt	$1,050,000
Employees	150
Customers	100
My Net Worth	$4,000,000
Revolver Expires	15 Months

The Litany

May 2002

"YOU SCREWED UP THE FRANKLIN PROJECT," the buyer for the prestigious
Oxford University Press said as lunch began at a Zagat Guide recommended
three-star restaurant. Buyers at Oxford, I noticed, were fond of pointing
out that they had been in business since the Middle Ages. I was fond of
muttering under my breath that it was unlikely that my customer from
New York—despite her crotchetiness, face like mis-extruded Play-Doh,
and cube-like plastic jewelry—was more than a couple hundred years old.
"And quite honestly, we're not so sure about working with you anymore."

The waiter politely pretended not to hear while awaiting my order of
pasta and water, which at fifteen dollars was about the price of one book
page. Larry, my salesman, had a small salad—another page. The buyer
ordered a bottle of wine—ten pages.

Larry, a Mormon, looked at me nervously, but not about the wine.
"Um," he said. I nodded encouragingly. "We didn't do the Franklin
project."

"Oh," the buyer replied, without being deterred. "Well, you still made
a lot of errors. What are you going to do about them?" She was sure we
made errors. Everyone made errors.

"Um," Larry said, "um, um—um, we actually haven't done anything with you in a while."

She stopped mid-wine-sip.

I jumped in. "We have instituted some changes in our process … People have been fired … hired …" She smiled and downed the Chianti.

This was what she wanted to hear. It didn't matter what we'd done or not. We were the vendor and they were the customer and they whacked us in the head. That's how it went. So I apologized for our mistakes, when we hadn't done any work at all, and the next week she sent us a book. Which, naturally, we screwed up.

My next lunch was less productive. "Well you know, I have to say that I view the world of typesetting as one of essentially limitless capacity," said Mr. P, a VP for another big New York City publisher.

Upon our arrival at this, his favorite midtown spot—once visited by the Pope—we had been ushered to a private upstairs table. The tuxedo-ed waiter watched Mr. P expectantly and said, in a thick Italian-waiter accent, "Ah, Mr. P—" He gestured as if miming the shape of a large martini glass, which was exactly what he was doing.

Mr. P hesitated and turned to me.

"Would it be wrong," I asked, "to order a beer at lunch?" I knew of his proclivity because Dan—always the premier lush spotter—had ID'd him years ago.

"Oh, no, that's fine," Mr. P said and gave a thumbs-up to the waiter.

The thing that came back on a silver tray wasn't a drink; it was a bucket. It was a swimming pool from the Playboy Mansion, and should have had a warning label, "No Diving." It was clear and cold and as big as Mr. P's head. He sent it back. Not dry enough.

"As I was saying, you've got the regular old suppliers here in America, the freelancers with their home computers, and every day an e-mail from another Indian!" The replacement drink arrived and passed three inspection sips that left it half full. "I saw a mandate go by that we are supposed to send out every job for three bids. Two to Americans and one to India." He narrowed his eyes conspiratorially. "The buyers tell me they sneak the Indians' pricing to the Americans so they can keep the business. But, oh," he said, noticing my expression. "It's not that you aren't very good at Clarinda." He lit a cigarette—only Mr. P's private table allowed smoking—and offered me one. I accepted, trying to gauge the acceptable amount of time to hold the hot smoke in my mouth to make it look like I had inhaled—anything for a customer.

"I think of you as one of my few friends in the industry. It's just that, you know, I'm not involved in the buying decisions. That's up to the, you know, buyers. I just manage the approved vendor list, and I've made sure to keep you on it. You know. And, well, that's what I was thinking about when you offered to take me out to lunch. In your travels around the industry," he waved his wrist towards the waiter for another round, put his arm on my shoulder, and leaned in closely, "have you heard of any jobs opening up?"

The following week Kathy from St. Paul, now my VP of production, and I met with two of Red Bones senior buyers in Columbus. McSwenson, ever vigilant about his account, had wanted to come, but his daughter had an ice skating competition. He had confidently told the buyers that the Gruffington calculus textbook was late because of Clarinda's software problems. In fact, it was late because they had neglected to get us the art files on time. Kathy and I smiled and took our beating while the buyers listed off other complaints on Gruffington, some real, some not, for a couple of hours.

To change the tone of the meeting, I showed them how SNAP kept track of their projects. I told them of my plan to have every typesetter enter what they worked on, the time, and how many pages they did. With that data, we would automate billing and status e-mails. We would link SNAP to a content-management system to allow them instant access to their files and archives—no more fireproof cabinets. They would be able track work from their desktops. "Isn't it amazing?" I asked.

"Well," the senior buyer said, sniffing, "It will be good when you solve your problems on Gruffington," and they left for lunch.

In the cab back to the airport I asked Kathy, "They've been doing this for a long time and are experts enough to be managing dozens of buyers, right?"

"So?"

"So, how did they let us screw Gruffington up? I mean—they know what goes wrong with art files. They do this for a living. Why would they let this happen? Are they that incompetent, or is this the only way they can justify their jobs?"

Kathy shrugged.

e

"How do you put up with it?" Rich asked after hearing me apologize on the phone for an hour to the Oxford buyer. We were in Clarinda's new New York offices—my apartment. Rich had easily convinced me to move out of Baltimore and rent a two bedroom-apartment in the East Village, down the street from the Hell's Angels' motorcycle club. It got me away from thinking about Dan, not that there was much time to think about him, with my having to take over and run the entire company.

Aside from the occasional roar of Harley's coming and going, and the couple of times club members came rushing out of the clubhouse with baseball bats when someone touched their bikes, it was a very safe street. The apartment had also been sufficient excuse to buy myself a textbook-thin plasma TV for the "office."

"'I've had my ass kicked up and down the East Coast by tougher guys than that,' as Dan used to say," I said. "And anyway, it doesn't matter. To get sales, this is the game. She reads me the litany, we screw up because she sent us the wrong stuff, which we don't complain about because they don't like us to point out their errors, and then she reads me the litany again."

"What litany?" he asked.

I closed my eyes, put my palms together, and intoned with the rounded syllables of a medieval monk, "You mes-sed up. I've seen some mistakes in my day, but this one is the one worst e-veeer. I don't understand how you could have done it. I thought we had explained this to you at the beginning of the prooo-ject. The pages, art, math, and your hair are all wrong. It was late. It was upside down. It was not at all what we would have expected from yoo-ou. The author is very upset and we won't make our print wiii-ndow."

Rich applauded a soft golf-clap with the tips of his fingers. "Very funny," he said, "but I thought you said the industry was changing because of the Indians."

"You mean the commodification of typesetting? Where skill doesn't matter, only how cheap your labor is?" I asked.

"Yes, that."

"You mean the question nobody wants to ask—how long can this go on with Americans lowering prices to match overseas? How even with our Manila labor we're still hard pressed to meet the customer's exaggerated expectations? Because the odd thing about an industry being crushed by outsourcing is that the fierce competition of dying vendors shoots up quality one last time before turning earthward once and for all? And customers are given a false sense of security that we can give Indian prices, American services, and never make an error?"

"Yes."

"You mean that despite giving customers more and more every year for less and less money, every publisher has endless complaints? Because there is overcapacity, if we win some of the scarce work, nothing we do is ever good enough?"

"Yeah that, too. So what exactly do you need salespeople for?" he asked.

"Oh," I replied.

"Like that salesman of ours who spends four hundred dollars a week on trips to New York and hasn't been selling anything," he said.

"Didn't Jakeway promise you a million dollars from McGraw by the end of the year?"

I nodded, the fun gone out of our conversation.

"And how much has he gotten?"

"Well let me just check on SNAP," I said. "Twenty-five thousand, and, wait," I saw Rich's glee that the data supported him. "That's just sold. He's got, well, another ninety thousand scheduled."

"That means all that work just pays for him, his benefits, and maybe half those lunches." He rolled his chair over to my whiteboard to add up the numbers in orange ink. "Leaves maybe ten grand to pay the people actually doing the work."

"You know as well as I do that it can take a year to build any kind of relationship. Jakeway's only been with us for a few months." As I said the words I recognized them as more received wisdom from Dan that I hadn't thought to question since changing course away from him.

"Do you know who he takes to lunch?"

I shook my head.

"I've been making him write it on his expense account, which he hates me for making him do by the way. Anyway," he capped the pen, "he takes himself."

"And we're paying for it?" I asked—recalling Hilda and her own private dining sales calls.

He nodded. "And what about McSwenson? Do you have any idea what he costs?"

Unfortunately, I did. We'd become Pearson's third largest typesetter out of over fifty companies, and the only one serving multiple divisions. Revenue had tripled to nearly three million a year, but our costs were out of control. McSwenson, aka 'the Cadaver,' who was about to turn seventy-two years old would take ten percent of that business, plus his base, for a total of over three hundred thousand dollars—rendering the work profitless.

He had become the highest-paid employee in the company, and maybe in the industry, because Dan had let his overly generous commission plan remain untouched for fear of making Red Bones unhappy. And to keep that twenty-year relationship secure, McSwenson made sure that communications to and from Red's people came and went through him. He had also ignored Dan's and now my requests to take on any other clients or even travel on overnight trips. "My wife likes me to be at home at night," he had repeated to me.

The most troubling was his interference with the rest of Pearson. Red represented only one division. To get McSwenson to allow Beth to sell to Guy Delaco and the other VPs in New Jersey, Dan had given him commission on Beth's sales. It was a plan hatched in a bottle of cognac— there was no way we could afford to pay ten percent commission to both of them. But it was another promise Dan had made that I was paying for.

"I know he called the New Jersey buyers after Beth's last visit and told them he's their salesperson. Apparently some of them dislike him so much that they canceled the books Beth had won," I said.

"You know what you have to do."

I did, and I thought about the image Jack had put in my mind of Dan standing behind me, performing an unnatural act.

Someone once told me that salespeople were the easiest people in the world to manage. If they sell enough, you keep them. If they don't, you fire them. Since it's clear to everyone what "enough" is, there isn't any problem when you have to fire them. They will understand. But the only way I could fire McSwenson and keep the Pearson account growing was with Red Bones' approval. With a third of our business, if he told me he wanted something my primary decision was whether to nod vigorously or ponder for a moment and then nod vigorously.

ℓ

In June, I had my annual audience with Red, which was our first meeting since I fired Dan. I took him to one of his favorite restaurants, a barn converted into an intimate, candlelit trattoria where we dined on fish from a corner table on a balcony above giant floral arrangements.

"I'm still thinking about that Cuba trip," he told me. In the flickering candlelight, Red's thin face and thinner lips took on the sheen of a too-whittled marionette. "I've been riding up to fifty miles on weekends with the local club."

I asked how he handled the biking when he went back and forth from Ohio to New Jersey so often. Perhaps I could swing that to a discussion of McSwenson's lack of willingness to travel on business.

"Women are the problem," he said. "I've got them in both towns and they both want me. But I'm not really interested in settling down right now. Not my style." I had no idea how to work firing McSwenson in with that.

He drove me back to the hotel in his rented Lexus—I had less than five minutes left. While trying not to squeal my suit on the plush leather, I reminded him he was my biggest customer and he had made it possible for us to be working with the other VPs. I told him McSwenson was costing us too much, and I needed him to be my advisor. I was asking the Don for a favor.

"Lou used to be very helpful," he said, his hands slowly turning the wheel through the leafy back roads of the wealthy north Jersey suburbs. "He was always there for us, but lately, with all the changes, he doesn't come out to visit as much as he should." We reached the hotel and he clicked the doors unlocked. "On the other hand, he's been a good friend to me so I'm sure you'll treat him the best way possible." I had gotten my authorization to whack the Cadaver, but as Red pulled away, I knew there would be consequences.

ℓ

Red said to "treat him well," so I gave McSwenson two options: be a

Typo

commission only salesperson with no base pay, or be let go with a promise that he would be paid commissions from May till the end of the year. Either way, he would get at least ten thousand dollars, which was much more than any of the fired typesetters got. I gave him a couple of days to think it over.

When I called him back he said, "I can't afford to live only on commission."

I said OK and sent him an agreement to be let go with his commission to be paid through the end of the year. I thought that by putting it in writing, I would avoid another Minnie. But this was the Cadaver—instead of a signed document, I got a call from Red, "You're not treating McSwenson with the necessary respect."

"What do you want me to do?" I asked.

"I'm not going to tell you how to run your business," he said and hung up.

"That's great," Rich said, "Thanks to the way Dan set things up, you, the owner, have to beg a customer to be allowed to fire a bad employee who is wrecking the company."

But what else could I do? Still channeling Dan, I had told both McSwenson and Red the truth about India, commissions and costs. Using those words against me, McSwenson complained to Red—and thereby jeopardized the very business that would pay him—because, after forty-three years at Clarinda, the Cadaver didn't believe that I could fire him.

While I pondered Red's requirement to be nicer, when I had nothing else to give, I received a call from Mr. C, the curmudgeonly World Book VP.

"I've been told Clarinda is doing badly. Very badly."

I told him it wasn't true.

"Well I have it on reliable sources," he said. McSwenson. "Tell me, who am I supposed to call about complaints I have with projects at Clarinda?"

I apologized and told him not to worry about who to call—he didn't have anything with us, and hadn't in a year. "But maybe you'd like to send some books to your new salesman? He's been trying to reach you for a couple of weeks now."

Mr. C. fell silent. It dawned on him that he'd been used by the Cadaver.

I sent another letter to McSwenson telling him all he had to do was sign, and stop complaining to customers, and the commissions were his. I sent a copy to Red.

When I didn't hear back from either of them, I assumed it was over. Maybe Red was waiting, or maybe he understood that his old friend McSwenson would only get the commissions if he kept working with us, or maybe he felt he had done everything he had to for him.

As for McSwenson, I found out what he was thinking months later when he finally sent me an e-mail demanding payment "or else." Unfortunately for him, since he had refused to sign, "or else" had already happened.

ℓ

I went to San Antonio to catch up with Jackie and·tell her what had happened with Dan. Her corner office had one window that surveyed her cubicled army of four-dozen production managers, and another that gazed out on an empty lot of tumbleweeds scheduled to become a golf course and condo development. TPC had been bought by Reed as part of the Harcourt takeover, and despite her assurances that the VP who had ousted us at Academic, Mosby, and Saunders was in a different division, I worried there would be trouble with what was now a third of our business.

"You did what you had to. But it must have been difficult. I know you really respected him," she said.

I nodded, glad she understood—that she felt some empathy.

"Well, you've been winning some friends here with your work and I think I might be able to swing Ohio to you guys," she said as a large man wearing a shimmering blue suit, expensive woven tie, and glossily shined loafers burst through the door. Breathing heavily and nailing his wayward comb-over back in place with his thick hands, he glared at Jackie. "Explain to me why you didn't answer my secretary's call!"

I had recoiled from the explosive sound of the door slapping against the wall, but she appeared unperturbed. "I'm sorry." Her voice was very soft and her expression unreadable. "But I didn't know she was calling for you. I didn't pick up because I was meeting with David here from Clarinda." He turned, realizing there was another person in the room for the first time, and slapped his hair down again. "Clarinda, as you know, is our largest and most valued typesetting supplier. David is the president of the company and he's here for his monthly status meeting with me." He did not smile. "David, this is Kevin, he's just come in from Reed headquarters as senior vice president to run production here in San Antonio."

He slid his hand one more time over his scalp and then extended it at me. I shook it, feeling his pomade wet my fingers. "Clarinda, yes," he said, not relinquishing my hand, "your company sucks, doesn't it?"

It was an odd word choice for a senior vice president, I thought, but I said, "I don't think that's the case. But if we did something troubling, I'd be glad to investigate."

"You do that," he said, let go of my hand, and to Jackie remarked, "Next time, make sure you're available when I call you."

After he left, she cupped her hand under her jaw. "Oh, David, I'm sorry. You don't know what it's been like around here."

A week later she called me in Iowa, and demanded, "I would like to know how you're going to handle the problems in Florida."

I had heard from Steve that the annual test review in Jacksonville with Florida's Department of Education had suffered because a high-speed data line to San Antonio didn't get installed correctly and somehow the blame had fallen on him. "I'm not sure what happened," I said, "We flew Steve down there, like last year, as a favor to you guys to compose test items on the spot. His job wasn't setting up the data lines. I'm sure you can help me clear things up with your folks."

David Silverman

"Yes, David, I understand that, but he volunteered to help during the meeting. And if he's going to volunteer, don't you think he shouldn't make mistakes?"

After the call, the Florida project, which we had been doing for years, developed intractable problems. Test items composed in Atlantic were sent back without requested changes. The problem would seem to be fixed and then reoccur the next day. After a couple of weeks, TPC's VP of Marketing made a rare visit to Iowa to investigate. If we were at fault, she would pull the contract. After two days of research, our habit of keeping every scrap of paper revealed that their editors had failed to forward the corrections to us. The VP of Marketing glanced at the evidence of our innocence, put the pages down, thanked Steve and his staff for their good work and left without further comment, but TPC's complaints continued.

After a project review meeting in San Antonio we were preparing to leave when Jackie made a surprise appearance. "You've been ignoring my request to keep our tracking system updated for Virginia," she said. "People are starting to notice here, and I'm afraid that this can't go on."

"Are you talking about the TOP database?" I asked.

Jackie cocked her head and half-smiled. "Is there another tracking database here?"

The TPC people had silently moved across the table, away from my staff and me. "I didn't forget. Your programmer said the system wasn't ready."

Jackie nodded. "TPC is fining you thirty thousand dollars, which I'll be instructing accounting to take out of our outstanding invoices." I was stunned. That was our entire profit on Virginia. "I hope this sends a message to your staff," she said and left.

In the hall, the Virginia project manager, a quiet woman wearing a pale lilac twin-set touched my elbow and said, "That was a rough meeting."

I nodded and thanked her for her concern.

"Well, I try to watch out for Clarinda. You know you've been making more errors than I've been letting Jackie know about."

She hadn't followed me out of concern. Like a vulture after the lion, she was taking advantage of my having to give into Jackie's demands. "What is it you'd like me to do?" I asked.

"Maybe a small gesture?"

She eyed my billing report expectantly. "Series three?" I said, trying to pick the smallest amount off the list.

She leaned over my shoulder, to check the amount—ten thousand dollars. "That will help your standing here a lot," she said, reaching to cross it off my list.

As the days went by, multi-indented e-mails copied up and down TPC's management chain filled my inbox, along with detailed "it's not our fault" responses from Atlantic. Mistakes TPC used to ignore or help us defend had become serious crimes, and our remaining large project, Massachusetts, had come under scrutiny. E-mails from Jackie claimed we were taking forty-eight hours or more to turn corrections we had contracted to do in thirty-six, and that, because of our errors, Kevin had personally taken over management of Massachusetts.

I was summoned to San Antonio for an official meeting.

ℓ

"That's a mighty fancy slide," Rich said, looking over my multi-colored bar charts. "You could get a job at Ernst and Young making these things."

SNAP provided me proof that we had been turning Massachusetts' pages in less than twelve hours—far less than the thirty-six expected.

"Proof," I said. "This has got to fix things for us."

He ran a finger along the second page, which showed the decline in TPC's business. We had done three and half million in 2001, but were on track for just two million in 2002. "I thought you said we were their favorites."

"The decline isn't our fault," I said and explained that TPC's customers were suffering the effects of the poor economy. While everyone agreed that testing was recession-proof—kids were still taking out their number two pencils—to save money, TPC had been recycling old questions. "Unfortunately," I said, "typesetting new questions is where we make money."

I showed him the data I had gathered on costs. The phone bills from Atlantic had tripled. From eight in the morning till ten in the evening we called them every four minutes—and that didn't include the e-mails. At the same time, regardless of TPC's complaints, for the past two months we had done hardly any work. The Atlantic plant was at a standstill. And before that, when we had been busy—to keep Jackie happy—we had run twenty percent overtime. Given the testing nature of their work, we faced a future of more lulls and droughts that would cause our profits to evaporate.

Additionally, the person we had put on staff in San Antonio, a former Marine named Pete, had, as Dan had predicted, been costing us a hundred thousand dollars a year. The only way to stop losing money was to increase volume and start sending work to Manila. My colorful slides were irrefutable. Jackie would have to see reason.

I called her to prepare her for PowerPoint deluge, and to tell her we needed to start charging something for Pete.

"You're lying to me, David," she said. "Health care costs are not fifty percent of someone's salary. They are thirty percent. That's the rule."

"Maybe at TPC. We're a small company. Our costs are much higher."

She grudgingly accepted half of Pete's charges, and said, "Send me your slides. I will put them in a packet for Kevin." Score another one for me.

The night before the San Antonio trip I developed a hundred-and-one fever. Lying in the shower at four in the morning, I accepted I would be ill whether I stayed home or went, so why not get it over with? On the flight I went straight to the back row and lay down across three seats. Surmising from the stares of the flight attendants, I suspected I looked grim in my crumpled suit jacket and tie, shoes on the seat, and shaking uncontrollably from the chills.

Upon my arrival, Jackie gave me the meeting agenda package. It contained none of my charts or my refutation of their complaints about quality and schedules. Instead it was about the database project she was fighting with another VP about.

At the meeting, my vision began to fog and my hands left moist circles on the desk as Kevin listened patiently first to Jackie's political pitch and then to my plea for more work. When we finished, he leaned back, folded his hands on top of his fly-away hair and moved on to his topic of choice: "I want more Clarinda staff in San Antonio."

I thought the fever had addled my hearing.

"You want Clarinda staff here?"

"A department of typesetters is the only way to guarantee turnaround times I need and cut costs."

"Move Iowa staff here?" I asked, recalling what had happened the last time I tried that, and—wait a second, he was insane. How could he expect that to work? When everyone else in the world was sending work to India he wanted to make San Antonio the new capital of typesetting? I forced up the corners of my mouth and said I'd be glad to look into that for him.

He grinned and leaned on his elbows. "Good. Now, we need to talk about increasing our volume discounts."

Hadn't I just told him TPC was doing less work with us? A volume discount for declining business? No fever was this bad. He wasn't just insane, he was pathological.

A month later Kevin was gone. Hoping the insanity had gone with him, I met Jackie at an industry conference appropriately held at Disney World. We walked the extra clean sidewalks beside a manmade lagoon and a make-believe turn-of-the-century American candy store.

I bought her an ice cream from a man with a handlebar moustache and we leaned against a railing while the nightly fireworks went off. "Is it over?" I asked.

"Oh, David," she said and kissed me on the cheek.

What did that mean?

e

My flight arrived at the beautiful city of San Francisco, the city I nearly moved to after college because of the burritos—drumhead tight tortillas filled with pork and things, and more pork, and why couldn't they seem to make them anywhere else? The weather was warm compared to autumn in the East. I got in a taxi and headed due south, directly away from San Francisco, burritos and any idea of fun. I was here for the Thomson Prepress Vendor meeting of 2002.

Both Thomson and Pearson had prepress vendor meetings in 2002. Pearson's meeting had been a dryer, much less organized shindig for half a dozen vendors in their New Jersey headquarters' cafeteria with deli sandwiches brought in on wheeled carts—no burritos in sight there, either.

Thomson had a much grander vision. The presidents of the twenty-five largest companies in the typesetting industry sat with their staffs at pink table-clothed tables scattered around the pink-carpeted ballroom beneath chandeliers designed in the late 1950s to look "mod." At most tables there hunched an old-line company president with pomaded hair, a grey suit, a yellow shirt, and a red tie, accompanied by his chief typesetter, a nervously overweight woman with curly brown hair, glasses on a chain, and a large insect shaped brooch with paste-jewel eyes. I had brought Ron, the estimating manager, Beth, our salesperson, and Kathy, from St. Paul. Aside from Ron we were half the age of our competitors, also Kathy didn't have a brooch, my suit was dark blue, and what little hair I had left had been reduced to a skin-tight buzz cut.

The buyers sat at tables along the side, keeping away from the unsavory typesetters, and the top corporate staff sat at a raised table in the front where they gazed down upon us like Khrushchev and the Politburo at a May Day parade.

Typo

The Cold War metaphor extended for the introduction of the new boss of the Thomson Corporation, David Thomson, who was presented to us in the form of a Canadian society magazine cover photo. The son of the old master, Lord Ken Thomson—a man alleged to have a line of credit large enough to purchase perhaps Disney and almost certainly Uganda, and who supposedly was fond of finding dented cans of tuna at the supermarket so that he could ask for a discount—David felt differently about money. The article described his latest acquisition, a painting worth thirteen million, which was more than the annual revenue of all but one of the typesetters present.

They had hired two consultants for the three-day event: one to facilitate the discussions and the other to entertain us with his thoughts on what we should be doing with our futures "now that typesetting is dead." We had come looking for business and instead got lectured about how we needed to reinvent our organizations of fifty-year old grandmothers into "knowledge warehouse workers." (To be fair, he didn't say "knowledge warehouse workers." He said some equally impossible thing that we couldn't have turned ourselves into.) He remarked, "typesetters are like watchmakers— you guys are all about skill." I scribbled a note to Kathy, "Don't most watches get made in China?"

The lead corporate buyer presented next. Standing on the dais with PowerPoint clicker in hand she said, "You are our core vendors. We can't stress how important you are to us as partners. But I think you already know because you've all seen an increase in work from us this year."

No, I thought, I hadn't seen any increase, but I wasn't about to raise my hand and single us out for ridicule. In 2001, we had done nearly a million for Harcourt and Thomson. In 2002, after Thomson bought Harcourt and closed several plants, we did less than two hundred thousand—our profit a slim twenty thousand that was in the process of being eroded by airfare and hotel charges while we listened to more praise from the other buyers.

At the close of the first day, we were left on our own while the Thomson people secreted themselves away for closed-door meetings and typesetter-free dinners. Ron, Beth, Kathy and I went to the hotel bar where I spotted

Rob Ranch by himself at a corner table. I hadn't spoken to him since our attempt to buy his company fell through in the distant past of Dan's dreams of world typesetting domination. Seeing me, he came over. He rested his hand heavily on the back of my chair.

"It was sad how it worked out between our companies." He leaned forward, bringing his face so close I could see the specks of grey in his moustache. "You are good guys, though. Good. You're a good guy, David, I always liked you." I shook his hand without saying a word and he walked away. He was drunk.

A half hour later he came back, and knelt beside me—first one, then both knees on the floor. He put his hand across mine and began quietly weeping. Ron, Kathy, and Beth looked behind them, at their hands, the ceiling, anywhere but at him.

His crying felt like it might quickly expand to sobbing or perhaps violent screams. "It's okay," I said. "I'm not mad at you. Times have been hard, but we'll be okay." He cried for a little while longer and then stood, patted me on the back, and stumbled off to his room.

The second day there was no sign of Rob as we headed off on a field trip to Thomson's glistening new offices overlooking the Santa Cruz mountains. I felt the way a Roman citizen must have felt on being called to the imperial palace and shown the new golden urinal acquired from last year's tax increases.

"What do you think?" a Thomson employee asked me, his badge proudly affixed with a yellow VP sticker.

"It's very nice," I said.

Back in the ballroom the lead buyer returned to her favorite subject. "We are partners. Like a father and son in a sack race," she said, and the PowerPoint presentation duly displayed cartoon characters in a potato sack. "And together we can cut typesetting costs." The happy cartoon couple was shown breaking the ribbon of "typesetting costs." I doodled an unclothed cartoon character in a barrel and then quickly scratched it out.

For several years, Thomson had sent us annual scale-pricing spreadsheets, and every year it took us two weeks to figure out the five hundred prices we were supposed to provide. Each year we lowered prices twenty percent—the amount the lead buyer had hinted strongly that we needed to drop them to remain a "core vendor." Clarinda had made gains with technology, training, and Manila, but even with the layoff, our main cost was still Iowa labor and my employees, quite reasonably, weren't looking for pay cuts.

Where did Thomson think these price decreases came from? They largely refused to use India, and whenever I mentioned our Manila plant, they cautioned me that they didn't want their books being mangled by unskilled workers—as if books didn't exist in Asia.

That evening I had sashimi with the consultant who had been facilitating the meeting (the knowledge warehouse guy had left the first day). Over a plate of food flayed from raw fish—the closer to alive, the better—I asked him how he liked working for Thomson.

"It's a good job," he said. "I tell them things they don't want to hear, they ignore me, and I get a check." This was a man I liked.

He explained, "Publishers have three costs: author royalties, marketing and production. They dare not cut the first two for fear of reducing sales. So they focus on the production costs. They've cut all they can already so if you ask me, this whole exercise of asking you guys in America for even lower prices while they pretend they might not go to India is like kicking the retarded kid in the wheelchair."

I told him that was a more effective image than my stickman in the barrel, and a magnificent summary of what I had been feeling.

"Great," he said, paying the check, "We'll put this on Thomson and you'll help me get them to understand that tomorrow at the wrap up session?"

The final day all of the vendors assembled at our tables, but many of the buyers' seats were empty. Their agenda accomplished, they had headed home. "We've had a good conference," the lead buyer said, "A lot has been accomplished and we have you, our core vendors, to thank for that. So, before we close, we wanted to do a poll and see if you had any comments to improve our partnership. We have a half hour, which should be plenty of time."

On cue, the consultant picked up a wireless mike and began edging through the tables. No one was eager to improve the partnership. When he got to me he stopped. I considered that I couldn't lose business that I wasn't getting. He continued to hover behind me. I tentatively moved my hand a millimeter and he brought the mike to my lips. I wasn't sure if my barrel was falling off or my wheelchair was whizzing downhill.

"To be quite honest," I said, as everyone turned to look—I'd sat at the furthest table— "You've gone through this process of asking us for scale pricing for several years now and gotten lower and lower prices. If you really want to save money," I looked up at the consultant, who smiled and nodded me on. "If you want a real partnership, assign us a volume of work. You've said you can't do that, but what do you have to lose?" One of my competitors gave me a covert thumbs-up. "There's no secret to my costs, or anyone else's in this room. We can work together to bring prices down. So why don't you just tell us what you want to pay?"

Thumb Man hid his digit in his palm, and all the typesetters looked up at the dais. "Well," the moderator said, looking at her boss, "thank you, but this is a meeting to discuss scale pricing, not about giving you volume guarantees."

The lead buyer might as well have said, "NO! We do not trust you. You're trying to steal from us by getting some kind of promise of work. Whatever benefits you hurts us. That is the axiom we live by."

Thumb Man raised his hand. In the hallway he had told me his first job had been picking cigarette ashes out of buckets of melted lead at a typographer in 1950. "Do you have a budget for your books before you send them out to us for bid?" he asked.

"Yes, we do. We have a rough budget, but you have to understand, that budget will get revised downward often," the lead buyer said.

"Okay, but do you have a line item for typesetting?"

"Oh, absolutely."

Typo

"Well, then would you consider taking that price, taking something off it and giving us that as what you want us to charge you?" he said.

"No, we couldn't do that."

"Why?"

"That number is secret."

Left behind by Thomson, the meeting transformed into an ad hoc typesetters' convention of owners, salespeople, and the consultant who had given me the mike. We had never felt as bonded as an industry, as we did squinting into the warm California sun sitting on the chaise lounges by the pool while waiting for the shuttle bus to the airport.

"You know that TV show where the cops get the guy on the ground and just keeping hitting him?" the president of a rural Pennsylvania company asked. "That's how I feel. Forty years of typesetting is enough. I'm going into software."

"You're just giving up?" I asked.

"I'll keep running my typesetting business until everything's gone to India, but how long will that be? A couple more years?"

He confided to me later that he had begun to secretly sub-contract work to India while firing his staff in Pennsylvania without telling the customer. The plan had worked until the Indians called his customer directly and said that they knew how to use the publisher's special software program. "Where did you learn that?" the publisher asked. "Only our key vendors are supposed to have that software, it's confidential." It had been a fiasco for the man from Pennsylvania.

The Thumb Man recounted an Indian gloating at another conference, "'For Reed-Elsevier we did half a million pages for two million last year!'" That's four dollars per page including alterations. When I had that work last year I'd gotten twenty-five a page. And this guy was ecstatic for his half million."

"That's because he made a million as profit," I said.

"You know the average rate for an Indian with a college degree in Bangalore is less than two thousand a year?" Pennsylvania said.

"I pay my Filipinos three times that, and in Iowa forty. How can we compete?"

Hundreds of thousands of pages of typesetting had moved to India, leaving the American companies fighting over the scraps left behind, and those scraps consisted of the hardest, gristliest, most complicated books there were. The more work the Indians took, the more we scrambled while trying to fire as few people as possible.

"And then Thomson makes me drop a couple thousand to come visit them when we are doing less work for them this year than last," Thumb Man added.

"But she said you'd seen an increase," I said.

"You were the one?" Thumb Man asked.

"No, I went down." We looked at Pennsylvania.

"Don't look me, I haven't seen a dime since they bought Harcourt."

"I asked," Thumb Man's salesman said. "I couldn't find who got more."

"Goldstone?" I asked. He shook his head. "Thumer's? Physical Comp? Western?" He shook no for each.

"I think I can answer that for you," the consultant said, putting down his coconut shrimp. "Before the meeting we asked the accounting department for data on what we were spending with you folks. They couldn't do it. They knew the total was eleven million or so, but Thomson is a multi-billion dollar company, and the accountants said that eleven million is just 'noise.' Losing eleven million doesn't even matter. So we just assumed you'd seen an increase. Besides the buyers thought it would sound good."

I divided eleven million by the twenty "core vendors." We should each be getting around half a million. We'd already gotten our shares; we just didn't know it! Half a million was enough work to pay for only about five to eight people at Clarinda. That's a reasonable account, but not with the expenses of dealing with them. If I did all the work in Manila with no sales expense I could make a profit, but my American competitors didn't have a Manila. Thomson was going to run every one of them out of business.

Maybe I didn't want to be a core vendor.

ℓ

"Is that all you called me for?" Red Bones asked.

I had called to see if he still harbored issues about my firing McSwenson and to go over his projections for our business—still a record setting three million—and because I needed more than that. I needed direction and I didn't know who else to ask. Rich understood business, but not the publishing industry. I couldn't call Dan. There was no one else who had been as close to our problems, and Red has always made a point of how he knew all about all his vendors—if not the whole industry.

"I need your help," I said and explained my situation. I told him about my millions of personal guaranteed debts, the revolver coming due yet again, about how Manila was trained and ready but it was hard to convince customers to let us send work there, about my own weariness from the practical and emotional turmoil still surrounding firing Dan, my friend and mentor, only five months before.

"Well I may have not been clear enough before," he said. "There were some missteps, some big ones, but overall you and Dan did a great job with Clarinda and I've been impressed with your determination. There's a man I played golf with last week and, if you'd like, I think he may be able to help you."

"Who is that?" I asked.

"A company I'd very much like to start using," he said, "Bookers, or as I like to call them, the eight-hundred pound gorilla of typesetting."

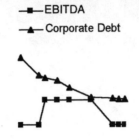

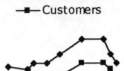

My Net Worth

Locations

Clarinda
Atlantic
Baltimore
St. Paul
New York
Manila

Revolver

Revenue	$9,000,000
EBITDA	$0
Corporate Debt	$1,020,000
Employees	120
Customers	80
My Net Worth	$4,000,000
Revolver Expires	11 Months

The Eight-Hundred Pound Gorilla

July 2002

TIMMY LOOKED OUT THE TWO-STORY REFLECTIVE GREEN glass window at the people in Union Square. Some were in business suits, maneuvering purposefully through the crowd while heading for the subway or a cab or, for the wealthiest, a waiting black town car. Others were in shorts, chewing gum and leaning against buildings, chatting with a friend over ice cream, or gazing in the windows of the W hotel, surprised to see Timmy, sitting on a large, backless cushion, starring back. "I miss New York," he said. "You just don't get women with legs like that walking around Fairfax, Virginia."

I tugged at my suit jacket that had gotten caught under my leg on the uncomfortable cube-stool and tried to smile. Tall with sandy blond hair, blue-grey eyes, and a hint of freckles, his boyish looks were disturbed only slightly by a more than average-sized nose. With corporately polished manners, and a smooth Maryland accent, Timmy was my best hope.

"When I ran Jimson Printers we had a corporate apartment in New York," he said, taking a sip of fresh squeezed orange juice from a leaded crystal glass. "And there was a driver waiting for us downstairs to take us to work. He'd sit there all day till I came out. You ever have a driver?"

I shook my head.

He was the president of the largest typesetter in the world, an Indian-owned company called Bookers—Red's half-ton typesetting primate. Dan and I had almost crossed paths with them many times and two of my salespeople had worked for them. What I knew didn't comfort me, but just as likely, my perceptions were colored by Dan's interpretation of those encounters.

One of our potential backers had been an Indian keyboarding company outside of Washington, D.C., run by a man named Sashi. Dan spent months discussing his plans for Clarinda and the roll-up of the rest of the typesetting industry. Sashi ultimately declined saying, "My nephew runs a typesetting company and he doesn't seem to be doing so well." A few months later, Dan and I bought Clarinda on our own and a company we had never heard of, Bookers, began buying typesetters almost exactly in the way Dan had been planning. Bookers, based in Virginia but with a giant production facility in New Delhi, turned out to be the firm owned by Sashi's nephew, also named Sashi.

I'll never know if the Sashis compared notes on our plans, but Dan certainly thought they did. Either way, I became fascinated with the company, checking their website and Googling to discover their venture capital backers. In late 1999, they bought two companies: the RFD group and Lincoln. RFD was a small company in Pennsylvania, but Lincoln, also in Pennsylvania, had been the largest typesetter in the country. Bookers rocketed from a couple million in revenue to sixty—all through acquisition. In 2000, Bookers bought ABC in California, adding another twelve million, and bringing their staff to over two and a half thousand employees—two thousand of whom were in New Delhi.

When Dan hired former Lincoln and RFD salespeople, I learned more. In the 1990s, Lincoln's owner engineered an ESOP takeover (an ESOP is an employee stock ownership plan and it means that the employees buy a portion of the company). When I had been looking for funding for Clarinda, several financiers suggested ESOPs, but Dan felt they were unethical. The Lincoln ESOP bought 49% of the shares of the company with the employees' money—their 401K money to be precise. That money went to the owner who retained the controlling 51%.

When Bookers came along they bought all the shares, giving the owner more cash. The bought-out employees recognized a fifty percent loss on their savings. Then Bookers fired half of them. According to Larry, our Mormon salesperson, "The bastard had swapped our retirement money into his retirement." It did not sound like "benevolent capitalism"—but where had that gotten me?

"Red Bones plays quite a round of golf," Timmy said. "You ever go golfing with him?"

I shook my head, recalling my lone terrible day of golf with Dan.

"Nice fella, cost me eighteen holes and I didn't get a single dollar of business. You guys must have quite a hold on your customers. So why do you want to sell?"

I'd explained that I had become involved with Clarinda because of Dan's passion for the business, and without him, I didn't want to be running my own company. I told him as much of the story about Dan's drinking as I thought he should know, and when he didn't respond, I said more about how Dan had been a father figure to me. Timmy nodded, and I decided not to mention any more reasons for wanting out—such as the fact that I was about to go through a second big round of layoffs.

"I think Red was right, we might be able work things out," he said. "Do you have any questions for me?"

I asked if he really was able to buy Clarinda or if the Indians were in charge.

"I understand your concern," he said, "I'd have the same question myself, even if I wouldn't necessarily ask it exactly that way. But yes, I make the deals. Sashi considers himself the founder of the company and he spends his time thinking about future strategy, not the details of the day to day. That's my job." I took a peanut from a black lacquer bowl on the cube table. "Think of him as a visionary looking forward to retirement."

"So I only need to convince you?" I asked.

Timmy laughed. "Absolutely! We've got the money and I've got the authority." He leaned back and opened his arms wide so that I could see the gold of his cufflinks emerge beneath his suit. "Why else would I move from New York to the woods of Virginia! I've financed and bought dozens of companies. I saw what Sashi was up to there at Bookers and I got him the money. I was the one who brought in the backers and I'm the one they're looking to for more deals." He looked in my eyes. "'Cause if there's one thing I know, it's how to make a deal. I am the master of the merger, and I can tell you right now, David, I know what an entrepreneur needs. I am going to make you very happy, maybe not extremely happy, but very happy. How do you feel about that?"

I felt, as Dan used to say, like "having him blow some more of that smoke up my ass."

ℓ

Two weeks later, Rich and I were on the road to Virginia in my Honda minivan.

"This thing really does say 'soccer mom,'" he said when I opened the automatic side door for him with the key chain button.

"I think it says, 'practical.'" We headed through the Holland Tunnel to the endless pavement of the New Jersey Turnpike. "You're probably going to squander your millions on a Porsche."

He nodded approval and tapped his fingers on the window.

"Bookers bought Lincoln and RFD for one times sales," I said. "That's nine or ten million for us."

"Really?" he asked.

"OK, minus debt, so maybe eight million."

"Nice. Four hundred fat ones for me and seven point six for you, or are you giving Dan his half?" The idea of presenting Dan over three million

Typo

dollars made me smile as we passed the chemical plants of Secaucus. That would show him who was more ethical. "Nice. But not going to happen," he said.

"Why not?"

"Nobody's buying this thing for eight million. You can't guarantee the sales."

"I can guarantee Pearson." Traffic had slowed for an accident—two SUVs, one crashed on the median, the other facing the wrong way on the shoulder.

"So maybe half of sales minus debt. That's still one point three each for you and your buddy Dan and seventy five K for me." Rich, like Dan, could do arithmetic more quickly in his head than I could with a calculator. "Still, I don't see them paying you one to two million."

"They'd want an earn-out," I said. "Pay me over five years or something."

"And how would they guarantee that? What if they lose all the business? Or decide that it isn't profitable? How are you going to audit their books?"

"So maybe half again?" I said. "Come on, that's only three hundred thousand left for me after paying back my father. What about all my hard work?"

Rich took out a map to look for a route around the Turnpike, which continued to jam after the accident. "So seven hundred fifty K up front and whatever earn out play they want? Get you out of the personal guarantees, pay your dad and give you enough money after taxes to not work for the three or four years you'll be tied up with a non-compete?" he asked, "That's the deal you want?"

"It's better than a stick in the eye," I said. "That's true."

"And better than owing two million in personal debt," he said.

It became clear to me what Rich, with his MBA experience, had been doing. This wasn't about the value of the company. It was about me forgetting my multi-million-dollar fantasies. What I wanted was what he had just told me to want. "I guess it is," I said, and focused on the sign that said, "Washington, D.C., 250 miles."

"The only question now," he said, "Is what does Bookers want?"

ℓ

"Now that's what I'm talking about," Rich said, pointing at the shiny new Mercedes with a vanity plate that read "Bookers." "I don't think that's Timmy's car."

Their offices were in a suburban office park at the edges of Washington that had been surrounded by fields a decade ago. Now they were swallowed by the sprawl of strip malls, bagel shops and tire repair places. Inside, the accommodations were no fancier than the outside, but we were seated and offered coffee by a woman who identified herself as "Sashi's personal assistant." On the table was an issue of *Inc.* that named Bookers as one of the fastest growing small businesses in the country—not hard, I thought, if the VCs bought it for you.

Sashi, a man who appeared to be comfortably becoming round, arrived first. He wore a pink, silky short-sleeved shirt. Although Indian by birth, he had been raised in Michigan and spoke without any accent as he introduced himself and handed Rich and me a business card that read "Founder and CEO." Timmy showed up a few minutes later.

"We had a little meeting with the VCs that turned into a big meeting," he said, looking very tired.

"What is your revenue?" Sashi asked cheerfully without waiting for Timmy to sit. He was literally bouncing in his chair, and not looking at all tired.

I explained our revenue picture.

"Pearson, absolutely, is that all from Red Bones' division?"

I explained the breakdown.

"Four divisions? Is that all of Pearson?"

As I explained the structure of Pearson and its trade and educational divisions, it became obvious that—unlike Timmy's description of the partially retired visionary—Sashi was very involved, though he didn't seem to know a lot about the customers.

"So tell me," Sashi said, "How many employees do you have in Clarinda?"

"About forty," I said.

Sashi looked at Timmy, "I thought you said they had a hundred and fifty employees."

"We have five other locations," I said.

"They have a Philippine operation that would be a good addition for us," Timmy said. "It would let us diversify overseas production like we've been talking about."

"Manila is our most profitable plant," I said.

Rich gave me a sidelong glance. We had both expected the meeting to be about Bookers putting a value on Clarinda, but Sashi acted as if this was the first he had heard of us. "What about cash flow?" he asked, leaning forward.

"We have a sixty to ninety day payment from the publishers, like anyone else," I said. "Is that what you want to know?"

"Absolutely not," he said, "I want to know cash flow."

Rich smiled and said, "We have a revolving line of capital from Household Finance at prime plus one. We have up to one point two million available and have been able to keep it closer to no more than seven hundred thousand on a regular basis."

Sashi nodded slowly. "So you have positive cash flow?"

Rich continued smiling. "Yes," he said. "Would you like me to go over our balance sheet?"

"Absolutely," Sashi responded.

As Rich explained in detail, Sahsi's questions indicated he knew less about corporate finance than I did. The meeting turned into Rich giving an MBA lecture on income statements and balance sheets. Timmy, with his background of mergers and acquisitions, would have easily known these things and could have briefed Sashi beforehand, yet he did nothing but follow along, smiling and nodding.

"You Americans," Sashi said, "It always surprises me that you can claim to be such good businessmen, but you don't know how to fight against someone who is really hungry to take away your business."

"But you are interested in buying us?" I asked.

"Absolutely."

I spent the drive back speculating what was going on between Sashi and Timmy. Did Timmy want Clarinda because it would give him leverage over production in India that was run by Sashi's brother? Or because he would get a bonus for acquiring another American company? Why hadn't he briefed Sashi? What did Sashi want? To show the world he could keep buying American companies? To add our revenue and cash flow to his to get him another article in *Inc.*? Did either of them intend to keep any of the American employees?

"It doesn't matter," Rich said, "What that meeting taught me was all that we've got to sell is our customer base and maybe Manila production."

"But I can't guarantee the customers will stay if we sell," I said. "That's the problem Ranch had."

"That's not entirely true—you've got Red. So what else can we promise?"

ℓ

The next week in Iowa, Rich came in my office.

"Maybe," I said, "I could get Jackie to put her commitment in the contract and make it dependent on Atlantic—that way she could guarantee that our Atlantic staff she likes so much would stay in place and I would have solid assets to show Timmy and Sashi."

Typo

I referred to the contract Jackie had put in place between TPC and Clarinda the year before, which according to Dan, "showed her bosses she was doing something." The negotiation process had been straightforward—I wrote some comments on her draft, she ignored them, and I signed.

"But what about her little kickback fund?" Rich asked.

"You mean the R&D?" I asked. Two percent of every invoice went into a "Research and Development" fund, as she called it. She had originally said it would be used for "soft money" development projects at Clarinda, but when I told Dan that, he had laughed and said, "She snookered you, my boy, but what choice did you have?" R&D fund purchases had included a $3,500 video projector Jackie kept in her desk, $10,000 to a database developer for a project unrelated to Clarinda, $2,500 for me to visit another vendor who was building a system to automate typesetting and thereby eliminate our business.

"So she spends it on herself, what do you want me to do?" I asked.

"The problem," he said, "is the unspent fifty thousand on our balance sheet combined with her one and half million in outstanding receivables." He handed me the list he had been holding. I was surprised to see some were over a year old. "Bookers' due diligence is going to uncover that half our line of credit is being used to carry TPC debts. Even without your overtime issue, the cost of money on those unpaid invoices wipes out our profits. You've got to get her to pay."

"Let me alone," I said, frustrated that Rich was destroying my simple plan to convince Jackie to promise future work rather than fix her past of pushing Clarinda around. "I know what you need."

"The customer isn't always right," he said and stuck a piece of gum in his mouth. I frowned, disgusted by the open-mouthed way he forced his teeth around the candy. "A business is in business to make money," he said, the gum clicking.

I crumpled and re-crumpled a piece of paper to make a sound I had control over. "Are you done?"

"If you happen to satisfy a customer along the way, well, all the better I guess."

"What the heck does that mean?"

"Did you want to be Vanderbilt, or did you want people to like you?" he said, and left, tossing the gum in the trash.

"Are you telling me you spent the R&D fund?" Jackie Dee asked.

"No. What I'm saying is we could really use your help in getting payables closer to thirty days." I had called her three Wednesdays in a row before she called me back on Tuesday evening. "The average now is one hundred eighty, and that's costing me a lot in interest on my line."

"I can't erase the R&D fund. The contract won't allow me to do that," she said. "You're putting me in a very difficult position."

"Please, let me explain why I'm asking to cut down the unspent balance," I said. "I have a company interested in buying Clarinda. When they do that they're going to look hard at all of our accounts and plants. You and I both want them to keep Atlantic going, but they've already told me they don't want to assume any balance sheet liability, and that's the R&D fund. They're a good company and a major supplier to your parent company. I've talked to them and they are ready to do whatever you need, including lower prices. I just need you to put the commitment for Massachusetts, Florida and Virginia you gave me into writing. I know how much you value Steve and the staff in Atlantic. This isn't about me, it's about them and their jobs."

"Are you threatening me, David?"

"No, no, no. I just need your help."

"We have a contract. I want you to remember that," she said, and hung up.

I sat down on my bed and looked down the street at the guy who covered the bikes in front of the Hell's Angels club when it rained. I *was* threatening her. If we stopped work for even a day, their business was at risk—her customers could fine TPC millions. Dan had told me holding work hostage was a typesetters' ultimate weapon and last recourse—like Daffy Duck immolating himself to win the audience's approval, I could do this trick only once. Jackie would never want to deal with me again, but she might sign and allow Bookers to take over Clarinda just to get away from me. If she accepted, I would win; if she didn't, we would both lose.

But how could I do it without violating what little I had held onto of Dan's benevolent capitalist ideals? The tiny robot of him was still in my head and it screamed as loud as it could, "Thou Shalt Satisfy The Customer!"

I went downstairs where Rich was sorting through invoices.

"Can they sue us for breach of contract?" I asked.

"Let me see it again," he said, and I pulled a copy. "Unhun, yes, yup." He flipped the pages rapidly. "What idiot let this thing through Legal?"

"Does that mean she can't sue?"

"For what? The contract doesn't promise any work. You can only sue for the value of the contract and this one has none. Are you going to do it?"

"I don't know."

I called Steve in Atlantic. "Are you sure she can't go a day without us?" I asked.

"Don't see how," he said. "They are sending work all the time and need it back in a couple of hours."

"Do you think they could find another vendor without your knowing?"

"I don't see how," he said. "I'd see the drop-off in work immediately."

"You're sure."

"I'm sure. Why are you asking?"

I couldn't not tell him. If I was going to sell the business and potentially lose TPC, I had to tell him. I explained my worries about the business, the hope for selling to Bookers, and the need to have Jackie commit work to keep Atlantic open.

"I'm sure I would know if she tried to leave us," he said. "And I'll keep an eye out for any changes."

I called Jackie, hoping that it would be easier for her to continue with Clarinda than without us. I wanted her to help me sell the company to Bookers in exchange for all the good things Clarinda and I had done for her. At least that's what I said in the messages I left her. Days went by and she didn't call back.

Finally, she called me. "You do what you have to," she said, "But I will not support your selling to Bookers. It is not in TPC's interest."

I hung up, it was nine at night, eight in Atlantic. I called Steve—he was still in the office. "Turn it off," I said.

I waited for the impact.

She had risked her company's business and millions of potential fines for a few thousand dollars in the R&D fund and the pride that no vendor would hold her work hostage—and she won.

"What do you mean she called and said 'send it back'?" I asked.

"I guess she found other vendors," Steve said. My weeks of fretting—instead of simply freezing the work—had given her the time she needed to find her own solution.

"Don't send anything till she pays her bills!" Rich shouted from the downstairs.

ℓ

"You need to sell to Bookers," Red said. I stood on the metal terrace-slash-fire escape of my apartment. A Hell's Angel tested the volume on his ride.

"What's that?" I asked.

"You need to sell," he said. Unlike Jackie, my friend and new surrogate mentor, Red, had given me a spreadsheet listing the books we would get, and he had gone to the other VPs at Pearson and helped me get lists from them as well. He had also promised Timmy that he would keep the work with Bookers after an acquisition, which was reasonable given that he had come up with the idea of them buying us. "You should not be trying to delay this deal."

I told him Timmy promised me a letter of intent, but we hadn't gotten it. I assured him I would sign almost any deal if they would just give me one. I reminded him about my millions in personally guaranteed debt and that my dreams were filled with worries about losing all my customers from the repercussions if the deal didn't close.

"Your reputation at Pearson is on the line here," he said.

I had told him everything, I said.

"If you don't do this deal, I will make sure you get no business from us next year."

I repeated that it was my every intent to sell. "However, without your business, I have nothing to sell."

I came in off the balcony and told Rich what had happened.

"He thought he was threatening you," he said. "He didn't realize that he'd pushed you clear off the cliff."

l

"You ever eat at a Cracker Barrel?" I asked Rich.

He shook his head.

"Me either." I pulled off the Interstate in Eastern Pennsylvania. It was a disappointment. The knickknacks on the walls: rakes, plows, tillers, were not only fake, there were very few of them, leaving big blanks of paneling. The same was true of my breakfast, a couple of small, unconvincing eggs and lots of open plate thinly covered in grease.

We were on our way to our second meeting with Sashi and Timmy, this time at the former headquarters of Lincoln typesetting in Lincoln, Pennsylvania. Like Clarinda, another typesetting company that named itself after a small town in a difficult-to-reach part of the countryside.

After a few wrong turns that sent us around the Lincoln tire factory and the Lincoln fitness equipment plant, we found it. All traces of the still prestigious Lincoln name had been erased, replaced by a giant Bookers logo on the building's side. Inside, the plant was much the same as Clarinda's—70s paneled décor and a carpet patched with duct tape.

Timmy had told me we would finally be getting a letter of intent, but in the conference room, he presented his plan without a piece of paper in sight. "I told you that you'd be happy and you will be," he began with an eye on Sashi. "What we do is make you a senior vice president in charge of our new publishing services division and we move the Philippine production into our New Delhi Group. And, Richard, I think you'd be perfect for that role of transitioning work to them," he said, and leaned back in his five-wheeled chair. "Now as for the financial details. I think we can get you a solid earn out after we let the company go into default."

"Default?" I asked.

"Default, bankrupt. We don't assume any liabilities, and that lets us move forward with money spent on you rather than on some silly loans. It's how we are handling the ABC takeover. I like to call it my 'no money down' plan." He smiled happily.

"But those loans are personally guaranteed by David," Rich said. "If you let the company go bankrupt, he goes bankrupt." I nodded vigorously.

"And this is not an option?" Sashi asked.

"No!" I said, too loudly.

"Well, let's look at the numbers again," Timmy said. "I'm sure we can work something out. Maybe you'd be happier in a senior technology role."

"I'm OK with whatever you want as long as it covers my debt," I said, knowing how weak Clarinda had become because of these negotiations. I began to worry that Bookers may have had plenty of VC backing, but after several expensive acquisitions, very little in the way of cash.

"OK," Timmy said, rubbing his hands together, "How much are the buildings worth in Iowa?"

"Nothing," Rich said.

"Nothing? How did you get a mortgage?"

"The bank put a value on them," I said, "but it's small-town Iowa. Who's going to buy them? If someone wants a five-thousand square foot light-industrial building in Southwest Iowa, they are perfect; if not, they don't sell."

"How long do you think they would be on the market?" Sashi asked.

"I have no idea," I said, and Timmy frowned. "Years, maybe?" Maybe I should have said a few months, but I couldn't imagine that happening. Lying never occurred to me.

"So," Timmy said, "how much are the buildings worth?"

I couldn't stand it. They had to buy. Timmy was a financial man, he didn't understand what could be done with production, and Sashi had bought his way to the top. They had to understand that Clarinda wasn't just another typesetter—that they needed me.

"But Clarinda is worth so much to you," I said. "There's our Manila plant, St. Paul editorial services, SNAP production tracking, and my knowledge of electronic publishing technology and operations."

I explained that I had learned from my conversations with them and the two salespeople who used to work for them that Bookers was hamstrung by the same problems as Clarinda—production tracking, efficiency, training, Americans sabotaging work sent overseas, and Indian production managers having no respect for the skill of their American counterparts. "I heard from McGraw about a book where your Indian production staff refused to make sidebars the customer wanted because they thought they knew better."

Sashi turned to Timmy, "Have you heard that?" Timmy half nodded his head toward his shoulder.

"Look," I said, going to the whiteboard, "You do fifty million with over two thousand employees and I can do ten with two hundred." Timmy perked up. No one had ever explained this to him. I excitedly wrote more numbers in green. "You've got revenue of $17,500 per person. $17,500 is OK if your employees cost $1,000 per year, but at Clarinda we were closer to $80,000 per person, including Manila—so wouldn't you rather have $79,000 profit than $16,500? One of my Manila employees does the work of ten of your staff in Delhi. Do you have an Internet browser?"

Sashi took us to the production VP's office. He also had a view of a tree next to a parking lot. On his computer I showed them SNAP. I pulled up our total sales, broke it down by customer, and then plant, and then individual employees. I told him how we planned to connect the whole thing to our own content management and customer alert system.

Sashi said to his production VP, "We have something like that in development, right?"

The VP responded, "Well, not exactly."

The next week Timmy sent a letter again promising a letter of intent, followed by a flurry of e-mails assuring me there would be a deal. Then Jack, our attorney, got a phone message.

"Two words, David, 'no deal.'"

I had thought I was getting them more excited to buy us. Instead, as Dan would have said, I was "pissing on everyone's parade." Sashi's pride made him believe he and his staff were the smartest guys in the industry. Sashi felt he was a winner and since I was trying to sell, I was, by definition, a loser. Who wants advice from a loser? A few months later, Timmy was gone, replaced by an Indian.

In Atlantic, Steve did his best to try to find work to keep the plant open. The TPC manager who had run the Florida project had moved to a rival testing company, and he had been talking to her about doing a big project. But after Jackie dumped us, she withdrew the offer. I called and asked why.

"Because TPC isn't using you," she said.

"Isn't TPC your competitor?" I asked.

"Yes."

"Didn't you leave because they weren't the best company?"

"Yes."

"Did we always get your projects done right?"

"Yes."

"Then why is our doing business with your competitor, who you left, a requirement for us to do business with you at your new company?"

"Well, it isn't."

"Great!"

"But we already found another vendor."

On the day I shut down Atlantic, Steve repeated his surprise. "Still don't know how she did it," he said. Then he got a job offer from Jackie. What choice did he have? His life and family was in Iowa, he didn't want to move, but Jackie had won and finally gotten the employee in San Antonio she always wanted.

ℓ

"Maybe someone else will want to buy," Rich said.

I nodded glumly, and pulled on one end of a rope toy while his brown pug puppy, Coco, pulled on the other. He had bought her just a few weeks before and she traveled to the office in a messenger bag strung over his shoulder because she couldn't walk that far. No more than a foot long, she growled as she tried to wrap her jaws around the half-inch knot.

"She loves it when you shake her head back and forth quickly," he said. I shook and the dog bounced up and down. "Look at it this way, as we lose customers Clarinda becomes less expensive for another buyer."

Coco jumped in my lap, trying to get at the end of the rope in my hand.

"TPC was a bad customer. Be glad we're rid of them. How about Pearson?"

"Red's not happy about Bookers, but if they send only a third of the work they promised that's over a million," I said. "And Red still loves Kathy and the folks in St. Paul."

"Three million," he said and made a face like a careful shopper examining a melon. "It's really not that bad a company."

I squinted at him.

"I mean it. Clarinda's not so bad compared to all the other companies I've seen. The profits are there, if it wasn't for all that debt looming over your head. But that's long-term and the monthly payment is only a few grand."

I put my hands on either side of Coco's head to cover her ears. "Mad, your daddy's gone mad, I tell you."

"I'm serious," he said. "Wouldn't it be nice if we could just run the business? If we can keep even half of Pearson and the other customers it wouldn't be a bad living for us."

"What are you saying?" I asked as he took Coco onto his shoulder where she began licking his head.

"I'm saying, how about we talk to Mike?"

Mike, Rich's friend the master salesman, didn't look the part. He had thick glasses, a tie that laid askew on his shirt, and wore sneakers beneath the frayed cuffs of his sat-in looking suit. He grabbed my hand and said, "So you're the guy Rich was telling me about." And while continuing to look me in the eye, he sat down on my well-traveled sofa. "Nice place. You want to get this company rolling again or what?"

He read a dozen papers and magazines cover-to-cover every day, and could as easily discuss the crisis in the Middle East as college basketball scores or the Tour de France. The rumpled suit was meant to distract—to make you feel at ease around a man who could recall any item from a discussion and e-mail it to you at two a.m.

"Give up? Why would you do that?" He looked at me as if I were deranged for even thinking such thoughts. "When the customer would benefit from working with your company? You would be doing them a disservice if you didn't give them the chance to use your company." He pulled up a sock. "Look, there is no reason Clarinda can't win business. I turned Airborne around when everyone else thought we were done. The message is 'Clarinda is Back!' How does that sound?"

"It sounds like meaningless marketing speak," I said.

"Is it? Really? Maybe I am just a jackass for thinking what worked for Airborne, a multi-billion dollar shipping company, would work for you. Maybe if you say it, I'll hear what's wrong with it," he said.

"I'd rather not."

"Go on, say it. I want to hear it," he said, pointing at me.

"Clarinda is back."

"Not like that, louder."

"Clarinda is back." He said it with me. Then he shouted it a couple of times—reminding me that sales was not about feeling sorry for myself. Effort, no matter how cheesy, not whining, sold customers.

"OK, OK," I said, smiling in spite of myself. He was right—I couldn't help feeling dragged along by the idea that we were back, and I was, for at least the moment, inspired by the idea that we could recover from all of the troubles by selling hard.

"So what's the deal?" he asked.

"Deal?"

"What are we offering? Sweetening the pot, bringing 'em in, getting back with the message about the best company in the world."

I suggested reducing the alterations charges for books done in the next three months. We needed books now.

"Does that save 'em something?"

"Probably twenty percent," I said.

"And if you waived the whole thing?"

"Forty percent."

"And that sounds?" he asked.

"Good?"

"Better than good, great, can you do it?"

I nodded.

"Done. Get me a list and I'll call 'em all tomorrow."

Free alterations. Take that India! Any revenue would backfill what we'd lost. How could anyone turn down free alterations from an American firm that they had been dealing with for years?

A week later, Mike had called two hundred buyers and we'd gotten exactly no takers. "It'll take more than that to discourage me," he said. "How about you?"

I told him I'd had my ass kicked up and down the East coast by worse than that.

"That's the spirit!" he said, clapping me on the shoulder. "The problem, I think, is education. They need to understand why they want Clarinda. Why do they want Clarinda?"

"Um," I said, "Because we have offshore prices with American service?"

"Excellent. What else?"

"Because we are honest about what is going on at Clarinda and the industry. We are moving work overseas, like everyone else, because we're forced to, but we're doing it the right way. I know other typesetters are sending the work secretly to India and firing the Americans without telling the customer. We won't do that. We tell the customer the truth," I said, and noticed I had been pounding my hand on the desk. "We pay our people in Manila more than double the going wage in the Philippines. And we are trying to keep as many Americans employed as possible. We also know more about the technology, and we are automating everything we can to further try to save those American jobs."

"I'll write it up and send it out. We'll tell 'em my consulting company has been hired by Clarinda to do an industry survey. They love that 'industry survey' stuff," he said, "and then I'll call 'em all again."

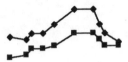

My Net Worth

Locations

Revolver

Clarinda
 Baltimore
St. Paul
New York
Manila

Revenue	$5,000,000
EBITDA	$0
Corporate Debt	$1,020,000
Employees	90
Customers	79
My Net Worth	$?
Revolver Expires	6 Months

Dem Bones

December 2002

"I DON'T KNOW WHAT TO DO," Kathy said on the phone from St. Paul. Since the layoff, I had promoted her from head of the editorial services to head of production for the whole company. I trusted her second only to Rich. "Red just left," she said.

"How did it go with trying to convince him to keep Pearson work with us?" I asked. "You're still his favorite, right?"

"I didn't get a chance," she said.

"What? Why not?"

"We all went out to lunch, a nice place, the place we took you when you came out." She began to sob. "Red stood up and said, 'Clarinda is not going to be getting any more work from Pearson. I wanted you to hear it from me. And I want you to also know that Clarinda is going out of business. And when it does, if any of you need jobs, you should give me a call. You know how much I care about all of you. And another thing—'" she broke off, crying.

"What?" I asked. Thoughts rushed through my head. *He said that? He couldn't have said that. Wasn't this the guy I had asked for help? Hadn't I confided in him and offered to do anything he wanted? Did this have anything to do with the Cadaver? There would be no biking across Cuba and camping in tents with him now. Was he really serious that if Bookers didn't buy us he would cut off Clarinda? How could he do that to my employees? How could he do that as a customer? Isn't that illegal? How could he say that he'd take away all the Pearson business? He couldn't speak for the other VPs, could he? Did he say anything about the other VPs? What about Addison-Wesley? We still had them, he can't take those books away. Can he?* But all I said was, "He did what?"

"And then," she said, still sobbing. "He said that you were a bad boss. He'd been right about you and Dan all along—you don't know what you're doing."

I called our New York lawyer, Jack.

"Look, the man's entitled to his opinion. I need you to understand that right now," he said. "But no, I don't think it's ethical and I think he's a fuckhead and it might be something you could sue over, but David, what would you get?"

"I don't know. It's wrong. Isn't that enough?"

"You can sue anybody for anything. Maybe it's worth a letter from me to his boss instead. Maybe that will cause the fucker some pain. Maybe it will get his ass fired or you'll get an apology, but as I look at it," he said, "I don't see it getting you back in with the customer. This is a one-way transaction, David. Exit only."

"Isn't there anything I can do?" I asked. "There's the other divisions of Pearson, and they don't report to him."

"Get the fucker on the phone. Tell him you talked to me. See if he'll relent. But this is not a get-your-hopes-up situation. He went out there to put a bullet in your head. I don't know why, or how it helps him, but he thinks it will so he did it. Not likely you're going to convince him otherwise if he flew all the way out there with this crap already planned out."

When I called Red, I was shaking. Why was I nervous when I had just had a customer tell my employees that we were going out of business and I was an idiot?

Typo

"David, good to hear from you."

"Really? If you're glad to hear from me, why did you go to St. Paul behind my back?"

"I was just telling them the facts."

"That I haven't been a good manager?"

"That is true. I don't think you or Dan have been good managers at Clarinda." He had been OK with me when I had gotten him lower prices, switched production to Superleaf, gotten his advice on firing McSwenson and listened to him on trying to sell to Bookers.

"Dan was a drunk, I told you that."

"And you were his partner."

I went to Pearson's New Jersey offices to try to rescue some business with the other VPs. I told them that Red had flown out to St. Paul to destroy my company, and that all I wanted was the work that they had already promised. When I arrived, Guy Delaco's secretary informed me he was sorry, but he couldn't make it to the meeting. The other two VPs, however, did meet with me, sympathized, and promised to send the work. Two weeks later, they met with Red and decided to drop us also.

The following day Kathy quit. "I've had enough of the publishing industry," she said. "I'm going to live with my sister in Maine for a while and rethink my career."

"You mean the one who lives off her husband's inheritance and smokes a lot of pot?"

"That's the one."

"What about your employees? We've still got the Addison-Wesley work, the bits from Thomson and IPC. I bet we might even be able to sell some more full service."

"You don't understand—I trusted Red."

I didn't want her to go, but I couldn't complain, and I did understand. I had trusted him too, and if I had the chance, I would do the same.

In December, I contacted Les Andover, the president of Corsairs to see if he would be interested in buying Clarinda. He was another Iowa competitor and the "favorite" vendor of Red's, as Red had told me many times. After I faxed over our financials Les called me back.

"You should probably know that I am opening a full service office at the end of the year," he said.

"OK," I said. "You should know we're almost out of that business."

"I know—" he said, pausing. "I'm opening in St. Paul. Kathy is going to be our manager."

So much for smoking weed in Maine. While I was trying to sell him Clarinda, Red had given him my business and convinced him to go after my employees. Over the next two weeks all but three of the St. Paul employees resigned to go work for Corsairs.

One of the departing Minnesotans forwarded a letter from Pearson disputing Clarinda's bills on three books. Inadvertently, she faxed the rest of the correspondence in which the Pearson buyer directed her to take the related manuscripts with her to Corsairs.

I called Jack.

"Let me get what you're saying," he said. "The customer disputes a bill they owe you, and then tells your employee to take those projects to a competitor?"

"Please tell me there's something you can do this time."

"Well not me," he said, and I sat down, defeated. "The police, however, have a word for this: stealing. Would you like me to call the cops and let Les know his new employee is in possession of hot textbooks?"

We got the manuscripts back. Score another one for me. Unfortunately, I was too many points down against Red for it to make much difference.

Shortly afterward, I received an e-mail from Corsairs that contained their weekly status update. Les had declined to purchase Clarinda, but he had sent us a book to do in Manila, as he too sought to reduce cost by going overseas. It had been easy to sell to him—his new employees in St. Paul could swear to the abilities of Clarinda's Manila plant, and I was in no position to be picky about rejecting a customer over a little thing like trying to destroy my company. The book was one of Red's, of course, although I doubted he knew Les had sent it to us.

Still, why send me the entire status report? Then I noticed it wasn't sent to me, but to an employee from St. Paul, and all her e-mails had been redirected to me.

Red had always held up Corsairs as the very best in the industry. He often said, "I only use Clarinda because Corsairs couldn't handle all my work." (Well, he'd solved that problem, hadn't he?) I didn't think Corsairs was so great—they were mailing me confidential status reports. And that wasn't the only time they were confused and disorganized. A few weeks into the book they'd subcontracted, I'd gotten a call canceling the project. About to have the material sent back, I decided to check with Les. He said it wasn't canceled, and he had no idea who called or why.

I pored over the status e-mails to see what made them so much better in Red's eyes. (Why not? It wasn't as if I was ethically bound to the competitor that took my business). There were less than twenty books on the report, each listed on a separate spreadsheet—a ham-handed use of Excel, that was like that stapler used to hold down the enter key in Atlantic. I considered how little those twenty books were worth given that Pearson had recently revised pricing with the succinct demand: drop them by forty percent or else.

I wasn't mad at Les anymore. I felt empathy for him. Les had secured Red's business by hiring my loss-leader full-service people, and they were about to be hammered on pricing. He had rolled over for Pearson just like Clarinda always had. That would have been okay if Corsairs had a Philippine operation like Clarinda, but I knew they weren't interested in owning a plant overseas because Les told me so. (Nor did he contact my employees in Manila to try to hire them away.) They were no better or worse than Clarinda. They were exactly the same.

The problem wasn't Corsairs competing unfairly with me. The problem was the customer. Red wanted to control vendors, but instead, like all the publishers, he was choking us. Just like TPC, Pearson paid sixty, ninety, and more than a hundred twenty days late, and they too arbitrarily discounted invoices.

Pearson owed Clarinda several hundred thousand dollars, most of which was more than six months overdue. That amount equaled the profit on all of Pearson's work with Clarinda. Put another way, Clarinda did work for Pearson in 2002 at cost. I didn't know who was worse off, Clarinda losing St. Paul or Corsairs getting them.

By January 2003, St. Paul was down to the last Minnesotan, T. T hadn't been offered a job at Corsairs. I went over the details of closing the office with her: turn off the utilities, return leased equipment, and finish the one last book—one of Red's. I asked if she had any final concerns or worries.

"I'm worried about the same thing you are," she said, "the customer."

"The customer?" I asked, trying to keep my voice level. "The customer that moved the work to a competitor? The customer that promised us work and then didn't send it? The customer that owes us hundreds of thousands of dollars? The customer that had worked so hard to make certain that we not only drown, but that we don't make bubbles on the way down? The one who is at this very second getting all of their files downloaded from Clarinda to be sent to Corsairs? That customer?" I banged the back of my hand against the table to let off my frustration. "I don't much care about that customer anymore. I care about getting paid. That's why we do this, right? To get paid?"

T said nothing.

"A business is in business to do work for money, not just to make a good product," I said. Had I taken Rich's beliefs to heart or simply stopped believing in Dan? I contemplated that during T's silent response—the chill of the cold winter air coming through the phone all the way from the land of ten thousand lakes.

e

When St. Paul closed, there was one unfinished project. Addison-Wesley hadn't been party to Red's plans to sabotage St. Paul, so their manager, Ethel, didn't know we were closing. "Really," she said, "I don't care. What I want is T, who we all trust here, to finish the project as you promised."

"Unfortunately, we stopped paying rent and there is no electricity, so I don't know how that's going to happen," I said. "The book's almost done. Why don't you let Debbie who's here in New York with me finish the project? I'll watch it every step of the way."

"I committed a lot of books to Clarinda. You made us a lot of promises. And I don't want my author finding out we've had to switch editors because your employees decided to quit." Another person demanding promises be kept. What about the promises Red and the other VPs at Pearson had made me?

"I would have been happy to keep doing your work. And so would have my employees. But that was out of our control."

Two days later, she relented to at least meet Debbie. I had hired her with the hope that having an editorial person in the city would be good for courting New York publishers. Now I needed her to help save whatever business we could.

"How did it go?" I asked when she got back from her meeting.

"I don't think they like me," Debbie said dropping her bag on the floor of my living room that doubled as her and Rich's office.

"Who couldn't like you?"

"They wanted to see my resumé. They were worried because I'd only done some K–12 books and never an anthology."

"Why does she need a resumé from someone who is just carrying messages to our typesetters for a couple of weeks? They've each been doing this for twenty years. Don't they know what to do?"

"That's the problem," Rich said, spinning around in his chair. "They think the process is hard and mysterious because if it were easy, why would anybody need them?"

At that moment, Ethel called. "Send the book back. We'll finish it ourselves."

Two days later she called again. "We don't have time to do it ourselves." I guessed they had too many meetings to go to. "I want T to finish it."

I explained again that T didn't have an office to work in. Moreover, if T decided she'd like to take out some frustration on Corsairs, Kathy, Ethel, me, or her ex-boyfriend then the manuscript might end up deep in the Mississippi. Why take the risk?

"Because I trust T," she responded.

In other words, she didn't trust me—but unlike Red, Corsairs, Kathy, and on and on, I was the only one actually trying to help. And in the same way I was finding it hard to act differently than my nature—so was Ethel. She called T directly and asked for her help. It was sad and awful, but Ethel had increased her risk of ruining the book and losing the author because she kept pushing in the only direction she knew.

"No thanks," T told her. "I've had enough of publishers." Unlike Ethel, T had, at last, learned to change.

My final conversation with Ethel revealed the truth of the situation to us both.

"I guess if I'm not going to be sending you any more work after this, I don't have much leverage with you, do I?" she asked. From the long pauses between her words, I could tell she was absolutely astonished at the idea, and so was I.

"You're right. However if you pay us the money you owe us, I might feel more willing to help," I said.

What she failed to grasp, and I had learned, was that I didn't have to give

Typo

the manuscript back to her. It was up to me. If I wanted to vent my anger and tear it up and feed it to Coco in tiny pieces, no one could stop me. Not that I would ever do such a thing, but I couldn't guarantee that they were able to read all the CDs when they got it back. It's amazing what one accidental scratch can do to those things.

ℓ

I had to find some revenue to keep the company going, and to keep paying off all those millions of dollars of loans I had personally guaranteed. From the Thomson meeting I knew other typesetters were sending work to India. So out of desperation, I called all the vendors I knew to pitch them subcontracting their typesetting to my Manila facility. It would be just like the old days when Dan and I did work for other typesetters back at Datadata. Maybe I could sell them cheap keyboarding from M&T as well—or maybe I could sell them the whole company.

My first two calls didn't go anywhere, and then I got Rob Ranch on the phone. I expected to be able to get something from him; after all, the last time I had seen him he'd been literally crying on my shoulder.

"You need overseas rates to remain competitive, and we've got a great group in Manila," I said. "What makes us different from those Indians is that you know we are trustworthy. We could do some books for you. Maybe even some keyboarding. Sure, I can hold—"

I heard the sound of a door close and then Rob got back on the phone. "OK, I'm here with Rita." Rita was his wife and business partner. "Can I put you on speakerphone?" Without waiting for my reply, I heard the hollow sound of an amplified empty room. "We were just saying, 'Thank God you called.'"

"I'm glad. We could get started with a book right away," I said.

"Not that," he said, whispering for no apparent reason. "I need you to save us."

Rob went on to describe his situation. He had nearly two and a half million in debt, much of it economic development loans, like the ones I had, but he had more, including (oddly for an Iowa company) September 11th relief funds. Worse, to make the past several payrolls, he had run up a quarter million in personal credit card debt. Now the banks and his own VP of Finance were closing in with a plan to refinance the business and fire him.

I said that I didn't know what I could do for him. I wasn't exactly in a position to come up with a couple million, but Rob was insistent. "Let me fax you my financials. We're both smart people. We can figure something out."

Looking at his balance sheet and income statement it was a shock to see how much price cuts forced by Indian competitors had changed his company. He hadn't turned a profit since Dan and I had been there two years earlier. I was not alone. But not being alone didn't make me feel better.

I asked Rich if there wasn't some way we could unite the companies.

He looked over the financials again. "You could fire all his staff, keep all the customers, and move the work to Manila."

I nodded.

"I'm joking," he said. "You're not serious about this are you?"

I nodded again, a little less excitedly.

"He would help us fire all his employees? Just like that, he's Mr. Tough guy, firing people?"

"He thought we could get a consultant to do it."

"And what would we pay them with? Carpet remnants and duct tape? Look I'm sorry. But, well, can he promise the publishers will stay with him any more that we could with Bookers?"

"Maybe we could get rid of his debt?" I asked, taking the financials back, looking for some trick, some way of joining our two drowning companies to make them float.

"By doing what? Letting him go bankrupt? Like Timmy's plan? If Ranch goes, Rob goes. Just like—"

"I know, I know," I said, still looking at the numbers. "Me."

I called Rob back.

"So I was thinking four million for the business, all in," he said.

"Um, well—"

"That's only one times sales. It's a good price. I wouldn't normally think so low, but you are a friend and I'd rather you than anyone else gets my company. Rita and I were thinking we could stay on long enough to help you get things settled and then maybe Florida. I've been looking at some houses, and—"

I interrupted. "I don't think we can do it."

"You have to. You're my only hope. My finance guy had the bank in here today. They want to buy me out for nothing. Fourteen years for nothing."

"Does nothing include getting you out from your personal debt?" I asked.

"Of course," he said, "But nothing else. Nothing for Rita and me. Are you sure you can't help?"

"Rob, I'm serious—I wish one of my employees had come up with a plan like your finance guy."

A couple of weeks later I spoke to him one last time. Rita had left him, and he was living by himself in an apartment down the street from his old company. He kept telling me what a good friend I was and how he knew he could pull it out with my help. Our conversation went around and around, and he sounded more and more like Dan, like someone who'd found his solution in a bottle.

I wasn't such a good friend to Rob. I called his finance guy and offered to sell him Clarinda. He was interested in Manila, but after what had happened with Bookers I told him I needed a letter of intent. He said OK and sent me a non-disclosure form—I could see where he'd whited-out "Non-Disclosure" and written "Letter of Intent" over it. I can't imagine what the finance guy's lawyer thought when he got his cc'd copy. I knew what I thought.

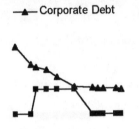

Employees
Customers

My Net Worth

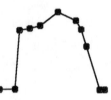

Locations

Clarinda
Baltimore
New York
Manila

Revolver

Revenue	$2,800,000
EBITDA	$0
Corporate Debt	$1,000,000
Employees	60
Customers	50
My Net Worth	$?
Revolver Expires	4 Months

Tire Fire

February 2003

"HI, THIS IS BANK MCGINTY," the voicemail repeated. "You don't know me, but I know someone who does. He was just in here working on his divorce and he couldn't stop talking about you. Says you're a good guy and that he's always been a sort-of father figure to you. Tells me to tell you that he's not drinking, and I can tell you he's looking good and fit. Good man, and he thinks you are somebody he should reconnect with. Why don't you give the old guy another chance? You can reach me at—" It was the first I had heard from Dan in a long time, albeit indirectly, but nevertheless my stomach turned at the mention of his name.

When the lawyers he hired after I fired him had first started to call, I'd been in a panic that he would destroy Clarinda and, at the same time, like the situation with my father, I still wanted to help him—believing that there was a difference between good old Dan and the drunk he had become.

But a combination of things had kept Dan at a distance physically and in my heart. First, there had been no time to think about him while trying to keep the company going, second, Rich had set up Jack to be our legal buffer with Dan's lawyers, and third those lawyers had all figured out

David Silverman   313

sooner or later that not only was Dan a drunk without any money, but that Clarinda had more debt than assets. Seeing that nobody was going to pay their bills, they dropped him, one after another.

Rich called Mr. McGinty for me. "No, Dan isn't the majority owner. Actually, we are not doing so well, and we were hoping he could reconfirm what assets he has against some personal guarantees. Uh huh. I see. Well I'll fax you what we need."

Bank never called back. Lawyers are capitalists too.

$$\ell$$

Francine, the manager in Baltimore, quit to go work for Port City Press. She couldn't see much future in staying, and I couldn't blame her. From fifteen people at its height, Maryland was down to four. In her resignation, however, I saw hope—and an excuse to close what had been Dan's pet plant. Even without Pearson, TPC, and Reed, we still had almost three million in work. If I moved all the production to Manila with just a skeleton of service in Iowa and New York, we could make it. I did the numbers, checked them, rechecked them, and showed them to Rich.

He nodded. "Yup, we could go as small as a million and keep paying down the loans. Just send everything to Manila, like Dan should have done in the first place."

"Yeah—" I said. "That might be a problem."

IPC, the company for whom I fielded that phone call for the receptionist two years earlier, and who had three hundred thousand in business with us, knew where we did each of their journals—some in Maryland, some in Iowa, and some in Manila. Dan had fought to spread the work to all the plants and I was left with the mess he had created. Journals depended on turning work daily. They would very much notice and mind.

"Wouldn't they mind just as much if we went of out business?" Rich asked.

I called Pat at IPC and offered him a twenty percent discount for letting me move his work to Manila.

"Twenty percent," he said, and as he did I imagined that he would enjoy telling his boss that he'd gotten me to cut prices. "I like the sound of it, but I'll have to get back to you."

"Of course," I said, and hung up wondering why a customer couldn't just say yes to a big discount. Next I called Mike, our freelance salesperson, who had been frustrated by his inability to get the attention of buyers, and told him to send out the whitepaper again. "I'm dropping prices and I'd like you to make the same offer to anyone you can find. We are now officially an offshore vendor. Can you sell it?"

"Sell it? As in, screw Red Bones, you're not going out of business?" Mike asked.

"Yes. As in, screw Red."

l

"That's right. Hire five more people," I told Fanta, "You're going to have a lot more work coming your way. You are the future of Clarinda. No, don't worry about the layoffs here. Yes, Francine knows. Yes, she wishes you well and she agrees you are running the best offshore operation there is." I had stayed up till four a.m. to talk to her. But just like when I had hired her from my hotel room at the Shangri-La, I talked, she stayed mute, and I tried to gauge if she was agreeing or had fallen asleep. "Are you still there? Good. Now with all the work coming over there I need you to do a few things."

I told her to start taking control of the administrative functions. Mai, the owner of M&T, had been out keyboarding vendor, but because she had an operating company in the Philippines and could more easily handle the basic accounting tasks, she had also being running our payrolls and handling the rent on our shared office space. However she hadn't been paying back the loan Dan had given her as an advance to build up her staff (to prepare for the work we had been so slow to send), and she wouldn't respond to my requests to bring her prices closer to India (even offshore keyboarding was under pressure from even more offshore places).

"Promise me you'll start taking over the payroll," I said. "I know Mai used to be your boss at Datadata, but remember, she's our vendor." The faint orange glow of dawn came in my window followed by the roar of the Hell's Angel's changing of the guard in front of their clubhouse.

"So how's SuperLeaf going? Does everyone like it?" I asked, shouting to be heard over the revving engine and hoping to end the conversation on a high note. "What do you mean it isn't that popular? Aren't you using it at all? But I'm about to send a bunch of journals and books that require it."

She began giving me reasons why she couldn't. I thought I had beaten the Clarinda culture, but here was yet another manager telling me training and automation would only slow her down—but this was not just another situation. If Manila didn't learn Superleaf I was out of options.

A week later Mai told me she didn't want us as a customer anymore.

"That wasn't the smartest thing for M&T to tell us," Rich said, and immediately put a freeze on about thirty thousand dollars of their bills. "Just about what she owes us on the loan."

That night I was up again at four telling Fanta to finish taking over accounting and payroll from Mai. Unfortunately, she told me, she hadn't started.

When the month ended, Fanta complained that she hadn't gotten paid, and, she told me, Mai reported our bank account was empty. "Mai doesn't know what to do about the payroll," she said. "So you will have to deal with her while we soldier on with production."

"No," I told her, "You've got to straighten this out. What can I do from halfway around the world?"

Our relationship with M&T had been too close. Rich called the bank and discovered that Mai had signing rights to our checking account in Manila. The account was empty because Mai had emptied it. Fanta's signature was supposedly required, and I wondered if she'd signed the checks—either duped or complicitly. I would never know. The bank refused to respond except to another authorized person, which they listed as Dan Coyne.

I spent two hours of the morning of February 1st yelling on the phone at Fanta. What little was left of the company continued to burn like a tire fire. "Rich tells me we sent enough money for the payroll. Have either of the January payrolls been made?"

"No."

"Why didn't you tell me before?"

"Because it's not my job."

"The people didn't get paid. We have to find out if Mai really stole the payroll. We need the records and we have to calculate what happened to all of the money we sent since it didn't make it into the pockets of our employees. You're their boss."

She sent some bank records and Rich calculated that more than eight hundred thousand Philippine pesos—sixteen thousand dollars—was missing. The best we could figure was that Mai had been stealing since November. Because Fanta had never checked any of the payrolls, Mai had been free to take anything. I asked why she hadn't she taken over the accounting payroll like I'd told her to.

She said she'd been waiting for "an official handover" from M&T.

"What did she want?" Rich asked. "A ceremony and a cake?" He wrote $16,000 on a scrap of paper. "That should have bought a lot of cake."

$$\ell$$

The day Fanta resigned I was in Maryland closing the office down. The previous night Rich and I had driven down from New York in one of the worst snowstorms in a hundred years—over eight inches—and all of it falling on us as we followed it south. By moving late in the evening, we avoided any possible issues confronting the landlord about the sixteen months still remaining on our lease.

It took until sunrise to clean out the office, using chairs as dollies to move files and what little equipment was left into my snow-covered van. The guy from the Salvation Army had refused to come. It wasn't worth his time, he told me, because he didn't have room for the used office furniture he already had—apparently we weren't the only company in trouble in 2003. Rich's dog Coco scrambled into a file cabinet to hide from the noise.

We spent a sleepless night in a miniscule room at the aptly named Microtel, Coco on Rich's chest, and me on a cushioned shelf under the cold window. We were back at eight to lock up for good and call Manila from the last connected phone.

Edward, the third shift (U.S. day shift) supervisor who'd been with Dan and me through Datadata and Bembo started by threatening me. "Maybe all of us will leave with Fanta," he said, in a soft voice muffled by distance and anger.

In the empty Baltimore office, surrounded by wires that ended in knots of discarded paperclips, rubber bands, and lint, looking at Dan's former offices and mine, the last vestiges of the man he had taught me to be dissolved. I let out a fountain of slow, loud words that, as I said them, reminded me of something Dan used to say—"You don't know what you're thinking until you say it out loud."

"Edward, let me remind you of all that's happened in the past year. Dan was a drunk and I had to fire him. We lost Reed Elsevier. We lost TPC. We lost Pearson. I shut down Syracuse, Atlantic and Maryland. Iowa has only a small staff left, and I am sitting on the floor. The books for our remaining customers are in Manila. You haven't heard or seen from me because I've been spending every waking moment keeping the company

Typo

alive. I trusted Manila because it was the only part of the company that seemed to be working correctly, and now your payroll has been stolen." From the corner of my eye, I saw Rich herd Coco to the door. "Did you know we paid Fanta double what we paid everyone else? Why? Because she's the manager, but she refused to help with M&T because she 'didn't want to get involved.' What do you think I should do, Edward? How am I supposed to pay the people if I can't get the money to them?"

The employees would walk without pay, he said. He was convinced that if all the work was in Manila, I would be forced to meet their demands.

"Edward," I said calmly, the anger gone, dissipated by my shouting. "You are free to do whatever you want. If you want to quit, go ahead."

A few hours later I had a message from Edward. The Manila staff was staying. I didn't bother trying to record the point for me—the total score was too depressing.

ℓ

"I'll be damned," Mike, said, calling a month after the renewed whitepaper push. "I've seen every kind of industry up till now, but this one, this one. I can't get anybody on the phone. No return calls. Never seen anything like it. Finally I get one today. One. A VP at McGraw-Hill in Ohio. First of all, how many levels do they have there? He tells me he's three up from the buyers and two down from the production chief? Don't tell me—it makes no sense. Cause he's apologizing. What's with that? Apologizing to me? Like I'm somebody? And then he's talking to me like I don't know who McGraw-fucking-Hill is. 'You know we have our own building in New York,' he says and I say, 'Really, is it, maybe, the McGraw-Hill Building?' and he's like, 'So you've heard of us.' He's talking to me like I'm his boss, and an idiot—so I ask him about the whitepaper, and he's telling me that he doesn't want to put Americans out of work. So I say what about the

Indians and he says, he doesn't use 'em, he gets the lower prices from the Americans. "As if that's really helping them," I say. He wanted to know if we could give him the discount and promise to do the work in America. I tell him what if we sent it without your knowing like the other typesetters are doing, like you told me, and if that's what he wants and he says as long as he doesn't know, but now he does and he can't use Clarinda."

He continued without a breath, "You know, I've worked in some low-end industries, staffing and shipping, so I thought you and Rich were just worn out when you told me that your customers were hard to deal with. When I talked to that guy I wished it was two cynics putting each other on, but it wasn't. He was the real crapola. If anything, you guys under-complained about selling to these guys. At first I thought be above board, bring 'em around with the truth, be innovative in this stagnant pool of a business, but now I know there's a reason why no one else in the industry was so open with customers before—it's not that they didn't think of it, it's that they thought better of it. I'm sorry, David, but I think we just made you the gopher that stuck his head out of the hole."

$$\ell$$

Pat from IPC finally called back. Twenty percent price reduction was good, but they were thinking sixty. I could agree or they would take the work to India. Cutting the prices meant having to fire the remaining Iowan staff immediately. If I did that, not only would we not be able to move the work to Manila (there would be no one to train them), we wouldn't be able to finish any work that was in progress for IPC or anyone.

I asked Pat if I could call him back.

"Sure," he said, "But my boss is ready to go to India."

ℓ

On a cold morning three and a half years after I had wired my father's life savings to Household Finance from the Charles Schwab branch in the former World Trade Center—the hopeful beginning of my personal disaster—I arrived at the bankruptcy attorneys' office in midtown. The meeting was Rich's idea. "Better to know your options, right?" he said.

The conference room table was huge, made of real oak and able to seat forty people. But other than the table the windowless room had little in the way of embellishment. There was no fancy multimedia projector, just a white board on an easel. We made no use of it.

There were five of us: Rich, three attorneys, and me. The attorneys were New York lawyers with every appearance of having come off a Law and Order episode.

"What is the debt?" The middle attorney asked.

"A million, or maybe two or more. It depends what we are able to pay with ongoing operations. We've got government loans, the revolving line from Household, the mortgages on the buildings, leases we are defaulting on in Syracuse and Maryland, and there are long term contracts for copiers and printers—"

"Personal guarantees?"

"It's a mix, but Dan also is guarantee—"

The attorney shook his head sadly and waved his hand for me to stop. "Total?"

"Almost two million," I said.

The younger attorney took notes on a regulation yellow legal pad, without any indication of surprise or not.

"Does Dan have assets?"

"Well, he's got a house—"

"Estimated value?" The middle attorney said and raised his thick eyebrows into his hair.

"It's got a mortgage, so I don't know—"

"Other assets? You or Coyne?"

"I've got a couch and bike," I said. "It's a nice one, but not worth a million." The younger attorney smiled, and continued writing. "But look, I really think there's a chance we can pull out of this. If I can sell a million in business, we can keep Manila going—I have just spent a few weeks getting them back on track over there—and we can—"

The lead attorney cleared his throat. The middle and younger attorneys turned to listen. "I don't see any moving parts here," he said. He looked right at me, his eyes locked on mine. I thought I saw compassion in his stare. "How old are you?"

I paused, not sure what that had to do with the company's potential bankruptcy. "Thirty-five," I said.

"You're a young man. You'll get over this," he said, "walk away." And he got up to leave.

"Don't file for bankruptcy?" I asked. The young attorney had stopped writing.

"Don't tell anyone," he said, moving to the door. The young attorney returned the pad to his case. "Collect what you can."

"What about me? Do I have to go bankrupt personally?"

"Maybe, but not much point worrying about it now, what comes comes." The young attorney sprang to open the door for the lead attorney, who turned back to me, and put his hand out. I stood to shake it. "Maybe think of a new career, have you thought about bankruptcy law?" He smiled, and walked out. "Who wants lunch?" I heard him say. "Maybe something Italian."

It really was the end, and I knew but didn't want to accept it. I walked the fifty blocks from the skyscrapers of midtown back to my home office in the East Village considering what to do. I didn't have a choice. I had to go back to work.

When I got back to the office, I called Pat and told him that IPC could have the sixty percent discount, but he had to wait until May.

He agreed, happily, eyeing the political gain of telling his boss that he had won a price cut and been able to keep the work with Clarinda instead of having to go through the pain of moving to a new vendor in India.

What Pat didn't know was that I asked for May because by then it would be a moot point. By May we would be gone.

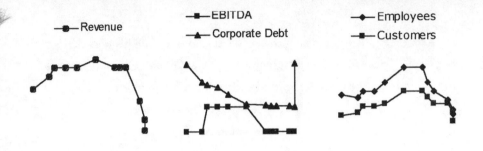

Revenue	
EBITDA	
Corporate Debt	
Employees	
Customers	

My Net Worth

Locations

Clarinda
Manila

Revolver

Revenue	$1,500,000
EBITDA	$0
Corporate Debt	$2,750,000 (With no more income, our balance sheet become completely one-sided. There were no more assets to offset the monthly debts from FedEx, Verizon, copier leases, and other vendor bills, including a $50,000 invoice from an Indian subcontractor.)
Employees	44
Customers	20
Locations	Clarinda, Manila
My Net Worth	about to become very negative
Revolver Expires	3 Months

Anger, Denial, Acceptance

March 2003

"**DON'T YOU WANT TO GET PAID?**" Henrietta, the owner of Blockheads Publishing Services screamed over the phone. "Isn't something better than nothing?"

"No." It was my turn to be difficult.

"You really screwed up the Fitsimons' project," she said, her voice suddenly soft, trying to cajole me into the old litany. "You missed the dates."

In my hand was the fax she had sent. "These aren't the original dates," I said. "Someone whited them out and put in an earlier one. Did you think we wouldn't notice?"

There was a pause, and then she started screaming again. "So, one of my idiot employees lied. What are you going to do about being late?" She was living in the past—a past where I would have just ignored anything she did, apologized and asked for more business.

"We aren't late," I said, and then began demanding myself. It felt good despite the fact that it would have been just as useful to reprimand a desk chair. "You have lied to us and it's unacceptable. You don't pay your bills and it's unacceptable."

She sputtered and hung up.

While I was enjoying my new found lack of fear, Mr. C from World Book called to request a download of every job they had done with us—hundreds of projects going back twenty years. Their price was seventy-five cents per page. I told him Clarinda's revised pricing: five hundred per download—a five-fold markup.

World Book was very slow paying (like everyone else) so, in exchange for up front payment, I offered him a big discount to three hundred fifty each. I figured he would see reason without my threatening—and potentially scaring—him by telling him the truth that for us to survive to finish the work, we needed the cash immediately.

Instead of thanking me for hanging on to his archives so carefully all those years, he was furious. After three calls and a letter explaining that our new price was, in fact, yes, five hundred per download, he tried his hand at Mr. Screaming Customer.

"We do not pay cash up front. We are a respectable company. And how dare you raise your prices when I need those files? I am faxing over download prices from our other vendors so you can see how stupid your pricing is."

"Our price is five hundred. If you don't want it, don't buy it." I said. "I'm certainly interested to see what our competitors charge, although I am curious how they will do your downloads when the files are at our plant."

Mr. C didn't laugh.

"You'll be hearing from me," he said.

I didn't.

At two in the morning that night I couldn't get to sleep. I knew Rich was awake because he'd responded to my e-mail, so I called him. "I don't get it. I told him as much of the truth as I could, yet he couldn't, wouldn't, or didn't believe me," I said. "Do you think I should let him know we're going out of business so that he can get his files back?"

"Why?"

"Because they will have to spend months and way more than the twelve thousand I'm asking for them to locate the printed books and get them converted to electronic files."

"So what?"

"So why can't he pay us? I could just tell him. Wouldn't that be the right thing to do?"

"Dead cat," he said

"Look, he's got to accept reason," I said.

"Like Minnie? McSwenson? Red? Why are you bothering?"

"It's another twelve thousand—didn't you tell me we needed to collect everything we could?"

"The cat's dead."

"What cat?"

"You, the company. In consulting we called it the 'dead cat bounce.' One last try, but you know," he said, "dead cats don't bounce."

$$\ell$$

As we tried to hail a cab, Rich and I pondered what was in the seven oddly shaped boxes slowly getting damp in the rain outside Mailboxes Etc. I knew they were mine because Shirley had kindly shipped my personal belongings from Iowa. I appreciated the effort even though I knew they weren't busy. Iowa was down to five people who were spending most of their time selling our office equipment: fifty cents for a wastebasket, two dollars for a chair, and a nickel per textbook.

But since I had already told her to throw away everything that was clearly junk—my files consisted of Ramen noodles and underwear—what was in the boxes? The three-feet-by-three-feet-by-five-inches box was a special mystery. In the dull light of late afternoon, I pried open the moist cardboard with a pair of orange-handled scissors and unpacked:

a. A chess set and deluxe Scrabble board I had last used with Dan at Brunner's in Clarinda.
b. A miniature tape recorder from a previous user of my Iowa desk.
c. Dirty laundry.
d. Laundry detergent for said dirty laundry, and one-third used bottle of Mountain Fresh Tide.
e. Box of tissues, one quarter used.
f. The sad fact that Shirley had packed up these things.
g. The sadder fact that she had nothing better to do.
h. The contents of the odd-shaped box: one bicycle tire.

On Monday, April 28th, 2003, I fired Shirley—the last of Clarinda's employees. She was surprised, but only by the reality of it coming down to a specific day. She wished me the best. I did the same, knowing that at least for her, it was over.

I was hardly off the phone when Luke called from Household Finance in Chicago. He was with the loan officer and they wanted to know what we were going to do—our revolving line of credit was due to expire in just over a month. I told him I'd decided to end the company, and that I thought there were enough receivables due from publishers to pay back the outstanding two hundred grand or so balance on the line.

Luke didn't need any explanation. He also wished me luck, and then he called Rolling Hills bank in Atlantic to tell them Household was exercising its contractual right to take control of our account. The company would end just the way Dan had originally feared. Without a line of credit, payroll would be impossible. The difference was, I knew it was coming, and almost was glad the revolver gave us a specific deadline for the end.

I had two months left on the lease on my apartment, and I would need every minute to collect the rest of Household's money—and anything I could towards the company's and my other debts.

ℓ

"Why didn't you tell us you were going out of business? You have a book of ours!" The buyer from Oxford yelled, the sound of her jewelry clacking faintly on the other end of the line. Screaming customer disease had begun to reach its final stages.

"That's why I'm calling you now," I said, and then pointed out—almost happy to annoy her with reason—I didn't have to call. I didn't have a job anymore. "I'm just trying to help you and get money back to Clarinda's banks."

"Send the book and we will review it. If it's complete we'll pay. This is the only way we do business with vendors."

I looked around my apartment. I had given my couch to Debbie, the New York customer service person I'd fired weeks ago. My kitchen table was piled high with computers I listed on eBay as "cash and carry." And I had just e-mailed a friend who admired my plasma TV that it could be his for half what I had spent.

"Unfortunately," I said, "I'm no longer your vendor."

I hefted the manuscript in my hand while she continued raving about how I owed her the book after everything they had gone through with us, what a terrible vendor we were, and how this was going to screw up her vacation.

The six hundred overly paper-clipped pages were a perfect example of how we lost money. Oxford had insisted we use the wrong software and as a result there were typographic problems throughout. The author, I had been told, was apoplectic because the horizontal bars above the algebra symbols were longer in the first chapters than in later ones. The staff in Manila had gone through the book character by character—repairing half a page an hour. The final pages I was flipping through had taken over two thousand hours to produce. A few hours less, and they might have gotten the book back before I had ended payroll in Manila.

"I'm not paying," she said, firmly.

"OK. If you change your mind, remember they are switching off the phones next Wednesday." I rested the book on the edge of my trashcan, ready to tip it in. Oxford's litany had become someone else's problem.

Pat at IPC, who only weeks before had thought he'd gotten the best deal of his life with the sixty percent discount, had a harder time adjusting to the sudden change in situation.

"Sorry," I whispered on the phone, "But the bank sent an auditor in here. He's here now going through my files in the next room and I've got to be quiet about whatever I'm telling you. If he even heard me offering to send files without payment he'd probably get me locked out of here."

"Those files are our property," Pat said, as he'd been saying for three days of attempted wrangling.

"Look, if you want them, I've got to fly out to Iowa," I whispered more quietly, "somehow break into the building the bank has padlocked, convince an ex-employee to come with me, 'cause I don't know how to download the files, and then get back here and sneak them to you electronically. And all I'm saying is you've got to pay before I can do that, and give me a little extra for the airline ticket and to pay the guy in Iowa who has been out of work since we shut down."

I heard him mutter to someone, his hand not covering the mouthpiece very well. "We want to talk to this banker, what's his name?"

"James Chen," I said. "But don't expect much. He really dislikes me and the customers."

"We'll be the judge of that," he said, clearly feeling empowered by the person coaching him. I tapped the side of my nose like Robert Redford in *The Sting* and transferred the call.

"James Chen, how can I help you?" Rich said.

"Surely, as a banker, you can understand our business needs those files."

"I don't know about that," Rich said, "But if you're entitled to something, you can have it when I'm done with my examination."

"How long would that be?"

"At least a couple of months."

Pat called back a few minutes later. "We can send you half the money for all the files and then the second half of the money."

Rich who had been listening put the phone on mute. "When they pay, send him half the files. Then he'll have to pay the rest before he gets anything more."

I nodded. "I know which ones he needs more and I'll save those till last." I took the phone off mute. "OK, Pat, and go ahead and send the money and I'm off to Iowa. Wish me luck." I hung up and reached between my legs to flip on the hard drive Jim had shipped out a week before that had every file for every customer. I would begin emailing the files as soon as the wire cleared. I was no longer a benevolent capitalist—I was a realist.

The last day, with the phone still ringing with debtors, I packed up my belongings to put in storage in my father's house. I wrapped my clothes and mattress triple tight in plastic to defend against the stench of his endless cigarettes, and put the ticket I had bought for Prague in my coat pocket. A friend of mine lived in the former communist state on less than six hundred dollars a month, and being a million or more in debt, I planned to emulate him with the few thousand in savings bonds my father had given me as a college graduation present—the irony that I still needed his money to survive not lost on me.

ℓ

In August of 2003, I was still in Prague—subsisting on dollar sandwiches and seeing what it was like to drink everyday for myself. Rich tracked me down. He had heard from Betty who'd heard from Ron who'd heard from McSwenson.

Dan was dead.

He'd known for a week or so and had been debating if he should tell me on the phone or wait till I returned. I went to an un-air conditioned basement Internet café and located Dan's obituary notice on the Baltimore Sun's website. He had died on June 10th. Almost exactly two years since we were in Iowa, and only a little more than a year after I fired him, he was gone.

My friend, my betrayer. The man I loved had already died, and now the body I hated had died. I had tried to help him and, more than anyone else, his rejection of that help led to drowning both of us. He had helped to kill Clarinda, and in return Clarinda had taken his life.

First I felt nothing and then later, nothing. I lay awake at night wondering at the nothing. Lying on a thin mattress on the floor in the cold communist-era concrete walled apartment, my eyes unable to close, I repeated out loud, "Dan is dead"—hoping that by speaking it I would solve the riddle.

I found no answers. My overused emotions of sadness and anger canceled each other out. It was as if I were standing between two giant loudspeakers turned to full volume but with opposite frequencies. In my heart, I could hear only the roaring silence.

When I came back to New York a month later I walked for hours or sat in bookstores—being unemployed and in debt didn't give me a lot to do during the days. On the clear autumn day of September 13th, I took Coco, now overweight, to the Union Square dog run. As I opened

Typo

a bottle of iced tea, my phone rang. Being on the lam from creditors and ex-employees, if I didn't recognize a number, I wouldn't pick up, but that day I did—we all feel from time to time like we are psychic, as if we can feel far away events.

"Coco, Coco," I call to the dog. She was speeding in circles through the sand with the other dogs—under benches, over the water trough, biting at dirty tennis balls. "Coco!"

"Is this David Silverman?"

But we aren't psychic. What we think is supernatural is just something we expected, but didn't want to happen.

"This is Officer Roberts with the Kingston Police."

We know what happens when the Jack in the Box handle is turned or the roller coaster stops clicking. Knowing doesn't lessen the impact.

"I'm very sorry to be the one to have to tell you this."

"Don't worry, officer, you're just doing your job."

"Your father passed away."

"I know. I mean, I'm not surprised. I mean I knew it would happen, I just didn't know the day." I took a breath of the Indian summer air. "I mean he's been drinking for many years."

"I'm very sorry."

"I know. Don't feel bad. I'm glad you found me," I said, "This is probably the worst part of your job, isn't it?" I couldn't help myself from treating the police officer like a long-lost Clarinda customer from the days when such things mattered.

The funeral home sat on the corner of Lafayette and Lucas, a corner my father passed on the way to the IBM plant every day for thirty-five years. It was also the corner we passed in the early morning when heading out for family vacations in the sky-blue Buick station wagon. As he frequently pointed out: "There's only one light if you turn down Emerson. If you stay on Washington, there's three lights. It's a waste of time and gas to sit through those lights." That morning, I had turned down Emerson.

Inside, the place was all doilies and Victorian frills separated by large swaths of empty pink carpet. As my sister and I signed forms and checks, I read the official cause of death: heart attack from alcohol overdose.

At home, in the living room, we put my father's cremated remains next to my mother's on the shelf. As I sat in the blue chair that I used to sit in for his lectures, I knew there would be no paying him back the two hundred thousand I borrowed. There would be no moment where he got to see his son succeed in business. There was nothing unexpected about this revelation, and therefore, unlike the events that had led me here, it upset me the most.

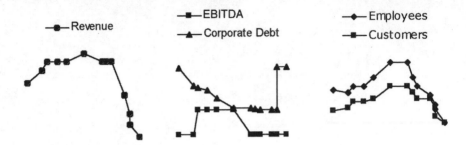

Revenue   EBITDA   Employees
          Corporate Debt   Customers

My Net Worth   Locations   Revolver

Revenue	$0
EBITDA	$0
Corporate Debt	$2,750,000
Employees	0
Customers	0
My Net Worth	-$930,000
Revolver Expires	expired

What You Need Is A Happy Ending

March 2005

HUNCHED ON HIS KNEES, RICH PULLED UP A wooden floor tile with the claw of a hammer. The square of birch broke into strips as it came slowly away from the glue. He tossed the bits in a plastic bag and then began on the next. Coco lay flat on the floor watching, her eyes trolling back and forth, while Kobe, her younger brother, barked from the edge of the DMZ between the exposed concrete covered with old glue and the new floor. "What do you mean a happy conclusion?" he asked.

"You know, a lesson," I said. "Something happy about the future."

He leaned back surveying the hundreds of tiles yet to be pried up. "You had a pretty good time in Prague, didn't you?"

I pulled Coco into my lap. "But maybe four months of heavy drinking isn't what I should be proud of."

Rich chewed on his tongue. "Well you had a year off, hanging around in New York, that's pretty good."

"I made five dollars doing standup dressed in an orange leotard wearing a Mexican wrestling mask."

"I thought you liked that."

"There was a certain pleasure in rolling around with a piñata on the floor of the city's finest dives." I pressed my voice to the front of my throat in a mock-Mexican accent. "El Orangina is confused by this term 'mid-life crisis.'" Coco licked my hand, her bristly fur rubbing against my arm.

"That third person referring to yourself is still weird," he said. "But you met Lilly with that shtick, didn't you."

"And you got me the job at Citigroup writing corporate policy." Kobe jumped in my lap as well—he wasn't getting enough attention. "But what if I had just stayed at IBM right out of college and you'd stayed at Ernst & Young? After sixteen years we'd probably have saved up more money, but had pretty much the same level of career we have now. I worked awfully hard and traveled pretty far to end up in basically the same place."

He threw three tiles in the bag. "Look, you didn't want to end up like your dad, stuck in one place. So you took a risk and lost—you accomplished a lot too. We kept that place running on sheer force of will for over a year. You can't forget that if Bookers had bought, or if just a couple of customers had stuck with us, we'd maybe have made it."

"You really think that? With Dan, the employees, the bank loans and the Indians?"

"That we could have made it?" He grabbed Coco with both hands and roughly petted her. She flipped herself on her belly in sheer ecstasy. "Nah," he said, scrunching his face up in mock financial calculation. "Not a chance."

In April of 2005, Lilly (my girlfriend of the past year) and I went up to Kingston for a Passover Seder with my sister and her boyfriend. Sitting in the repainted living room, my sister and I recalled—for the first time since his death—my father the way he was when we were growing up: the stupid jokes he would make about the fancy dishes we used once a year, the way he presided over the meal, the love that he had for us.

After dinner I sat in the quiet room listening to the ticking of the miniature pendulum clock my father got on his twenty-fifth year with IBM. The question still remained in my mind. *Did I contribute to the fall of Clarinda or could I have stopped it? Or was I, as Dan said, "watching the circus from the best seat in the house?"*

Looking back, it's clear that typesetting was going overseas. Dan was crazy for trying to increase employment in America, but there was no reason to fire everyone on the first day. We could have gotten work to Manila, and kept most of the American jobs if sales had grown or even stayed steady. But Dan's drinking meant that effects of mega-publishers buying in bulk, technology changes allowing Indian competitors able to send and receive work electronically (and therefore at no cost), and employees unwilling or unable to use technology themselves to compete on a global scale, turned what was a severe change in the industry into an un-survivable "perfect storm."

I don't know if Dan, or anyone, could have overcome the other obstacles, and that's because of my own failing. I believed my father and then my father-figure Dan so completely that I was trapped in my own downward path. I wanted so badly for them to be right—for the world to reward me for knowing all the elements of the periodic table and π to fifteen decimal places. I wanted the employees and customers to applaud my seeking of opinions from them before making decisions—rather than using the information I gave them for their own ends. I wanted what I thought everyone deserved—if I was the best son I could be, my father would always be there to be pleased.

I was wrong. Capitalism is about making money. Benevolence is a feature of companies that have enough excess profits to afford it. IBM survives today because the old IBM employee recreation center with the Olympic-pool and discount hamburgers that my father valued so much has long since been abandoned and become overgrown with weeds.

That night it rained, and when I awoke, hearing the patter of water on the roof in my old bedroom, I remembered a piece of my childhood I had forgotten.

The hurricane was coming. "The first one to come this far North in a hundred years," my father had said. We watched the TV news showing the white circle of clouds ascend the Eastern seaboard and into the mouth of the Hudson River.

My father opened all the windows. "We need to equalize the pressure," he said.

All afternoon I could feel the heaviness of the air rising and then, just past dusk, the rain came. A wall of water that I swear I could see move up the street: the Piantanidas, the Schatzles, the hedge, the sassafras tree, the maple and then the whole world was wet.

My father and mother dashed from room to room to make sure rain wasn't coming in and adjusted each window to the proper height. My sister—wearing her pink and white housecoat—watched the windows in the living room. "OK in here!" she yelled.

Then the power went out. The battery lights my father had plugged into strategic outlets on each floor switched on. I saw the kitchen light up with emergency glare. "Good thing I tested them," he said, as my mother lit candles and placed them on a plate to catch the wax. And then, the rain stopped.

"The eye of the storm," my father said and put his hand on my shoulder. He opened the screen door and we walked outside onto the street. The Flicks came out and so did the Winters and the Schatzels. Down the block, I could see the Sweenys and the Piantinadas.

The air was a mix of fresh leaves and Caribbean autumn swept thousands of miles north. There wasn't the faintest breeze.

"Look up," my father said, "You can see the stars."

I did and there was the Little Dipper.

"And Orion's Belt, the hunter. You see the three stars?"

All my life, I had never seen Orion. Other than the Little Dipper, all the stars looked the same. But that night I saw where he looked without pointing.

"Yes," I said—even then, eight years old, I knew someday I would point out Orion to my own son.

The wind began again. Everyone walked back to their houses, but my father and I didn't go inside. We stood on the front stoop, just under the awning of the roof as the rain came back—roaring up the street with lightning and thunder.

"Take a good look, David," he said, "Who knows when you'll see something like this again?"

Appendix: A Brief History of Typography

"I want to talk about the story of Wapping partly because I like talking about it, but also because Wapping is a microcosm of the issues that face us now. It puts them all in a nutshell." Rupert Murdoch, November 1989, New York City

Movable type was invented by Johann Gutenberg in 1440. Before then monks copied books by hand—which took, unsurprisingly, years. He melted lead into the shapes of individual letters, combined them to form lines of type, and then pages. The process of sticking the little lead blocks together was called typesetting. The lead was slathered with ink, mounted on a modified wine press over a sheet of paper, and printing was born.

Gutenberg's press was so good that it remained pretty much unchanged for centuries. In the 1700s, Ben Franklin printed *Poor Richard's Almanac* with movable type. At the Franklin Museum in Philadelphia you can watch them turn out pages just as Ben did. You can even ink a page yourself, if your girlfriend isn't tugging at you to get lunch.

By the early 1900s there were more than 100,000 people employed as typesetters, and machines such as the Monotype and Linotype automated constructing lines. Type text on a keyboard and *voilà*, a line of lead type would be melted on the spot. Inventors tried to make up whole pages automatically, but mechanical contraptions weren't up to the task. Mark Twain lost almost everything investing in such a machine—his own "dot. com" business.

Lead pages are heavy, take up lots of space, and are a real problem if you drop them, especially on your foot. In the 1960s there was a significant departure from the technology of the Middle Ages: photolithography. An image of the page was made with a camera. The resulting film (no different than a regular photograph) was placed on top of a metal plate and bathed in chemicals that ate the metal wherever there wasn't type—leaving a surface with raised type. The plate was inked and used to print.

The process was called "cold type" because in wasn't like melted lead which was, um, hot. In the 1970s computer-based typesetting systems appeared. They cost millions of dollars and were difficult to use, but technology advanced furiously. In the late 1980s, *Time* magazine collaborated with two programmers to create software called QuarkXpress that did typesetting using the new Macintosh desktop computers. What had taken days with knife and film using older methods could be done in seconds with a Mac and a mouse. Quark and similar systems such as Atex made a fortune for the programmers. However, fewer people with less skill were needed to make pages.

It was at this juncture in technology that Rupert Murdoch bought the prestigious *London Times* newspaper from Lord Ken Thomson of Thomson Publishing. Lord Ken was no fool and after one labor strike too many (the journalists struck just two months after getting the printers back to work), he decided to cash in on the value of the word "prestigious."

The *Times* was still being set in hot lead. Every other major newspaper in American and Australia was using the newly developed photocomposition systems, but the printer's union in London resisted change successfully— thereby, in their estimation, protecting jobs.

But Murdoch was not impressed with the union. He recounted, "Many of them, for example, ninety percent of the News of the World publishing department, had other jobs. Some worked for rival publications, some were cab drivers or car mechanics, one owned a vineyard, another was a mortician." Composing and printing the *Times* took "three times the number of people at five times the wages" of his other papers.

While appearing to negotiate with the unions, he secretly set up a new computer driven factory in the town of Wapping in the docklands of East London. The offer to the unions was, as it was designed to be, unacceptable. When they struck, he dismissed them all and pulled the wraps off of the new plant.

There were literal riots. Almost two thousand police were dispatched to protect the barbed wire-fenced Wapping. Delivery vans loaded with scab produced newspapers would be launched at high speed at unexpected intervals to thwart protesters attempting to block them. It was a spectacle and it altered the world of British publishing forever. The newspaper the *Independent* emerged made up mostly of dismissed *Times* employees, but, Murdoch pointed out, they used the same electronic production methods he had pioneered. Nobody wanted to go back to the old ways.

It's easy to point the finger and say that Murdoch was a greedy capitalist.* On the other hand, a newspaper, like any other business, has to make money. Would he have been less evil if he'd kept the *Times* going until a competitor emerged and drove them out of business? Would the world applaud him then? There was no solution to the problems at the *Times* without many losing their jobs, or losing to less expensive competitors. It was either the whole company or the printers.

In Prague, I met a man from Australia who had been in Wapping in 1986. He'd worked for one of the technology companies that supplied the new plant. He told me he crossed the picket lines to train "unskilled brick layers and gardeners" to become typesetters using the new-fangled computers. He recounted to me that he did his part for all involved: strikers, new workers, his company, and Murdoch, by getting himself "piss drunk" every day and doing as bad a job as he could. That way, he proudly told me, the change he'd been dragged into wouldn't be his fault.

I smiled, thinking how well he would have fit in in Iowa.

Glossary and Compendium of Typesetting Miscellany

Art
: Also known as graphics or pictures. Simply put, the stuff on a page that isn't text. Art often holds up the typesetting because author's photos often need to be retouched and line drawings need to be redrawn to make them consistent to the style of the book design (color, line width, fonts for labels).

Book Design
: The layout of the information on the pages of a book. Such questions are book design questions: Do new chapters start with a big roman numeral on a right-hand page, or do they start with a blue stripe and a reversed Arabic numeral? What font is the body text? How much room for footnotes is allowed before the flow to the next page? Should art always be on the outside edge of the page?

Cold Type
: Cold type was neither particularly cold, nor exactly type. Cold type was any process for making pages that didn't require hot lead. The first systems, which used photographic images of letterforms exposed over photographic film to make negative images of pages that could then be made into positive printing plates, were called phototypesetting. The earliest in the 1950s were complicated electro-mechanical contraptions. In the 1970s minicomputers began to be used in conjunction with complicated electro-mechanical contraptions, and in the 1980s desktop publishing emerged. By the year 2000, the entire process could be done from initial data entry to printed book by computer.

Composition
: see *Typesetting*.

Copyediting	Copyediting is any editorial review of a manuscript. Copyediting may be light, medium, or heavy. A light copyedit is usually limited to a review of punctuation and grammar. A medium copyedit focuses on reviewing for sentence structure and sense. A heavy copyedit often requires rewriting. Editorial marks are done with different color pencils to indicate who has made the edit: the author, the editor at the publishing house, or the editor at a copy-editing firm (such as Clarinda's St. Paul facility). Copyediting is still primarily done with colored pencils on printed manuscripts. However, more and more editing happens electronically and is called "online" or "softcopy" editing.
Correction or Alteration (Alt)	Changes made to a manuscript after it has been laid out as final pages. Corrections are charged for "by the line," which dates back to hot lead when individual lines had to be reset by hand with movable type or photocomposition where errors had to be cut out of the photographic film and then corrected text pasted back in. With desktop publishing corrections are much easier, and by charging by the line, it is a rare opportunity for profit by the typesetter.
Cut and Paste	'Cut and paste' was originally a term from photocomposition. Individual columns of text set on photographic film were cut into appropriate lengths and then pasted together with art to make final pages. Errors were cut out of the film and corrections pasted in. People who performed these tasks were sometimes called 'film strippers' and at least one lady at Clarinda was denied a credit card on the basis of this being her listed profession.

Desktop Publishing (DTP)	Desktop publishing is a generic term for personal computer based typesetting software such as QuarkXpress. It is generally used in contrast to older minicomputer based "batch" composition systems such as Xyvision or Penta. However, nowadays there is no real difference between the systems as all of them can run on desktop computers and all can work in network environments. Desktop publishing also is used in contrast to word processing software which doesn't have the page layout features of typesetting software.
Double Keyboarding	Double keyboarding is a process for reducing errors in entering data into the computer. One operator types the hard copy page that is to be made electronic and then another operator does the same. A third operator uses computer software to compare the two files and fix any discrepancies. There are variations on this method that use two, three, and four operators, and include triple-keyboarding (mostly used by non-English speaking operators such as in China) and double keying with proofing. Double keying supposedly guarantees 99.995% accuracy or higher—which isn't really all that accurate, as it equates to an error every six pages or so. It is used primarily to convert huge amounts of printed material (like converting all the U.S. tax law cases into a CD-ROM database—a project I worked on).
Educational Publishing	Educational publishing is all those books you got in school and never read: textbooks, standardized tests, workbooks and so on. In the United States, educational publishing is driven by the government textbook review boards in California and Texas. Because they buy so many books and other states allow books to be chosen by markets as small as an individual district, these two boards end up setting the standards for the rest of the country. The dominant educational publishers are Pearson, McGraw-Hill, and Thomson.

Film

Film is used during the printing process to create metal printing plates with raised type that will then ink actual paper. It is a replacement for directly inking hot lead type and then printing with that. Photocomposition is the typesetting process for making film without the need for lead.

Font

'Font' is the way the letters look. Here's some trivia about fonts you can whip out the next time you want to give somebody heck about their document: In Roman times, when words were inscribed in stone, the finishing chisel mark produced small lines at the end of a character, now termed *serifs*. Later, with calligraphic style pen, serifs became part of the writing style for another reason— instead of letting the ink blob at the end of a stroke, it was finished neatly with a serif. *Sans serif* (no serif) typefaces did not appear until the early 1800s—then it was discovered that the little serif lines actually aided legibility, the explanation being that they lead the eye from one character to another. The words 'uppercase' and 'lowercase' come from the fact that the different size letters were stored in the upper and lower drawers of the California job case that was used for storing lead type. *Times* font was invented in 1931 for the London *Times* newspaper to pack as many letters in as small a space as possible, while maintaining readability. *Arial* font was invented in the 1980s as a cheap replacement for software developers who didn't want to buy Helvetica. Microsoft was one such developer. (For a professional graphic designer, Arial is just like Helvetica in the same way two cans and a string are just like a telephone.) *Book Antiqua* font is, like Arial, a knockoff off the more expensive Palantino. But, unlike Arial, Microsoft eventually paid the font designer, Hermann Zapf. So if you check your font choices (starting with Office 2000), you get both Book Antiqua and Palantino.

Full-Service	'Full-service' refers to a company that provides all of the functions of a publisher's production editor as an outsourced business. This includes project management, copy editing, book design, management of typesetting, and rights management for copyrighted art. Clarinda's full-service division was in St. Paul, Minnesota.
Galley	A *galley* was a single column version of a book that was essentially partially typeset to the point just before cutting and pasting (in photocomposition) or page composition in a composition box (hot lead). The galley would be reviewed by the publisher and author for errors at this stage because the cost of making changes in final pages was much higher than at the galley stage. With desktop publishing, there is no galley stage, but some publishers will call proof pages (see *proof pages*) galleys, and some publishers simply won't understand that galleys don't exist and get mad at you for suggesting otherwise.
Hot Lead or Metal Type	Gutenberg's invention in 1440 or so. Also called 'movable type.' It allowed the reuse of cast lead letters in building lines, blocks, and pages of text, thereby eliminating the need to rewrite every copy of a book by hand. So good, it forced spelling to become consistent for the first time in history. So good, it lasted until the 1950s. Actually, it is still used in less developed parts of the world and by the occasional typesetting nut who is convinced that the uniqueness of each letter somehow makes it look better. And here's a little fact to throw around at the next cocktail party you are attending with people you'd like to impress: the saying "mind your 'p's and 'q's" comes from the fact that lead type had to be set in reverse (from right to left) like a mirror.

HTML	'HTML' is the typesetting language of the Web. HTML is a set of tags for telling an Internet browser what to do with text. For example \word\ would cause a browser to show the text in bold, "**word.**" HTML is a direct descendant of SGML (see *SGML*), which is a direct descendant of the original computer typesetting systems such as Penta, Xyvision, troff, IBM DCF/Script, and so on.
Keyboarding	'Keyboarding' is typing of manuscripts or corrections to manuscripts into the computer. In the past, all manuscripts arrived from the authors' typewriters and had to be keyboarded. Nowadays manuscripts arrive "on disk" (the term is used even for e-mail), but corrections are still often marked on the hard copy printout of the manuscript. These corrections need to be keyed. Keying was traditionally done by homeworkers, such as the wives of farmers, and paid on a piece work basis. Keyboarding today mostly happens overseas. (See *double keyboarding.*)
LaTeX	LaTeX is a descendant of the math typesetting language TeX developed by computer scientist and church organist Donald Knuth. (When I met him he was playing an organ at a cathedral in Boston and was quite good, I might add.) LaTeX is just one, albeit popular, variant of TeX. TeX, like open source software, allows for individual user customization. It is therefore very powerful for an author who might have invented their own mathematical notation to write their journal articles, and very difficult for a typesetter who is used to the click-and-drag world of QuarkXpress to take the highly marked up and programmer-oriented TeX and compose said article into a journal's official style. TeX disks sent in by authors were lovingly referred to by such typesetters as 'coasters,' and an opportunity to provide some work for their favorite keyboarder.

Legal Publishing	Legal publishing includes all the material published by the courts and legislatures of the world. Legal publishing is dominated almost entirely by Thomson, Reed Elsevier, and Wolters Kluwer. Legal publishing is as close to a license to print money as is available. Given their regular but complex information structures, legal publishers were the first to switch to computer-based typesetting systems in the 1970s, the first to make online databases in the 1980s (Westlaw and Lexis-Nexis), and the first to make CD-ROMs in the 1990s.
Macintosh	Macs have better typesetting ability than PCs because of the native ability with graphics and multiple fonts. That was true in the 1980s, and hasn't been true since, but it doesn't stop people from believing it. Realistically, though, the Macintosh made typesetting at the desktop possible with a machine that cost $5,000 instead of $100,000 and thereby convinced an era of publishers that they could bring typesetting in-house—not realizing the real costs of typesetting were people, their management, office space, and the constant need to upgrade those Macs and their software. Most New York publishers abandoned their in-house efforts shortly after setting them up (unless, like McGraw-Hill, their typesetting was in rural New Jersey), but not before training a generation of freelancers who they could then use without any of the costs of management, office space, or computer upgrades to do production work. As for typesetting companies, they were squeezed into the market segments that required complex but regular page designs, such as professional, reference, university, STM and legal publishing.
Manuscript	A *manuscript* is the thing that the author thinks is a book, but isn't yet.
Page Makeup	see *Typesetting.*

Penta	The batch composition system software company that Dan Coyne went to work for as president. They zoomed to millions with their IPO and then zoomed back down again when they couldn't keep up with technology changes. See *Xyvision*.
Plates	Plates are pieces of metal with raised type where ink can stick. Inked plates are pressed or rolled against paper or another roller (offset printing) to actually print. Plates can be made from photographic film in a chemical etching process, or made directly from computer files in a process called direct to plate, DTP, which, confusingly, is the same acronym as for desktop publishing. DTP is sometimes also called computer to plate, CTP. And, to further add to confusion DTP can mean direct to press, a process which removes the need for plates at all and turns a giant printing press into essentially a laser printer. Direct to press is sometimes called computer to press, CTP, which makes reading a printing industry trade journal utterly confusing. Technology change in printing is slowed down by the enormous capital investment in printing presses—a six-color Heidelberg can cost millions—but it also advances sometimes surprisingly fast. In 1995, Dan Coyne said film would last for another twenty years. In fact, it was all but gone from professional publishing by the beginning of 2001.

Printer	Printers are the folks with the big machines that put ink on paper. These include R.R. Donnelly, World Color, and my friend Pete with his sheet-fed Multigraphic press over a pizza shop in the Bronx. Printers in Ben Franklin's day did both typesetting and printing, because both happened from the same piece of hot lead. In the 21st century, printers rarely do typesetting, preferring to get final page images either on fim or preferably in an electronic format such as a PDF or PostScript file. The economics of the typesetting and printing business are fundamentally different. Typesetting is about skilled labor and profits are primarily made by being more efficient in the use of technology or finding cheaper labor. Printing is about the efficiency of the printing press and the primary issue is getting enough work to keep the presses rolling. Any printer worth his ink stained hands can tell you how much his press costs for every minute it isn't churning out pages.
Professional and Reference Publishing	Professional publishing is information used by, well, professionals. This could be a doctor, lawyer, or candlestick maker. Professional publishing is composed of part STM, part university, part legal, and part educational (post-graduate) publishing and partly unique items such as dictionaries and encyclopedias.
Proof Pages	Proof pages are fully laid-out pages that contain the authors' manuscript in the design template of the book or journal. Proofs can be sent either hardcopy or as "softcopy" files such as PDFs, which is considered terribly modern by any editor born before 1990, and they will ask you to send print copies of your proofs to make sure they match the softcopy. Other than looking for design errors or typos, the primary reason for checking proofs is to verify that colors are correct and there are no errors like printing yellow on top of black without "knocking out" the black area so the yellow can be seen.

Publisher "A desk and a phone," as Dan Coyne would say. Publishers find authors or information to publish or republish, contract for its production (typesetting, printing, or webpage layout), find buyers or subscribers, and then market the product. Publishing used to be considered a "gentleman's business," but the economics of business led to many publishers being acquired by large multinationals that trimmed their book lists (how many poetry books do you really need anway? they asked themselves) and implemented MBA style management. The result has been that large publishing companies dominate the industry, make huge profits, and do not publish a great deal of diversity, but instead focus on the 10% of their list that generates the most sales. This has, however, opened an opportunity for small publishers to fill niche markets. Reduction in production and distribution costs (such as the offshore typesetting and printing that helped kill Clarinda), allows independent publishing to have larger lists, produce books on-demand, and be able to provide diversity to the market while making a profit (some people want a lot of poetry books or even a book about typesetting). One man's loss is another's gain.

QuarkXpress	The desktop publishing program of the 1980s. It was invented in a joint effort between the software company and *Time* magazine. Since it was built for the complex page layouts of magazines, it is very inefficient for use with text that "flows" across many pages, like science journals and textbooks. For example, Quark has no native ability to make footnotes. Because Quark was point-and-click and WYSWIG (what you see is what you get), it was easier to get to know than "batch" composition systems like Xyvision that were code driven, and it could be used for a wider variety of page layouts with less customization. Thus, Quark almost entirely supplanted all the batch systems even though it was ultimately slower at producing pages—a perfect example of a mass market tool winning out over a better, but more limited market, product. The conflict between the supporters of the two kinds of systems resulted in most typesetting companies, like Clarinda, having multiple typesetting systems and a workforce that knew how to use one or the other, but rarely be efficient with both.
Queries, Author Query (AQ), Editor Query (EQ), Printer's Error (PE)	Queries are questions on the manuscript from an editor to another editor (such as a copyeditor) or an author, or indications of an error to the printer. In this case printer means typesetter. Queries can be either written on the manuscript, or attached via Post-It notes which tend to fall off so that editors cover them with too much tape which makes them unremovable stickies.
Redacting	Redaction is sometimes considered to be a synonymous term for copyediting, but in journal (and other periodical) publishing it specifically means matching a manuscript against house style. For example, redaction would make sure that all references to the United States are written as U.S.A. instead of US, U.S. or USA.

Scientific, Medical, Technical (STM) Publishing

STM publishing includes scientific journals, books published by professional societies (like the American Vacuum Association—not the Hoovers, but the scientists who study nothing), monographs published by professors, and so on. STM material is often published by a professional society in partnership with a major publisher, such as Reed Elsevier. The society provides the material and the dedicated audience (all the members of the society) and the publisher provides technical production capability to make both print and online publications. Because the audience for the information is well defined, and often gets the material, such as a journal, by default with their membership dues, it is an extremely profitable publishing segment. If you are a dentist, you will get material from the ADA, making it even more of what is essentially a monopoly than legal publishing. In the 1990s a major portion of the STM market was swallowed by three major publishers: Reed Elsevier, Wolters Kluwer, and Thomson. Other publishers, such as John Wiley and the American Physical Society, represent very small portions of the market. However, they are still large in their own right, and the APS is big enough to provide publishing services, such as typesetting and print buying for its member societies. STM publishing was the first to make significant use of offshore copy editing and typesetting.

SGML	SGML stands for 'standard generalized markup language.' It is the descendant of a generalized typesetting language developed at IBM called GML, which stands for Goldfarb, Moshe and Laurie, the inventors of the thing. SGML was adopted by the US Defense Department's CALS initiative—an acronym that isn't worth trying to decode. The point was that military equipment came with tons of documentation—the rumor was that a destroyer would sit ten feet lower in the water because of all the manuals—and they wanted to be able to reprint and reuse parts of the documents and make electronic manuals that could be more easily carried, used, and updated than giant binders of paper. The problem was that all the manuals were typeset using all the different composition systems of the day: Xyvision, Penta, Miles 33, and so on. The goal of SGML was a universal text coding scheme. The result was a lot of hope by my former employers that there would be a mass conversion to SGML (and they would be paid to do a lot of it), the dashing of said hope because it was in no one individual company or military unit's interest to pay for all that conversion, and the ultimate demise and then rebirth of SGML as HTML (see HTML) and XML, which is used nowadays, even by Microsoft.
Trade Book Publishing	Trade books are the kind of book you see in Barnes and Noble. They include novels, cookbooks, how-tos, children's books, and so on. Trade books are usually typeset in-house at the publisher, by the printing company, or by freelancers. Some are done by typesetting companies, but the layouts are either very simple, very consistent (the *Dummies*-type books are done using Microsoft Word templates), or so unique (like the cookbook) as to require a freelancer to do all the careful individual work.

| Typesetter,
Typesetting,
Composition,
Page Layout	Me! Actually, not me. A typesetter is a person or a company that takes manuscript pages and then lays them out to the design of the book or journal with all the fonts, page numbers, colored boxes and so on that the designer wanted. Typesetting originally referred to the actual setting of the bits of lead type into a 'composing stick' for each line of type. That hasn't been true for a long time and although the words 'typesetting,' 'page layout,' and 'composition' are now interchangeable and done with software, people still respond when I say I ran a typesetting company with, "Isn't that done with computers now?" as if I had been waving around a bit of lead in their faces. Given that most people spend a good part of their jobs fighting with Microsoft Word or PowerPoint to make a document look right, you'd think they understand there's more to making a book than just typing it. But they don't.
University
Publishing	University publishing programs include all types of publishing. Oxford University publishes everything from poetry, to trade books, to highly specialized material such as the *Encyclopedia of Dance*. University publishing does not mean small. Harvard University's business school publishing program is so large, it is a separate business from Harvard's main publishing program and from the business school itself. One of the largest university publishing programs is at the University of Chicago, which does publishing services for other, smaller universities.

Word   Word's definition has been absconded from being a bunch of letters separated by a space by Microsoft for their word processing program that by trying to be all things to all people at all times tends to do bizarre and unexpected things every time you try to do anything. It can do a lot of the functions for composition, but does not handle complex pages with art, math, and fine typographic control (like line and letter spacing) as well as QuarkXpress. The need for these fine typographic controls in the majority of published material is a matter for the kind of debate that makes people argue over Captain Kirk versus Captain Picard.

XML   XML is the descendant of SGML that is used for technical documents and is the new language of the Web. XML fixes what was wrong with SGML in terms of being able to practically implement it. One of the key inventors of XML was Jon Bosak, who I sat next to as he prepared his speech for the SGML conference. I remarked that I had had my speech at the previous years' SGML conference struck from the proceedings because I'd said SGML had these problems. He sympathized that I had a big mouth.

Xyvision   A batch composition system that tried to reinvent itself as a WSYWIG point-and-click system to compete with QuarkXpress, but never pulled it off, and thereby watched their stock sink to the penny level while the inventors of Quark rolled around in piles of money. A reminder that it is better to make something people want to buy than to be the first in the market.